Behind the Bench

INSIDE THE MINDS OF HOCKEY'S GREATEST COACHES

Behind the Bench

INSIDE THE MINDS OF HOCKEY'S GREATEST COACHES

Craig Custance

TRIUMPH
B O O K S

This book is available in quantity at special discounts for your group or organization. For further information, contact:
Triumph Books LLC
814 North Franklin Street
Chicago, Illinois 60610
(312) 337-0747
www.triumphbooks.com

Printed in U.S.A.
ISBN: 978-1-62937-244-0
Design by Patricia Frey
Page production by Meghan Grammer
Photos courtesy of the author unless otherwise indicated

For Cassie

CONTENTS

FOREWORD

I don't usually make a point of going back and watching the biggest games of my career. I tend to hang on to the big moments. I don't necessarily remember every detail about every game.

But I do enjoy it when I catch them unexpectedly on television. It's fun when you turn on the TV in the summer and all of a sudden one of those games pops up on the screen. It's like catching your favorite movie halfway through and watching it all over again. It brings the emotions of those games rushing back.

As I watch, I start to remember exactly what I was thinking on the ice. You start to recall the small moments that changed the course of the game. You start to think about what might have been if things had gone differently.

I'll give you an example.

When we won Game 7 of the Stanley Cup Final against the Detroit Red Wings in 2009, there was a Niklas Kronwall shot late in the third period that could have changed the outcome if it had gone in.

I was sitting on the bench right behind Kronwall as he shot. I think it hit the crossbar or the post. I remember the feeling I had on the bench in that exact moment. Every time I watch, that exact feeling returns.

It's that feeling of uncertainty—did it go in or didn't it?

I remember being on the bench watching and feeling sick to my stomach.

The coaches in this book have all been through so many important moments like that, so many key situations. Playing in a few of those games for these guys, you learn a lot about what it takes to win. Chemistry is a big thing. There's a trust and a belief in what you have to do to succeed. And building that chemistry always takes a bit of adversity. The best teams all have to go through it.

The best coaches help guide you through it.

In 2009, I remember Dan Bylsma joining the Penguins and bringing a lot of energy when he arrived. He made sure guys enjoyed coming to the rink. We had such a young team and there was a lot of pressure on us, especially having lost in the Stanley Cup Final the year before. Expectations were so high.

He came in and made sure we enjoyed the ride along the way. He emphasized that with his personality and how he handled everyone. That played such a big part in us being able to win.

From Mike Babcock with Team Canada, I've learned what happens when a coach has absolute clarity in what he's trying to accomplish and is confident he can do it. It's so important to understand what is expected of you as a player and to be pushed. In the short-term events we've competed in together, he always made it clear what he expects from every single guy on the team. That allows you to head in the right direction right away. Everybody feeds off his confidence.

There are a lot of decisions you have to make as the Team Canada coach. There are a lot of line combinations. I remember him asking me about the forwards I was most comfortable playing with during the 2010 Winter Olympics in Vancouver. Just thinking through all the options was crazy. Look at that roster. It was unbelievable. I would have played with anybody. But I do remember talking a little about Eric Staal because he was so good at holding on to the puck down low and I like to play down there, too. So that's what we did.

Ultimately, a coach has got to have the right instincts and trust the decisions he makes. As a player, you can see Mike Babcock has that.

You begin to trust it. You believe in it and then you're willing to do whatever it takes to win.

Playing for Todd McLellan in the World Championships was another a great experience. I was pretty sour about being eliminated from the Stanley Cup playoffs by the Rangers that year, and the experience in Prague ended up providing a big boost to my preparation for the next NHL season.

For the first meeting we had as a group with Hockey Canada, Todd McLellan gathered all the players and our families together. He made it clear that he wanted to make it feel as much like a family as possible. I was playing with a couple guys from Philly in Claude Giroux and Brayden Schenn who I had never played with before. We had competed in the playoffs a couple years prior and they were great battles. Todd made sure all of us were coming together as a team. We were there to win but he wanted us to enjoy the experience in Prague as well, which we did. That was a big part of our chemistry throughout the tournament. The whole experience was awesome.

And now, winning two Stanley Cups with Mike Sullivan has helped me truly appreciate him as a coach. He's just so honest and consistent. Whether we've won three games in a row or lost three games in a row, he's looking for the exact same thing. He evaluates every situation the same way. He just wants guys to work. He wants guys to compete and play their roles to the best of their abilities. He has high expectations but he's fair, too. When guys are doing what they're asked, what has been clearly explained to them, they get rewarded. As long as the message is clear and the expectations are fair, that's all you can ask for from a coach.

A lot goes into being a good leader but it starts with having a good group. All of those teams had great groups. It's about understanding that everyone can lead their own way. It doesn't have to be a rah-rah guy. It doesn't have to be a guy who spends 10 hours at the rink. It's about understanding the different personalities in the room and the importance of each guy. It's about understanding that guys are going to have different opinions but it's still a team.

That takes a strong group. It takes a strong organization.

It takes a strong coach.

In the NHL, coaches are viewed by wins and losses. That's just the business. But to me, the best coaches are the ones who get the best out of all of their players. If each individual guy feels good about his game and is playing to his peak abilities, everyone comes together and can do their thing. The best coaches are those who can get the most out of their players and have that mutual respect no matter their perspective.

The coaches in this book all have different perspectives. They see things in different ways. There are always going to be some things that are consistent and similar but ultimately each leader is his own person with his own personality.

That's what makes each person's story so cool.

—*Sidney Crosby has captained the Pittsburgh Penguins to three Stanley Cup Final victories, in 2009, 2016, and 2017. He is a two-time winner of the Hart Memorial Trophy and the Conn Smythe Trophy, as well as two Olympic gold medals and a gold medal at the World Championships.*

PREFACE

There's a great perk that comes with being a hockey writer: after NHL coaches finish up their media responsibilities on the morning of games, they often stay behind to chat.

That's when the real conversation happens. These guys love talking hockey. They're looking for an edge or any information you might have. Often, they want those around the game to have a better understanding of what goes on during games.

The recorders and cameras are shut off and it's at this point when you get the real insight about players or a decision from the previous game. Or sometimes you just get great hockey stories.

I love those chats.

I have an affinity for coaches. I'm passionate about the relentless effort it takes to win at the highest level.

To me, coaches are a little more relatable than the players. I'll never be able to duplicate the extra gear Connor McDavid finds on the ice or the sheer beauty of a one-timer from Alex Ovechkin or the way Sidney Crosby can absolutely will his team to a victory.

But coaches, I can relate to. The way they study their craft, the way the coaching world is like a tight-knit club where they protect and defend each other. In many ways, the writing world is the same way. I imagine most professions are the same way.

The closer I get to NHL coaches, the more I realize we all can learn from them. We all can benefit from their stories, from the paths they took, from the lessons they've learned.

That's the genesis behind this book.

* * *

Years ago, Ken Hitchcock was coaching in Columbus and was chatting with a few writers after his media availability. I learned more about hockey in those 15 minutes than I'd learned attending games that entire season. I was just starting out and couldn't believe this was accessible to someone like me.

I mentioned to my friend Aaron Portzline at the *Columbus Dispatch* just how great it was that Hitchcock would take the time to do that. He answered that Hitchcock even took local media members in and showed them video clips of games so they'd get a greater understanding of what was going on.

That stuck with me.

The leadership and coaching geek in me could think of no better way to spend a couple of hours. I desperately wanted to do the same thing; I just needed to find an avenue to make it happen.

And here we are.

Some of the best coaches in hockey agreed to sit down and watch film of their crowning achievements, their signature games, with the conversation to be shared with hockey fans and leadership junkies in this book. We watched games that clinched Stanley Cup victories. Olympic gold medal games. Even a final from the World Championships.

The idea was exhilarating to me. The execution was overwhelming. The hockey calendar now stretches from September to July, so I had about a two-month window to pull this off. I promise you, there were many times I wondered if it would happen at all. There were some close calls.

Thankfully, things worked out, and the payoff is in these pages. There are stories I'd never heard before. Moments the coaches hadn't relived since they originally happened. I'm indebted to every coach you're about to hear from for making this happen.

I hope you enjoy reading it as much as I enjoyed living it.

CHAPTER 1

DAN BYLSMA

Game 7 of the 2009 Stanley Cup Final

It's 10:45 AM on a rainy spring day in Pennsylvania and I'm nervous. Part of it is because I'm sitting in a 2007 black Town and Country minivan with a giant crack stretching the entirety of the windshield, parked in front of a house in an upscale neighborhood about 15 minutes north of downtown Pittsburgh. I'm sure I'm being judged by everyone driving by.

I'm early to meet former Pittsburgh Penguins coach Dan Bylsma at his house, so my solution is to drive to a more modest section of the subdivision and wait. I feel like I look suspicious. I'm waiting for a knock on the window at any moment from a neighbor wondering what in the world I'm doing parked there.

I'm also nervous because I realize I haven't perfected my plan for the day. Bylsma has graciously agreed to sit down and watch one of the best playoff games in recent NHL history—Game 7 of the 2009 Stanley Cup Final between the Penguins and the Detroit Red Wings. He's the first coach on my list, mostly because he has the time to do it. He's between jobs and I know that won't last. We're going to spend a few hours reliving the game that launched him from a virtual unknown to a Stanley Cup champion.

He offered to get a DVD of the game from the Penguins and I turned him down because he was doing enough just allowing me to visit his home—I didn't think he needed to do my legwork. At this point, I wish I'd let him.

This meeting came together quickly in April. As one of ESPN's hockey writers, I was approaching our busiest part of the season—the Stanley Cup playoffs. Bylsma, at this exact moment, was between head coaching jobs. I also knew his employment status wouldn't last and my intuition was right. Soon after we wrapped up, he was named the head coach of the Buffalo Sabres.

So I crammed this film session in when I could. Before he got crushed with the demands that come with being a new coach in a new city. Before he changed his mind about helping with the book. In the rush to get it done, I didn't have time to get a hard copy of Game 7 on DVD, kind of an important part of the process.

The solution to the DVD problem was to download a digital copy of Game 7 from iTunes onto my laptop at an investment of $3.99. On the way to Pittsburgh, we—my wife, three kids, and a 14-year-old golden retriever, all accompanying me on the road trip because it was spring break for the kids—stopped by my sister's house to grab her AppleTV, and that was that. (Later, I'd discover just how lucky I was. Not a single other game I needed for this book was on iTunes. It was just completely random luck that this one was.)

Now, minutes away from sitting down with Bylsma, the worst-case scenarios are running through my mind. *What if he doesn't have a wireless network? What if his TV doesn't have an HDMI port? How does AppleTV even work?*

It was closing in on 11:00 AM, our predetermined meeting time. I started the minivan up, thankfully without drawing any attention from the neighbors, and turned the corner to Dan's house.

It's a beautiful brick colonial, newer construction, but nothing that screams a millionaire NHL coach lives there. If anything, it's a house with a modesty that reflects the coach living inside.

Any apprehension about the meeting evaporates almost immediately when Dan answers the door. He's wearing a tracksuit, and if he had skates and a whistle, he could jump on the ice for practice.

It's his golden retriever puppy, Dutchess, who truly breaks the ice and eases my nerves. She seemed to sense my own golden and was immediately on my side, jumping up for a greeting.

"How old is she?" I ask, walking through the front door.

"Just over a year. She gets excited when new people come over," Dan answers, then turns his attention to Dutchess. "Dutchess, down. Come on."

Bylsma turns his attention momentarily away from the dog, her tail wagging. "Would you like a cup of coffee? I'm having one."

I accept the offer and try to casually throw out the question that is going to make or break the entire afternoon.

"You have wireless, right?"

"Yeah. I'll get the password."

And we're off.

I start connecting the laptop wirelessly to his big screen, hoping he doesn't mind I've switched the plug of his television from one wall to another to get everything to fit.

He takes a phone call and I realize that he may be in between coaching jobs, but a coach never stops coaching.

"If they make the long pass, it's a mistake," he says during the phone conversation. "It's a mistake for them. It's a 2-on-1 or 1-on-1."

I start wondering if every coach talks like this during phone conversations.

Bylsma is a great coach because of his attention to detail. You can hear it just from listening to one end of one random phone call.

It's an attention to detail that came from maximizing every ounce of talent he had just to make the NHL as a player. To stay there, he had to be willing to learn details about the game those who had more skill didn't need to master.

Along the way, he took exhaustive notes, writing down coaching styles and drills that worked or didn't work in pages he added to a three-ringed binder. They are journals with entries that span years and which he still references.

"He wasn't going to outskate somebody," said Tom Fitzgerald when we chatted on the phone a few days earlier. Fitzgerald, who played 17 seasons in the NHL, was one of the assistant coaches on Bylsma's Cup-winning staff in Pittsburgh. "He needed stick position, foot position, angles—that's what Dan was all about. Those are the things he believes that hockey players have and more importantly demand that they play with detail."

Bylsma wraps up the phone call just about the time I miraculously get Game 7 to flicker up onto the flat screen in his living room. The only slight hiccup is a screensaver that keeps popping on when the game is paused, a screensaver composed entirely of photos from my sister's family vacations. I hope he doesn't mind seeing my niece and nephew at Disney World.

I'm sitting on a large couch, with my laptop set up on a stuffed ottoman in front of me. Dan sets down a large cup of coffee next to the laptop and settles into a seat to my left. Dutchess, much to her disappointment, is gated in the kitchen behind us.

Behind Dan's chair is a small table along the wall with a large copy of *The Art of War*.

I cut the family vacation screensaver short and begin the broadcast on the screen in front of us.

The voice of NBC's Doc Emrick kicks in, a voice that would accompany the entire visit:

"No change in either lineup for Game 7 from Game 6. What will be tonight's lasting memory? Game 7s have long memories. The Red Wings are 11–1 on home ice this year, 20–3 the last two playoff years. Trying to be the first to win in back-to-back years since they did it themselves in '97 and '98."

"Were you nervous?" I ask as the intro to the game kicks in and Doc rattles off reminders of just how good the Red Wings have been in Joe Louis Arena during this era.

"I wouldn't use the word 'nervous' at all," Bylsma says. "There's a certain amount of angst. It's Game 7, someone is going to win a Stanley Cup. We got down 2–0 in the series, we got punted in Game 5, we scratched out the win in Game 6. We had a chance to win the Stanley Cup in Game 7. There was a lot of talk about how it can't be done, you can't beat the Red Wings at home."

Detroit had one of the last powerhouse rosters of the salary cap era, in part because the Wings added Marian Hossa on the cheap to an already great team. They had Henrik Zetterberg and Pavel Datsyuk in their prime. Nicklas Lidstrom, the best defenseman of his generation, playing half the game. Chris Osgood, who knew how to win the big game, in goal.

And it was Mike Babcock, a coach with a Stanley Cup ring won the previous season against these Penguins, against…Dan Bylsma, some guy who was coaching in the AHL five months earlier.

Shots of both coaches flash on the screen.

By no means does Bylsma look old now but it's stunning to see this version of him on the screen—young, inexperienced behind the Penguins bench. He's wearing a suit, a paisley tie, and a white dress shirt. His arms are folded and he's pacing slightly back and forth.

Then it cuts to Babcock—his thick head of hair, eyebrows pushed down in intense resolution.

"You really look younger there," I say.

Bylsma laughs.

"I wasn't blessed with Mike's hair."

Because his team wins this game, because he coached Sidney Crosby and was the star of HBO's Winter Classic documentary and soon established himself as one of the game's best coaches, it's easy to forget how meteoric Bylsma's rise to this moment was.

Our setup in Dan Bylsma's living room to rewatch Game 7 of the 2009 Stanley Cup Final.

He only had 25 regular season games as an NHL head coach on his résumé before the Penguins' playoff run, although his record in those 25 games was an impressive 18–3–4.

Bylsma was as an AHL head coach for all of 54 games.

Dan's older brother Greg was also working his way up his own organizational ladder, this one at Herman Miller, a Michigan-based furniture maker. Even as the successful big brother, Greg had gotten used to being referred to as "Dan Bylsma's brother." That happens when a sibling makes it into the NHL.

In February of 2009, Greg was promoted to CFO of Herman Miller. It's a big deal, running finances for a company that had revenue of $1.6 billion in 2011. He finally had a moment that eclipsed the accomplishments of his little brother.

"I called him up, having lived in the shadow all those years, and said, 'I think I finally beat you. I'm finally ahead of you,'" Greg said. "Three days later, he goes, 'Guess where I'm coaching tonight?'"

Penguins GM Ray Shero had fired Michel Therrien and promoted Bylsma to head coach to get the Penguins into the playoffs.

"I had a pretty good run for three days," Greg says with a laugh. "All of a sudden he's coaching the team that Herb Brooks coached."

And on the screen in front of us, he's 60 minutes of action away from winning a Stanley Cup. The hockey world might not have given the Penguins a chance but the guys on the bench in front of Bylsma believed. He'd instilled that belief months ago.

* * *

The Red Wings and Penguins are feeling things out against each other in the first period of Game 7 and our conversation shifts to leadership and exactly how he empowered a group of players sitting outside of the playoffs into the one playing for a Stanley Cup in front of us.

Bylsma is the youngest of the four Bylsma boys, so to understand his personality and leadership style, you first have to go to the backyard of his childhood home. It was the battleground for whatever sport was in season. It also wasn't a democracy.

Scott is the oldest of the brothers and with that came power. He decided what was going to be played unless he could be convinced otherwise.

"I could say, 'We're going to play football' or 'We're going to do this.' Danny was the youngest—he couldn't say that," Scott said. "He had to get older people to see his direction or see what he wanted to do in a different way than I did as the oldest."

In Scott's eyes, leadership is the ability to get people to do the hard things necessary to be successful in such a way that they might not even realize they're working hard. It's convincing them to do things they might not otherwise want to do by convincing them they're having fun.

"That's the real secret of a leader," he said.

I share Scott's leadership theory with Dan and he gets it immediately. One of his philosophies in life is that he simply doesn't do things unless he enjoys them. That philosophy carries over to the way he runs a team.

You see it in the way his teams practice—at a high pace but always fun. Bylsma is usually right in the middle of it, throwing a shoulder into a player as he skates by or holding a shootout contest at the end of practice as players stand at center ice and cheer.

"I'm not a huge fan of the words 'hard work.' Hard work to me is eight hours of shoveling stones or digging a ditch. That's hard work. Getting after it playing hockey, practicing—even that to me is an enjoyable thing," Bylsma says. "I want to create an environment and an atmosphere where people want to work and want to learn and want to get better, improve, and grow. I want to do that for the team as well."

I thought of Bylsma's comment later while standing just outside the visitors' dressing room at Scottrade Center in St. Louis next to former Penguins forward Matt Cooke. He'd just wrapped up an extended practice for the Minnesota Wild during a playoff series against the Blues. At this point in his career, he was a guy who was in and out of the lineup on the fourth line.

On Pittsburgh's championship team, he was part of a line with Tyler Kennedy and Jordan Staal that was critical to the Penguins' success. They wouldn't have won the Cup without that trio.

We were leaning against a wall in the hallway when we began to talk about Bylsma and that great Penguins team. His immediate smile confirmed the connection was still there.

"Dan didn't come in and demand things. He didn't come in and scrap everything," Cooke said, sweat still beading on his face. "More than anything, he supported the group that was there. We came up with a list—I don't know if Dan mentioned this. I don't know if I should say it."

"If you don't want to say it, it's got to be good. C'mon, say it."

"It was called the Woody List."

Cooke explained.

"It was doing things that excited your teammates. Taking a hit to make a play. A big save. A clear on the penalty kill. A faceoff won at a key time in the game. Obviously a big goal. Any of those things that are immeasurable to teams that everybody on the bench sees—it creates momentum. It jacks everybody up. It supports your teammates. We didn't have that at the time. I think that once the team recognized it, that those things matter to wins and losses, that it matters this much to each guy on the team, it brought a respect level that wasn't there."

The Woody List.

"Who came up with the phrase?" I asked.

"Dan. Ask him what it means."

We wrapped up the chat and I pulled out my phone to text Bylsma.

"Can't believe you failed to mention the Woody List," I type into my phone. I mean, we only sat in his living room for *four hours*.

"I didn't tell you everything," he shot back. "It only seemed like it."

I laughed. But there's some genius in the Woody List, because on that list are the most miserable aspects of winning hockey games. Nobody wants to step in front of a shot coming in at 100 miles per hour or expose themselves to the big hit along the boards to keep the puck in the offensive zone a moment longer.

What the Woody List did was celebrate those who did and encourage others who might not normally participate in the harder parts of the game to do so.

When that Penguins team was clicking, everybody was making those contributions that don't show up later in the box score.

"That's the true sign of the team, and understanding that and knowing however you're going to contribute, it's going to have an impact," said Penguins captain and superstar Sidney Crosby. "The best example of that is guys like Petr Sykora and Miro Satan blocking shots. Syky broke his foot. Guys got out of their comfort zone to win games."

* * *

On the screen in Bylsma's living room, NBC analyst Pierre McGuire is standing next to Red Wings coach Mike Babcock for an in-game interview.

Our conversation shifts to Babcock. It's at this point that I learn about the journals Bylsma kept throughout his career, the ones that detailed drills and techniques Dan's coaches used in practice—good and bad.

The NHL coaches who impacted Bylsma most were Andy Murray, his coach when he played with the Los Angeles Kings, and Babcock, for whom he played in Anaheim. From Babcock, Bylsma learned how to clearly spell out and articulate the foundation of a team.

With my eyes on the screen, I steer the conversation toward the team battling the Red Wings.

"What was the foundation of this Penguins team?"

Bylsma stands up from his chair. "Push pause for a second."

I reach toward my laptop and a moment later the screen freezes. In a minute the family photos screensaver will appear on the TV.

Dan leaves the room, looks in his office for a moment, and then disappears into the dining room.

His voice echoes from the other room: "I hid everything since you were coming over."

A moment later, he sits on the couch next to me holding a binder with a USA Hockey logo on it. Bylsma was the coach of the American Olympic team that finished fourth in the 2014 games in Sochi, Russia.

In this binder was the foundation of that team. The identity.

He opens to a page and I see the words "Who We Are" in all caps and underlined. Below that are six phrases, each with bullet points under them.

Bylsma starts reading.

"Fast. Aggressive. Smart. Patient. Smothering. Great defensively."

The last bullet point comes under "Great defensively" and reads, "This is the key to winning the gold."

After coming up with the identity of the team, Bylsma structures his entire practice around those words, making sure everything they do is working toward improving one of those areas.

"What we do in practice, you're going to have these elements. You're going to hear me say the word, 'Fast.' We're going to play quick. Neutral-zone transition, ready to skate, middle-lane drive, attack mentality. Aggressive, relentless on the puck—we talk about hunt and pursue, we're forechecking, we're physical, we grind down. You're going to continually hear these same words from me."

With the Penguins, he didn't want the words to come from him. He wanted them to come from the players. They provided them in a team meeting that helped shape the identity of that championship team.

Bylsma is the kind of guy who exudes confidence. He's a guy who never thinks he's out of any competition, even if evidence suggests otherwise.

His brother Scott tells a story that captures Dan's mindset perfectly. The Bylsma family does a lot of golfing. Scott and Dan had just finished nine holes of golf and Scott was absolutely on fire. Everything was falling for him.

They made the turn and were walking toward the 10th tee when Dan asked for an update on their scorecards. Scott had opened up a four-stroke lead.

"I'm only down four?" Dan answered.

In that moment Scott saw a change in his brother. Something washed over him that suggested he knew it was still close enough to bear down and win in the next nine holes.

"His body changed. It was bizarre," Scott said. "He just looked at me, like 'Oh, I can get that.' I was like, 'Oh my god, I'm going to lose this.'"

When Bylsma was hired in midseason to replace Michel Therrien, the Penguins had just lost to the Toronto Maple Leafs by a score of 6–2 in a game in which they entered the third period with a 2–1 lead. It was the last straw.

It all happened fast and Bylsma didn't do a lot of contract negotiating when he was offered the job. When you're the AHL coach getting promoted to one of just 30 NHL head coaching jobs, that's not the time to take a hard-line stance.

But he revealed the confidence he had in one request. He met with Ray Shero, then the Penguins general manager, in his office.

Shero offered a bonus of $25,000 if Bylsma somehow got the Penguins into the playoffs that season. At that point, they were five points out of the final playoff spot in the Eastern Conference.

Bylsma accepted and left the office. Five minutes later, Shero heard a knock on the door. It was Dan, with that one last request.

"What if we win the Cup? Can I have a bonus?" Bylsma asked.

"What are you thinking?"

"$100K."

"Fuck, I don't care," Shero answered, adding that he'd have to check with ownership.

It was a long shot. But that's Bylsma. Down four strokes at the turn? No problem. Outside of the playoffs by five points with 25 games remaining? He's thinking Stanley Cup.

A few games after joining the Penguins as their coach, Byslma gathered the players for a meeting and they talked about the perception of the team. It wasn't all too dissimilar to conversations Mike Sullivan would have with a different group of Penguins years later when thrust into a Bylsma-like resurrection of the same franchise.

Bylsma gave the players a voice.

They talked about how they wanted to be perceived. They talked about how they wanted to play. It wasn't Bylsma giving them an edict. It was a conversation, orchestrated by the new coach but with the voices of the players very much at the center.

"What was the perception of the Penguins at that point?" I ask Bylsma.

"There was talk about our players, talk about our teams, how you could play against the Penguins," he replies.

More specifically, Ruslan Fedotenko said the words that connected most with how Bylsma wanted the team to play.

"I don't have the words exactly verbatim," Bylsma says. "Grind down, play in the offensive zone. Wave after wave, not paying attention to the score. Nothing is going to stop us from coming at you. Playing fast, aggressive. Playing in the offensive zone. Being hard to play against. Ruslan Fedotenko hockey."

Ruslan Fedotenko hockey. Byslma could write "RFH" on the white board in the locker room and the team knew what he meant. Words that helped created the identity of this team, phrases the players themselves volunteered.

Fedotenko laughs on the other side of the phone line when reminded of this story years later.

"Yeah, I remember," he said. "I was just answering Bylmsa's question. He put me on the spot and I was like, 'Oh shit.' I don't like to be the center of attention. But, okay."

In another example of how the coaching lineages run through the generations of players and coaches, Fedotenko thought for a moment and tapped into what he remembered working so well in Tampa Bay, where he won a Stanley Cup under John Tortorella in 2004.

It's what makes hockey great. It's what makes coaching and mentoring great. These moments passed down from era to era.

Fedotenko shared wisdom in that moment that Tortorella would have appreciated.

"The whole thing is to play for each other, to be accountable and not play individually. Not for the points. You need to play for the guy next to you," Fedotenko said. "We want to play aggressive hockey. We want to initiate, not retaliate. We want to set the tone."

Until that point, the Penguins were thinking too much on the ice. They were passive, too timid. Too many shifts were spent trying not to make a mistake.

It was time for the Penguins to be the aggressor.

"So teams had to adjust to our play and not for us to adjust to the other team," Fedotenko said. "That sums it up. At the time, when you're in it and breathing it and living it, you remember all that stuff."

It was how the Lightning won. It was how the Penguins would win.

* * *

The screen in Bylsma's living room cuts to a shot of the Joe Louis Arena rafters at the conclusion of the first period, as the broadcast goes to commercial on a question from Doc Emrick: "Eleven Stanley Cup banners in those rafters. Will there be 12?"

"Nope!" Bylsma answers.

In all, the first period is a good period for the young Penguins.

"The next period is much more memorable," Byslma says.

It's early in that next period that the Penguins score first, the goal Byslma wanted so badly.

Red Wings defenseman Brad Stuart has possession of the puck behind Osgood and sends a pass up the ice that ricochets off the skate of Pittsburgh's Evgeni Malkin, right to Max Talbot. Talbot beats Osgood and the Penguins are on the board.

"One of the things we always felt like was an area we could do something—Detroit is a close support breakout," Bylsma says, going into coach mode. "They're always going to make a pass. Our sticks were very important, more so than being physical and trying to kill them. This was one of those situations. We forecheck, we get a stick on a puck. We always know we can get an opportunity this way against the Red Wings. It turned into that for us."

Play continues and there's a shot of Bylsma behind the bench. He notes that he's wearing his lucky tie, the one his son brought down for him from Wilkes-Barre for his first game in Philadelphia. The Penguins won and Bylsma pulled it back out for the big games.

He's sure he wore it for Game 7 against the Washington Capitals in the second round of the playoffs that spring. That was the epic series in which Sidney Crosby and Alex Ovechkin went toe-to-toe for the first time, including the game in which both had hat tricks. It concluded in one of the most anticlimatic wins in NHL postseason history, with the Penguins steamrolling the Capitals 6–2 in Washington for a Game 7 win.

"We took off after that," Cooke said of beating the Capitals. "We celebrated like idiots in the dressing room. We felt like that could have been the Stanley Cup Final. That was an unbelievable series."

After that win in Washington, the players were packing up their gear when Cooke heard music coming from the coaches' room attached to where the players were packing.

It was Bylsma and the Penguins coaching staff singing Bon Jovi's "Living on a Prayer."

It's one of those moments that remained with the players for years.

"You can hear them screaming, 'Whooaaaa, ohhhhh, we're halfway there!'" Cooke said. "Dan was raw. He was enjoying every minute of it."

Bylsma has a question he asks during big moments: "Who is going to wear the cape?" Going into Game 7 against Detroit, he might have wagered on Ruslan Fedotenko being the hero. Fedotenko had the track record, scoring two monumental goals for the Tampa Bay Lightning in their 2004 Stanley Cup clincher against the Calgary Flames.

Another safe bet might have been Sidney Crosby, one of the best to ever play the game and a player who was entering his prime as an NHL superstar.

That notion ends with 14:35 remaining in the second period when Red Wings forward Johan Franzen drives Crosby into the boards near the penalty boxes. It's clear Crosby is in pain immediately. It's a struggle for him to get back across the ice to the Penguins bench. He immediately heads down the tunnel for treatment.

A moment later, Pittsburgh's Hal Gill gets a penalty and the Red Wings go on the power play. It's as perilous of a 1–0 lead as you can possibly have in a hockey game.

"When Sidney Crosby gets hurt and tries to take a shift in the second period, he just can't go," said Tom Fitzgerald, a Penguins assistant coach on that team and the person charged with keeping tabs on Crosby's injury the rest of the game. "You're wondering, 'How are we going to do this?'"

For the players, the feeling was different. They checked to make sure the injury to Crosby wasn't anything career-threatening and then returned to the task at hand. That's how focused and locked in that group was in that moment.

"We believed we were so close, so we rallied," Fedotenko said. "Being a veteran who had already been through it, it's never one person. It's never one player."

Every few minutes, Fitzgerald would go down the bench and check with Crosby: "How are you doing? How does it feel?"

During a TV timeout, Crosby hopped over the boards and gave it a skate.

"There was no push," Fitzgerald said. "Nothing in him. Sid just felt that we had healthy bodies to carry us rather than going out on one leg."

In the moment, Bylsma didn't think the injury was particularly serious. Then he heard from the trainer that Crosby wouldn't be available the rest of the second period. Possibly more.

On the TV in front of us, the Penguins are playing on without Crosby, pretty effectively. As the second period winds down, I raise the question Bylsma was asked often in his tenure behind the Pittsburgh bench.

"What was it like to coach Sidney Crosby?"

He takes a sip of coffee and pauses before answering.

"Everyone says, 'What's it like to coach Sidney Crosby?' I don't know what they perceive the person to be but it's something like a god. You've dubbed him the best player in the game and now you're asking the question—what's it like to coach him? I don't really view him like that. He's no different than coaching any other player."

He isn't but he is.

When Bylsma was an assistant coach for Wilkes-Barre, he was in Penguins training camp helping Therrien organize practice. Bylsma was running a drill and looked up to see Crosby staring at him, listening intently. If it had been any other player, he wouldn't remember this moment. But it was Sid, and he does. Clearly.

"There's 87 staring," Bylsma says. "That was like, 'Oh my gosh.'"

So what stood out? Crosby's unquenching desire to get better. The best example Bylsma can think of is this: for a long time, Crosby didn't kill penalties for the Penguins. But he still attended every meeting for the Pittsburgh penalty kill.

"If you want to try to trick him or motivate him, indicate that he's not the best at something," Bylsma says.

Bylsma motions toward one of Dutchess' bones, and points at the couch across the room. If we invented a game where you had to bounce the bone once and get it to land on the couch, Bylsma explains, Crosby wouldn't leave the room until he mastered it.

The hardest thing about coaching Crosby is that people care about how you coach Crosby. It becomes a thing. Nobody asked him how he coached Mark Eaton during his tenure behind the bench.

There's an outside perception that is attached to coaching Sidney Crosby. We saw it years later when Crosby wasn't producing under Mike Johnston, Bylsma's replacement. People immediately wondered if Johnston was the right coach for Crosby. This isn't usually a consideration with other players.

I continue to talk about Crosby but I'm cut off. The game, and the Penguins' destiny, is about to change.

"Here it comes," Byslma says.

The Penguins are clinging to a one-goal lead. Their captain is hurt. It doesn't matter that Pittsburgh is outshooting and out-chancing the Red Wings at this point.

It's midway through the second period when Chris Kunitz wins a battle and chips the puck up to Max Talbot for a 2-on-1 with Tyler Kennedy against Niklas Kronwall.

Talbot buries the shot and the Penguins are up 2–0.

The moment sparks a thought. A picture. It's Bylsma's favorite picture and he wants to show it to me to make a point.

We stop the game and head down to the basement. Bylmsa is in the process of packing so there are moving boxes everywhere. He's not sure if the picture he wants is even down here. It could already be packed.

"I've got to have it somewhere," he says.

In the basement, there are 13 hockey sticks leaning against the wall—a couple of his own, a couple from Jarome Iginla, a Sidney Crosby stick, a Mario Lemieux stick. You could put a nice down payment on a house with the proceeds from selling these sticks.

There's a giant canvas photo on the wall, the classic post–Stanley Cup team photo, with players laying all around the Cup, each holding up one index finger. In the team photo, Bylsma is standing right behind Fleury, his goalie who came up so big during that run, with a giant smile on his face and a white championship hat on.

There's also a sign that once hung on a wall for the team that reminded the Penguins just exactly how they needed to play. It had the words "Team Identity" at the top with bullet points below them:

Fast/Speed

Gritty/Tough

Hunt

Preparation/Detailed

Tough to play against

Initiating

In other words, Ruslan Fedotenko hockey.

There's a shelf with a framed, autographed Kirk Gibson photo on it, next to a Detroit Tigers mini helmet signed by Gibson, one of Bylsma's childhood heroes. There are a few Pittsburgh bobble heads and a Sidney Crosby statue still in plastic nearby.

Bylsma continues working his way through the memorabilia, looking for the photo taken the moment Talbot scored that goal.

The picture he wants to show me is nowhere to be found. It's a picture of him on the bench after Talbot's goal.

"I think of it because the other day, I was watching college hockey and a team scored a similar goal and the coach is going apeshit on the bench. Trying to grab everybody and get them him back into order," he says.

Bylsma's reaction was the opposite.

Talbot scores and the players on the bench celebrate. Ruslan Fedotenko has a huge smile and is looking up at the scoreboard. Pascal Dupuis is smiling while watching his teammates celebrate on the ice.

Bylsma's arms are crossed, a reaction that looks more like the first row of Red Wings fans behind him than the players in front of him. The reaction was the result of conversations he had early on in his coaching career.

"I was informed that I was too animated," Bylsma says.

He doesn't say who told him the first time. When Todd Richards told him the second time, while he was an assistant in the AHL, he took it to heart.

"Your demeanor as a guy behind the bench rubs off on your team. I've seen many teams where the coach screams and yells at the referees and the team yells at referees. I've seen teams where the coach is a sarcastic son of a bitch and it rubs off on players."

We head back upstairs to watch the third period.

* * *

The visiting coaches' room at Joe Louis Arena is cramped. The cinder block walls are coated with layers and layers of paint left over from the Scotty Bowman era, when teams would arrive to a room filled with the fumes that come with fresh paint.

There were no paint fumes in this series but quarters were still tight.

Bylsma and his staff crammed into the coaches' room and the memory stills brings a smile to his face. During the second intermission of Game 7, the Penguins were 20 minutes away from winning a Stanley Cup and Bylsma remembers a very animated Mike Yeo taking over the meeting.

Bylsma stands up in his living room and does an imitation of his assistant coach pacing and giving out instructions.

"He gave me like 20 reminders. Like, 'We've got to get the puck deep. Make sure—in and out.' On and on and on. I'm like, 'Mike, please, take a deep breath. I got it.' Every time we get in that room, we laugh about it. He literally gave me 20 reminders."

When the clock hit 10 minutes left in the intermission, Byslma left the coaches' office to talk to the team. He shared some of the 20 reminders that Yeo rattled off but Bylsma also didn't want to overload the players.

When the Penguins opened up a 2–0 lead, he already saw his players naturally shifting into a more conservative mode.

Shift lengths were dropped considerably, some coming in around 25 seconds. All the reminders coaches give players about protecting leads, the players started doing automatically with so much on the line.

"Lines were getting jumbled up, we were rotating centermen through. We talked about making sure you're aware of who you are going with, who you're going for," Bylsma says.

During the intermission, Crosby received treatment from the medical staff. He still hadn't given up hope of playing and Bylsma made sure the lines of communication were open between Crosby and Fitzgerald.

If there was a faceoff in the offensive zone, Bylsma decided he'd give Sid a shift.

On the television, Phil Pritchard, the keeper of the Stanley Cup, is pulling the trophy out of its case and placing it onto a table. Wearing his white gloves, he takes a white cloth and starts polishing it.

Exactly 9:35 into the third period, Sidney Crosby re-enters the game for the first time in the final period. He takes the faceoff against Pavel Datsyuk and wins it.

We watch.

"Here's where you send out Sid in the offensive zone," I say.

"It's really the only chance I had."

"So, it's 10 minutes into the third. Are you watching him or watching play?"

"I'm watching him."

"What were your impressions of that shift?"

"Honestly? I didn't think it was too bad. But again, I'm not going to talk to him here. I told him that. Or I should say, Fitzy told him that. I think Fitzy is talking to him right now. Fitzy is now telling me right now they had the conversation."

It didn't go well.

"He's done?" I ask.

"He's done."

"Nine minutes left."

A few minutes later, the Red Wings are buzzing in the Penguins zone.

The puck again finds its way to Detroit defenseman Nicklas Lidstrom, who sends it across the ice to Jonathan Ericsson, who rips a puck past Fleury.

In his living room, Bylsma lets out a whistle. It's a one-goal game again.

We're both quiet as the Joe Louis Arena goal horn sounds multiple times.

"It doesn't change a whole lot. Obviously, you're like 'Whoops.' It makes it more interesting but it doesn't change a lot. We've got to keep playing," Bylsma says.

The intensity of the game grabs us both. A couple of minutes go by and nothing is said. We're watching as though we don't know the outcome. The players on the ice are playing it somewhat safe, exactly what you'd expect in a one-goal game with the Stanley Cup on the line. Nobody wants to make a mistake.

"I feel like we're watching a Devils game right now," Bylsma jokes, invoking New Jersey's conservative scheme from the 1990s. "Everyone is playing position."

Bylsma remembers being concerned about faceoffs. Crosby, his best guy in the faceoff circle, was hurt. Craig Adams, Jordan Staal, and Evgeni Malkin were all under 50 percent. It's one real edge the Red Wings had in this game, and at this point Bylsma admits he was thinking about what he'd do if the Red Wings tied it up, how he'd get the players' spirits back up after blowing a two-goal lead.

The Joe Louis Arena crowd is now standing. With less than three minutes to go in the game, there comes a moment I'd long forgotten about, even though I was watching from the press box.

Red Wings forward Dan Cleary sends the puck up to Niklas Kronwall at the right point, who quickly skates in for a better angle and fires a wrister. It beats Fleury and the crowd momentarily goes crazy. Everyone thought the game was tied.

But the puck deflected off Jordan Staal, over Fleury's right shoulder, and it hit the crossbar. The fate of so many people changed thanks to the deflection of the puck. It's amazing how often this happens in hockey, in these moments.

Watching it play out on television, Bylsma lets out another whistle.

"Wow. It's amazing how close…" I start.

"Life is," he finishes.

"Opinions are formed on people, on coaches, on players. On that shot."

"On that shot."

Much later, I had a conversation with Andy Murray that showed just how close life came to being dramatically different for Bylsma.

Listening to Murray talk, I heard echoes of Bylsma's theories and strategies. One of the things Murray believes strongly in is the notion of having multiple interests. It's something he stresses to the players he's now coaching at Western Michigan University. He wants them to focus on academics so they're prepared when their hockey careers are finished.

He saw that parallel interest in Bylsma. Murray remembers telling Bylsma to start thinking like a coach as his playing career was winding down. Bylsma took down everything in a notebook. He was constantly preparing for what was coming next.

"He wasn't going to be a guy who was going to be done playing at 36 and not have something to do," Murray said. "He was preparing all the way through."

It reminded Murray of a story. He asked me if Bylsma mentioned the interview at Shattuck–St. Mary's School in Minnesota.

The boarding school that was once the home of guys like Sidney Crosby and Jonathan Toews was looking for an assistant coach for the bantam team. Bylsma was looking to break into coaching shortly after his playing career was over.

Murray had a home there and helped arrange an interview for Bylsma. He picked him up at the airport in Minneapolis and they talked about how Bylsma would be able to get his kids into the school, sketching out what his future might be like as a coach at the school.

Bylsma met with school officials but he didn't get the job. They wanted someone with more experience. Shortly after that, he was hired to work in the Penguins organization.

It was the life equivalent of a shot ringing off the crossbar. If Bylsma had gotten that job, his life today might look very different.

But that's not even the point Murray wanted to make. His point was that Bylsma got an opportunity early on and all his work, his parallel preparation, meant he was able to take advantage.

"It's being ready when that time comes," Murray said. "He was ready."

* * *

There's 1:17 remaining in Game 7 and the Red Wings call a timeout. The telecast cuts to Penguins GM Ray Shero watching from the press box with an intense look on his face.

Pierre McGuire pipes in from between the benches:

"His father, Fred, won two Stanley Cups with the Philadelphia Flyers. Ray Shero had to make the courageous effort to bring in Danny Bylsma. That was not an easy thing to do. He did it."

The Red Wings pull goalie Chris Osgood and go on the attack. They have less than one minute to try and tie this game to win their second consecutive Stanley Cup.

Detroit wins a faceoff and Marian Hossa gets a decent look but the puck ends up under a pile behind Fleury. A whistle blows and there's one last faceoff left with 6.5 seconds remaining. On the telecast, NBC's Eddie Olczyk suggests that Bylsma should use his timeout.

"No," Byslma answers while listening. "I had my players on the ice. They knew what they were going to do. A timeout gives [Detroit] a chance. We're not tired. I have my faceoff guy. They know what they're supposed to do."

Henrik Zetterberg wins the faceoff and the puck ends up on the right point, where Brian Rafalski fires it into a mass of bodies in front of Fleury.

Two seconds left.

The puck kicks out to Nicklas Lidstrom, who has a wide-open net.

"I just know there's enough time," Byslma says, watching it unfold. "I don't know what happens after that."

Fleury pushes over and makes the save of a lifetime. Penguins forward Craig Adams jumps on the loose puck.

I called Adams to get his perspective of that moment. He explained that it was his job to be in the shooting lane in front of Lidstrom, but when the shot was blocked, he thought the Penguins had possession, so he collapsed toward the middle.

"Basically, the winger's job if you're collapsing to the middle, no matter how deep you get, if you're 60 feet away from the defenseman, you're between him and the net," he said. "Because I thought we had the puck, I'd drifted over six or seven feet to the left. A shot goes on [Fleury],

In a span of six months, Bylsma went from being the head coach of the Wilkes-Barre/Scranton Penguins to Stanley Cup champion. (AP Images)

a rebound goes to Lidstrom out wide. Instead of going directly out at him, I'm going sideways. Everything is happening in slow motion. Everyone knows what is going to happen. He's going to get it and shoot it."

Lidstrom glides in and fires a shot at Fleury.

"I end up diving head-first, which is not a great way to block a shot in most circumstances," Adams said. "In that situation, I'm praying for it to hit me in the face. I dive head-first and wasn't able to get in the shooting lane. Thankfully, Flower also dove head-first and made a great save. Because I dove head-first, the puck just came right to me when I was on my stomach, which was pretty lucky."

The voices on the telecast go quiet. So does the Joe Louis Arena crowd. All you hear are the screams and yelps of the Penguins jumping and celebrating as they pile around each other.

There's a shot of Hossa on the Red Wings bench with a blank look on his face. For the second consecutive year, he's on the wrong end in this moment. He squirts water into his mouth and then looks down.

The Penguins continue celebrating. Hugging. Then, Doc Emrick sums it up:

"A coaching change with the team in 10th place in mid-February. Eighteen wins in 26 games to finish the season. They went from 10th place out of the playoffs to fourth. And then in the postseason, 16 wins out of 24. Knocking out the defending champions."

The handshake line begins and there's a shot of Crosby going over to Bylsma to give him a hug rather than joining the line immediately. Crosby then gives Mike Yeo a hug as his teammates work their way through the line. It was a decision by Crosby that people in Detroit are still upset about, that he didn't get in the handshake line quickly enough. By the time Crosby jumps in the handshake line, some of the Red Wings have already left the ice.

Crosby shakes hands with Mike Babcock, who praises the young captain.

"You played great," Babcock said to Crosby. "That's great leadership by you."

There's a shot of Bylsma shaking hands with the Red Wings players, his hair messed up amidst the celebration.

"Someone tell me about my hair, for God's sake," Bylsma says as his image flashes on the screen.

We wait for a shot of him and Babcock, his former coach in Anaheim, a guy he credits as a major influence, to shake hands. It never comes.

"We might not have shook hands. I might have gotten pulled out," Bylsma says. "I remember we met under the stands the following year. I think that was the first time I talked to him after that."

"What was that meeting like?"

"Normally, we talked in the summertime. We didn't that summer. When we got there, he got word over and we met before the game and chatted. There wasn't a huge, you know, significance other than—I think when you win, you accept graciously…"

He doesn't finish. Evgeni Malkin wins the Conn Smythe and a shot of him accepting the trophy is on the screen.

NHL commissioner Gary Bettman grabs the microphone with the Stanley Cup behind him on a table. As Bettman speaks, Bylsma reflects on just how difficult it is to get to that moment.

"People don't understand how hard it is to win the Stanley Cup playoffs," he says. "As a player, I barely even sniffed a chance to compete for it, let alone when I did, you go through four rounds and then you lose in the Final, as I did. That was my only sniff. As a coach, yeah, we had a good team, good players, but it doesn't mean anything. So many people get hurt, survive and play, and get injured…"

Crosby grabs the Cup, gives it a kiss, and starts skating around with it. Then he hands it to Bill Guerin.

The celebration continues.

Players, friends, and family jammed into a visitors' dressing room at Joe Louis Arena in a party that lasted until 2:00 AM. The plane ride back to Pittsburgh went by in a blink.

The players and coaching staff arrived at the airport and there were limousines waiting for them, moving the party directly to Mario Lemieux's house.

When Bylsma got the job in Pittsburgh, his brother Scott bought two cigars for Dan. The first was to be smoked when the Penguins made the playoffs. Scott had one back home, and they enjoyed it together over the phone.

The second cigar was for when Dan won the Stanley Cup. That one was sparked at Lemieux's house the night before the Stanley Cup parade. Dan isn't the only Bylsma who thinks positively.

But before the party got to that point, while the players celebrated like crazy in the cramped Joe Louis Arena dressing room on the night they first raised the Stanley Cup, GM Ray Shero quietly walked out by himself to the Penguins bench. The Red Wings championship banners were hanging above him. He was surrounded by empty red seats.

That's where it all started to set in for the GM. The incredible rise from outside the playoffs to Stanley Cup champs. They quieted that rink against one of the great teams of their era.

Two minutes later, Bylsma walked out of the celebrating dressing room and stood next to Shero on the bench.

They remained in silence for a moment before a thought popped into Shero's head.

"Our interview was 10 minutes before I hired you," Shero said.

"Yeah," Bylsma answered.

"Let me ask you a question."

Shero and Bylsma are both Americans. If you're coaching players eight years old and under, you need to at least be certified Level 1 by USA Hockey. If you're taking a group of 14-year-olds to a national tournament, you have to be Level 4 certified.

"Do you have a coaching certificate through USA Hockey?"

"Yeah," Bylsma answered, and then paused. "I'm a Level 3."

Shero shook his head and laughed. Then they went back to join the celebration with the players in the dressing room.

CHAPTER 2

RON WILSON

Gold Medal Game of the 2010 Winter Olympics

I was on a plane that felt way too small, headed to Hilton Head, South Carolina, to see Ron Wilson, former coach of the Anaheim Ducks, Washington Capitals, San Jose Sharks, and Toronto Maple Leafs.

The ride was noisy and turbulent enough to make my stomach drop, and I'm a person who actually likes to fly. The woman next to me was leaning forward and hugging the seat in front of her. We were sitting in the ninth and final row. A flight attendant brought her some water to wash down a Xanax. I'm not convinced it ever kicked in.

There was a young couple in front of us, and the girl had pulled her hoodie tight around her face. Later, she and her boyfriend took selfies of their scared faces during a bouncy descent into Hilton Head.

I had put on my headphones to help drown out the lady next to me, who was giving her fellow passengers a play by play of each turbulent bounce.

It was around that time that I started thinking, "Ron Wilson had better make it worth it."

We'd agreed to sit down and watch the 2010 Winter Olympic gold medal game against Canada. Wilson was the only coach I asked to sit down and relive a loss. I'm grateful he agreed.

Wilson moved to South Carolina years ago when his daughter was attending college there, lured by in-state tuition. The golf courses didn't hurt either.

We agreed to meet at his home at noon on a mid-February Friday that was just sunny and warm enough to make me feel guilty about keeping him off the golf course surrounding his home.

On the way over, I called a friend who has known Wilson for years. Frank Provenzano was the assistant GM in Washington when Wilson was the coach of the Capitals. He was there when the Capitals advanced to the Stanley Cup Final in 1998.

I explained that I was en route to Wilson's house and asked him for any last-second questions that might get the coach going.

"Ask him what it was like to get a call from President Clinton after losing in the Stanley Cup Final," Frank answered.

It's one of the great practical jokes I've heard because it took guts to pull off so quickly after the Red Wings had swept the Capitals. Frank, who does great impressions for a former hockey executive, played the role of Clinton, and the call came into the coaches' office after Wilson and the Capitals' season had just ended. The Red Wings were still celebrating their Stanley Cup win.

I laughed at Frank's suggestion and told him I had every intention of asking that question.

Then our conversation shifted to Wilson's legacy. He never did win a Stanley Cup; that series was the closest he came. His biggest successes came internationally, where he won the 1996 World Cup, expertly guiding the Americans to the championship. He was just as effective in the 2010 Olympics, where he took a team nobody thought would finish with a medal to within an overtime goal of beating Canada for Olympic gold on its home soil.

He did it by instilling his swagger and confidence on a young group of Americans.

"He was really relaxed," said defenseman Ryan Suter when we chatted about Wilson in the lobby of the Wild's team hotel during a trip to Columbus. "He was so calm, so mellow. He had a very good presence."

In all, Wilson earned 648 wins as an NHL coach, No. 10 on the all-time list at the time of our chat. He's the only American coach to win medals in four different international tournaments—the World Cup, Olympics, World Championships, and World Junior Championship.

"What other American coach has a stronger résumé than Ron's in terms of winning? Not many," Frank said during our phone conversation on my drive over.

"He was born in Windsor, wasn't he?" I asked, the only flaw in Wilson's red-white-and-blue legacy.

"Yeah, technically he's Canadian."

"We claim him in America."

"He's got a burr in his ass over Hockey Canada. Poke that. He's all about USA Hockey."

Wilson lives in a beautiful tan colonial in a gated community about 20 minutes away from the Hilton Head beaches.

There's a small rock laying on the ground next to his "W" welcome mat with the words A LITTLE PIECE OF HEAVEN engraved on it. He can step off the back porch and golf. In February. Yeah, heaven.

I knock on the door and wait a beat.

This is always the moment of truth. I had spent months arranging these meetings, booking travel, finding a day that would work for everyone, and then when you knock on the door there's a possibility the guy who opens it completely forgot about it. For a second or two, that's my concern—I'm already figuring out flights in my head to extend the trip if I have to. This is how my mind operates, in the four seconds it takes for Wilson to answer.

He opens the door, with a smile and extended hand. He's wearing khaki pants, a white USA Hockey T-shirt, and a navy USA Hockey jacket.

"Nice to see you. We've got some nice weather today," he says.

"It's awesome out. I almost forgot what this is like."

Michigan winters, in my defense, are very long.

"It's not like this all the time. We've had ups and downs. It's been as cold as 40 degrees, a couple days ago. That's cold for me."

He leads me down a hallway, past a bedroom on the right with bunk beds for his grandkids. The kitchen is on the left, and a beautiful black player piano is straight ahead.

Instead of sheet music, there are CDs lying across the front of the piano, with a John Denver disc in the middle.

There are really interesting things everywhere you look, including a rather large telescope facing one of the windows and binoculars sitting on the table behind it.

The centerpiece of the room is a coffee table that is itself a piece of art. The legs appear to be small tree stumps and the top is the carving of three board games—a Monopoly board in the center, with chess and backgammon boards on either side.

Sitting on a glass table next to the couch is a black Bible with Wilson's name engraved on the front, right below a Toronto Maple Leafs logo.

The television is sitting on a built-in wooden shelving unit, surrounded by family photos and a few books. The books, like the game board table and telescope nearby, suggest that the occupant of the house is an adult who still has some little kid in him. Or at least someone with grandkids.

There's a book titled *Hallowed Ground*, on the best places in the world to golf. There's another that is a history of USA Hockey, written by Kevin Allen. Then there's *Trains* and *The Art of Walt Disney* and *The Ultimate Encyclopedia of Knots and Ropework*.

Hanging on the wall is a framed picture of a tiger in the snow, a gift from the Vancouver Canucks in 1997.

I'm not so concerned about getting the game and my laptop hooked up. Wilson has always embraced technology. I'm confident he's a guy who can work his way around a computer network. My suspicions are confirmed when I ask about wireless networks and there are two waiting to go.

I click on the one named "Ronald Wilson's network" and it occurs to me that I wouldn't have the slightest clue how to rename a network.

He sits down on a brown leather couch next to me, in front of the television that will soon be playing scenes from 2010.

I don't mess around. We're breaking the ice with humor because that's how Wilson has always coached. He's a guy who uses sarcasm, sometimes biting, as a way to get his message across.

He did it with the Americans he coached in the 2010 Olympics. If they were expecting an intense coach—and some were—they got something else.

"He was very, very approachable, which I did not expect," said forward Bobby Ryan. "I found the most interesting thing is he hung in the players lounge, and he kind of just was around. You got to trade stories with him. It was pretty cool. I really enjoyed my experience with him."

Not exactly Wilson's reputation.

"[Phil] Kessel was like, 'I've never seen him like this,'" Ryan said, laughing. "He was definitely different."

With that in mind, I begin our session with the Clinton impression story. I have to hear his version of the post–Stanley Cup prank, partially to see if Frank is telling the truth.

I let him know that I chatted with Frank on the drive over to his house that morning.

Wilson starts laughing. Really hard.

"He got me on that one," he says.

Wilson starts sharing the details of the practical joke.

It was June 16, 1998, and the Red Wings had just swept the Capitals in the Stanley Cup Final with a convincing 4–1 win at the MCI Center. It was a gutsy time to pull off a practical joke, but really, when is there a better time?

In on the joke, the Capitals PR guy told Wilson that President Bill Clinton would be calling both coaches after the game, starting with Scotty

Ron Wilson is proud of his connection to USA Hockey, and it shows.

Bowman. Wilson was told that if the phone in his office rang after the game, it was Clinton.

Wilson watched from the home bench while the Red Wings celebrated the Stanley Cup win. He watched the presentation of the trophy. When he'd had enough, he walked to his office.

"Sure as shit, that phone rang," Wilson says. "I pick it up and someone on the line says, 'This is the White House operator, stay on the line please, the next voice you hear will be President Bill Clinton.'"

Only it was not Bill Clinton. It was Frank Provenzano. And that wasn't the White House operator. It was another member of the Capitals PR staff.

At the time, the Capitals coaching and management staff had a remote-control fart machine they used on unsuspecting people walking down the hallway of the Capitals offices. This turned out to be an important part of this story.

"He finally comes on," Wilson says. "He has that accent—'Hello, Coach Wilson, this is Bill Clinton.' It doesn't sound like Bill Clinton to me, but what am I supposed to say? He's going, 'Coach, we're really proud of you. It's too bad you lost.' Blah, blah, blah. He finally goes, 'There's only one other thing I want to say to you, Coach Wilson.'"

The last thing Wilson heard from the other end of the line was a long, loud fart.

"I go, 'Thank you, Mr. President.'"

Wilson loves the story. There aren't many NHL coaches who would take a joke like that with such grace and humor right after a season-ending loss, let alone retell it with a laugh and clear admiration for the execution.

A sense of humor is a big part of Wilson's ability to communicate with his staff and his players.

"In order to be myself, I have to be funny," he says. "That was part of it. I didn't want to just kill my sense of humor when I coached. I wanted the players to see I could bust balls with anybody. That was one of the things I did a lot. I made humor one of the things I used with the team."

That was part of the strategy with the young American team that went to Vancouver in 2010. Wilson's approachability and sense of humor would help ease the pressure. Wilson and GM Brian Burke also made every attempt to place the pressure on the shoulders of the Canadians and not the Americans.

Burke was confident he had built a team capable of winning gold, but you never would have known it by the public declarations from everyone involved.

"We decided, hey, let's not duck this underdog thing," Burke said. "My public statements were, 'Why are we even in this tournament? Why did we bother to come? Nobody is giving us the chance.' I think the team fed off that. We talked to the team and said, 'Look, we're going to play this card publicly but we don't believe it at all.'"

"We thought the team could be pretty good, and we were," Wilson says.

This is where he first mentions Phil Kessel, a player with whom he had a contentious relationship during their time together in Toronto.

"I didn't think Phil played well at all," Wilson says. "I don't know how much he should have been on the team. I don't know how much I was really getting along with him going into that Olympics. Phil was on my shit list, big time. I was giving him a hard time in Toronto. He played a fairly big role on our team but not [the U.S. team.]. He was on our third line and that's where he should be—on the third or fourth line. He didn't really compete that hard."

Team USA assistant Scott Gordon remembers pulling Kessel aside for a moment during the Olympics to try and explain Wilson's frustrations with him.

"I just said to Phil, 'He just wants you to work,'" Gordon said. "'He wants you to work and compete. These are high stakes. You have to give a little more than you're giving.'"

A few months after I sat down with Wilson, Kessel would win a Stanley Cup with the Pittsburgh Penguins. He'd win it on one of the best third lines in hockey.

From memory, Wilson starts talking about the line combinations he kicked around in Vancouver. He loved Joe Pavelski and said there was some disagreement from management about whether or not he should be on the team. Wilson fought for him.

"He's not an elegant skater. He really struggles to skate," Wilson says. "He knows how to do everything well, though. You can put him in any situation and he won't let you down."

Wilson initially wanted Paul Stastny to play on a line with Patrick Kane but saw right away that it wasn't going to work out. Both players liked to have the puck.

"Patrick Kane wants the puck all the time. He's a center playing the wing," he says. "The first game we had them together there was no chemistry at all."

The chemistry instead developed between Ryan Kesler and Kane.

I grab my laptop and pull up a copy of the roster. He starts looking at the names and offering thoughts on each guy as he goes down the list.

He loved Ryan Whitney. Great guy.

He thought Brooks Orpik played great in the tournament. Same with Jack Johnson and Erik Johnson.

He remembered a healthy debate among the coaches about whether or not to include Chris Drury and Ryan Callahan on the roster.

"They were warriors, Callahan and Drury. I couldn't ask for more. Any big shift we needed, I'd put those two on the ice with David Backes. Backes is a warrior, too."

He loved Dustin Brown.

"Getting Dustin Brown to check isn't a problem. Trying to keep him out of the penalty box, that's a problem. He's really mean and really strong."

Wilson takes a closer look at the roster on the screen. It's like he's thinking about some of these guys for the first time in years.

"Patrick Kane was unbelievable. So was Zach Parise. Bobby Ryan played well, too."

I take one more crack at getting into the Phil Kessel debate before hitting play on the game.

"Did you ever have a 'come to Jesus' meeting with Phil before the Olympics to clear the air?" I ask.

"You never have a 'come to Jesus' meeting with Phil. He's impossible to talk to."

I hit play and the introductory music begins. This is the same video I'd later use to watch the same game with Wilson's counterpart in this one, Team Canada coach Mike Babcock. There are no commentators on this recording; it's just a raw video feed, which is fascinating because there are times we can hear the voices of the players on the ice.

"Have you watched this game since that day?" I ask.

"No. I actually haven't."

Not that I blame him. I'm half surprised he agreed to watch it again in the first place.

Until this game, everything had gone right for the Americans in the 2010 Winter Olympics. They beat Canada early in the tournament in a game that announced their presence. They hadn't lost a game until this one.

Mike Babcock flashes on the screen. Then there's Wilson.

"You don't look too nervous," I say.

"Believe me, I'm nervous. Obviously we beat them once already. I know, chances are, it's our turn to lose."

There's a shot of the fans and it's a mass of red-and-white jerseys, draped in Canadian flags, with only the occasional American fan to break the sea of red.

Team Canada had nearly the entire building in its corner, aside from actor Vince Vaughn, shown in his red, white, and blue. Fans in Canada had been waiting for this moment for a long time.

This is where Burke and Wilson's strategy to make this game bigger than the players on the ice helped provide focus.

At the U.S. orientation camp in Chicago months earlier, USA Hockey brought in wounded warriors from the U.S. military to tell their stories and make a connection with the players.

One of those veterans was Michael Thornton, a Navy SEAL who earned the Congressional Medal of Honor for his bravery and service in Vietnam.

Thornton's story stuck with Wilson.

"They had landed in a place somewhere in Vietnam. They thought they were in U.S. territory," Wilson says, telling Thornton's story while pausing occasionally to watch the action on the screen. "They landed in what they thought was an abandoned area and it was loaded with Viet Cong soldiers. It was just hell to pay. They were getting shot at and in the end, Mike ended up getting shot in the ass. Just like Forrest Gump did in that scene in the movie. It was just like it. He said to our guys, 'Trust me, you get shot in the ass, you don't think it hurts. It fucking kills.'"

Another soldier who spoke to the players was the commander of an armored vehicle that got trapped on a bridge and had a grenade dropped into it. Somehow he survived but his leg was shattered. He managed to get out and shoot the guy who dropped the grenade in the vehicle. Then he passed out, woke up in a hospital in Germany, and eventually had 20 or 30 surgeries on his leg before he finally told doctors to cut it off. Hearing these stories made playing hockey against Chris Pronger seem a little bit more manageable.

Suddenly, these American hockey players weren't just playing for each other or hockey fans. They were playing for the soldiers they had connected with.

"It was unbelievable. It was the best thing we did for the team," Wilson says. "We had a player adopt each guy, and they had cards, almost like hockey cards, of the soldiers."

The players also had personal items from the soldiers to bring to Vancouver.

"It could be anything. Lucky T-shirt. Lucky underwear. They couldn't believe they had all this stuff," Wilson says. "Most of these guys had some serious injuries. It was really unbelievable."

During the Olympics, those mementos from the soldiers were in the Americans' dressing room, a constant reminder to the players that they were playing for something much bigger than themselves.

"You realize that what you are playing for is much more than just us guys in the room. It put it in perspective what kind of impact us doing well in the tournament or trying to win the tournament, how it can affect so many different people," Team USA forward Ryan Callahan said. "The other thing is it showed just how much passion they had for protecting our country. They put their lives on the line and it showed us we have to have the same passion."

Callahan connected with a soldier who gave him a patch ripped off the vest he had worn in combat. There was a letter telling his story that came with it.

"It's pretty incredible what they go through and what they do and really don't get enough recognition," Callahan said. "We're playing a game and the spotlight is on us. The media is on us. It almost doesn't seem right. It gives you extra motivation."

Not that they needed any additional motivation at this point in the gold medal game. Wilson is sitting on the couch, the grandfather clock near him occasionally gonging the advancement of time, watching the game with the intensity of someone who hasn't seen it in years.

The conversation gets quiet because he's really into it now. I try to spark it a little bit as the first period unfolds.

"Are you satisfied at this point with how play is going?"

"Oh yeah."

Babcock is shown on the screen.

"What's the challenge of coaching against Babcock?"

"I don't think there's any challenge there. He's like any other coach. I didn't think he outcoached me. Their team won in overtime on a little bit of a flukey goal."

Another long silence.

Jonathan Toews scores. It's 1–0 Canada.

"It's no big deal," Wilson says, now very much into the game. "They scored a goal. Stay calm."

It's as though he's back coaching the players on the screen in front of him.

"Stay calm," he repeats.

Coaches learn a lot about their teams in times of adversity. Over the course of a long season, most coaches don't mind the occasional rough patch. It's an opportunity to see how players respond to a challenge, which ones dig in and which ones check out.

Already in this game, Wilson had a sense of who came to play in the biggest game and who couldn't handle it.

"I thought all our guys competed hard," he says. "We didn't have any weak links on our team. In this game, I remember one of our defensemen wasn't ready. By the third period, I had him firmly on the pine."

"What do you mean, he 'wasn't ready'?"

"He just didn't make a lot of good decisions with the puck."

Wilson hasn't mentioned the defenseman by name but we're talking about Ryan Whitney. It was a Corey Perry goal that ultimately did him in.

"I figured, and understandably [because] I messed up on the Perry goal, I wouldn't be out there again," Whitney said when we chatted about it later.

"When he played, I thought he was too nervous," Wilson says. "Or at least, I was too nervous. Every time he had the puck, I was like, 'Holy fuck.'"

Wilson did appreciate Whitney's transformation into a positive force on the bench. Whitney knew he wasn't playing much, but during television timeouts, he'd take a twirl on the ice, shouting over to the bench to let them know he was ready. He constantly encouraged teammates.

"He was really good about that," Wilson says.

So, at this point in the game, Wilson was figuring out the players he was going to lean on. It was apparent that a young Patrick Kane was absolutely thriving in that environment. Kane was as good as anyone on the ice in this game—on either side.

"I was never nervous when Patrick Kane was on the ice," Wilson says. "I can tell you that."

The second period kicks in and the pace to the game is incredible. About five minutes into the period, just moments after Team USA successfully killed a Canadian power play, Team Canada forward Eric Staal is called for interference. At that moment, the American power play is connecting at a strong rate of 28.6 percent.

Wilson and I watch as Canadian goalie Roberto Luongo casually turns aside a Brian Rafalski shot, followed immediately by Canada clearing the puck.

The Americans regroup. Parise skates the puck in deep but is knocked to the ice by Chris Pronger. The Canadians clear again.

There's 40 seconds left in the power play.

Jack Johnson carries it into the offensive zone, attempts a pass that is intercepted. The Canadians clear again.

This is repeated again and again throughout the American power play until it expires and the crowd is as loud as it's been since Toews opened the scoring.

Not long after that, Corey Perry scores the goal that essentially ends Whitney's night. It's 2–0 Canada.

"Is that the last time Ryan Whitney sees the ice?" I ask.

"Basically."

"Things, at this point, aren't going great for you guys."

"Now, I'm a little worried. It's 2–0. It's basically halfway through the game."

The crowd is mockingly chanting American goalie Ryan Miller's name.

"I'm not panicking. Find a way. We just needed to keep shooting the puck," Wilson says. "I kept saying, 'We have to score one goal. That's all we have to do. Score one goal.'"

We continue watching. The pace is incredible, which makes for great entertainment, but not necessarily great conversation. We're both into it. We might as well have grabbed some popcorn.

Then comes a moment that highlights Wilson's frustration with Phil Kessel. Mike Richards flips a puck toward the middle of the ice in front of Ryan Miller. For a moment it sits there, free for the taking in the biggest game of most of these players' lives.

Kessel reaches out with his stick and gets there first. But Canada's Eric Staal arrives a moment later, looking to separate Kessel from the puck. In avoiding the hit, Kessel leaves the puck up for grabs. Staal fights through and works the puck to Richards, who then finds a streaking Sidney Crosby in the slot for a quality scoring chance. The puck sails wide of Miller but I can see Wilson's frustration with Kessel in that moment.

"There's Phil," Wilson says. "He bailed again."

The clock is ticking and it doesn't look good for the Americans. There's nine minutes left. Then eight. Then Ryan Kesler gets the puck with speed, shooting down the middle of the ice. He enters Canada's zone and slides the puck over to Patrick Kane. Kane fires a shot and Kesler gets a little bit of a stick on it, beating Luongo. Just like that, the Canadian lead is cut in half.

The goal horn sounds on Wilson's television. The replay cuts to Kesler.

"That's a nice goal. I forgot how well Patrick Kane played in this game," I say.

"He was the best player on the ice. For sure."

"So you're feeling better now?"

"Now, I'm definitely feeling better."

We start chatting about the path Wilson took to get to that moment. Wilson's first NHL coaching job was as an assistant under Pat Quinn in Vancouver. It was Quinn who taught him the importance of preparation and trusting those who work for you.

"He really trusted me," Wilson says of Quinn. "Pat was such a players coach. Everybody viewed him as someone who must be laying the heavy hand down in the room, but he wasn't at all."

Wilson used those lessons of preparation to impress Jack Ferreira in an interview that landed him the head coaching job of the Ducks back in 1993. Ferreira wasn't even going to interview Wilson, but another candidate got sick so he gave him a shot.

Wilson drove an hour and a half into Washington to meet with Ferreira.

"I had everything planned out. I had books on all the teams," Wilson says. "I had a booklet for him. I told him how important it was to do all the right travel. I understood the travel and how difficult it is."

The television in front of Wilson cuts to some of the celebrities attending the gold medal game in Vancouver. There's a shot of Gordie Howe. William Shatner. Vince Vaughn, again. All the things you don't see when coaching in the middle of the action.

"This is the first time I've seen this. I had no idea who was at this game," Wilson says.

In addition to the celebrities, almost two entire countries watched the game on television that night. As the game reached its peak, 34.8 million viewers in the United States were tuned in, making it the most-watched hockey game since the 1980 Miracle on Ice game against the Russians. In Canada, an estimated 80 percent of the country's population watched at least part of the game.

"You don't realize it at the time, but it's like the Super Bowl of hockey," Wilson says. "That's what we get to participate in. You look back on it, you realize how special it is."

The Americans continue pushing.

"All of a sudden we're playing a lot different. A lot freer," Wilson says.

The second period ends. The numbers flash up on the screen. Canada is up 2–1, holding a slight edge in shots on goal, 25–23. Both teams are 0-for-2 on the power play. The Americans hold a 20–18 edge in faceoffs.

Wilson's message to his team during the second intermission was simple: keep playing the way you did in that final stretch of the second.

"You have 20 minutes to tie it," Wilson remembers saying. "You don't have to go out there in the first five minutes and do something."

* * *

As highlights from the first two periods play on the television, I take the opportunity to start talking about Toronto. When Wilson was hired by the Maple Leafs in 2008, he was one of the game's most-respected coaches. He'd taken the Capitals to the Stanley Cup Final in 1998. As the

Wilson speaks to his 2010 USA Hockey team, one that would fall just short in the gold medal game against Canada. (AP Images)

coach in San Jose from 2002 to 2008, his Sharks teams were always in the running for a Stanley Cup.

After he left Toronto in 2012, he couldn't get another job in the NHL.

There's a widespread assumption that then-Leafs GM Brian Burke had something to do with Ron Wilson going to Toronto, since they were so close, but Wilson was actually hired before Burke had even arrived. Wilson says Toronto executive Cliff Fletcher was the driving force behind him becoming the head coach of the Maple Leafs.

When Fletcher first called Wilson, the coach said he wasn't interested and sounded sincere about it. Two weeks later, Fletcher called him back and convinced Wilson to make a trip to Toronto just to hear him out.

They spent a day together and Wilson asked what the job paid. Fletcher's answer came in at about half of what Wilson thought he deserved.

"I said, 'I made almost a million bucks last year in San Jose. I'm not taking a pay cut to come here,'" Wilson says.

Eventually, Fletcher said he could match his salary demands.

"I was like, 'Oh, fuck,'" Wilson says, laughing.

This all happened shortly after Wilson had been fired by the Sharks, a decision he's still unhappy about. When San Jose GM Doug Wilson gave him the news, he said he knew he'd be hired again immediately.

Wilson's prediction turned out to be true, but he concedes now he had no idea what he was getting into when he was hired in Toronto. The constant media attention was something he'd never experienced at that level.

"I thought I'd be able to handle it. I never had any problems before at all," he says. "It's just the sheer volume of it. You've always got three or four cameras there every day. You have seven, eight, 10 media members there every day. My mistake was I dealt with those guys every day. I didn't send my assistant coaches out there. I thought I could handle it myself. It got ridiculous after a while."

"Did you read it or is it just the questioning?" I ask.

"It's the questioning. I could anticipate what some of the questions would be. I would have someone lead off the questioning. It was our color guy on TV. He would always be the first one and he'd ask a softball question. I would try and get the rest of the questions to go along that line."

I laugh because I've seen this tactic at play in a media scrum.

"We're too smart for that Ron, c'mon."

"Oh, I know."

When I sat down with Mike Babcock a few months later, he shared his own strategies for dealing with the Toronto media. Both he and Wilson believe it's better for the coach to try and control the message.

Wilson's tactic was to plant questions. Babcock tries to steer the conversation right away.

"When I walk into a room with you guys, I always have a plan," Babcock said. "Especially if we played shitty."

Sometimes, Babcock admitted, he'll throw in a diversion.

After one loss during his first year in Toronto, he met with the media and immediately made a joke about one of the media members. TSN's Mark Masters had mentioned on Twitter how he left his wife in coach during a flight to take a seat in first class. Masters, naturally, took heat on social media for his lack of chivalry.

Babcock added to the heat at the outset of his press conference, starting it with his own question: "Who is the guy who left his wife in the cattle car?"

Nobody was talking about the Leafs' loss after that—just Masters' questionable life decisions.

"I got out of there before we talked about the Leafs," Babcock said.

"Are we that easily duped?" I asked.

"It's not duped. You guys are just looking for something to write. What I try to do is have a plan. When things are bad, I come in and say, 'Boom.' I tell you right away it was bad. I don't let you ask me. I tell you. I go right to it. So, I'm in control. Not you. And then I try not to put gas on the fire."

As we watch the game, I ask Wilson if he truly wanted the job in Toronto when it was presented to him or if his hesitancy was just an attempt to drive up the annual salary.

"I didn't really want the job at the time," he says. "Then it was a negotiating ploy. It was a smart one on my part. I didn't think I'd last in Toronto longer than two years."

"Based on the roster?"

"I just didn't think it was possible to win anything in Canada. The pressure was getting to feel ridiculous."

"Do you still feel that way?"

"Yeah. It's going to take a special team to win that plays in Canada."

I asked Babcock, who is currently right in the middle of trying to build one, if winning in Canada is even possible.

"You can," he answered. "Just watch."

* * *

There's now five minutes left in the third period as Babcock and Wilson go head to head on the screen in front of us. The Americans are starting to run out of time. At this point, Wilson says he's dividing ice time in his head to make sure he has the right guys on the ice in the final minute.

The goal was to get Zach Parise, Patrick Kane, and Ryan Kesler as much ice time at the end as possible.

With just over one minute to play, Wilson calls a timeout. Miller is on the bench for the extra attacker. Wilson has a dry-erase marker in one hand and a white board in the other. On the board are the numbers of the six players he wants on the ice. He puts Jamie Langenbrunner and Kesler in front of the net, Kane near the right circle, and Parise on the left. The numbers for Ryan Suter and Brian Rafalski are on the blue line with a black line drawn back and forth between them.

"I'm trying to get them lined up for a one-timer. I want Ryan Kesler right in front of the goalie," Wilson says.

In that arena that night, this was the point at which I remember members of the media on press row packing up their computers, fully convinced of a one-goal Canadian win.

Canada wins the draw and sends it down the ice. Wilson's plan during the timeout was immediately scrapped. There's another stoppage in play with just under a minute remaining and now Mike Babcock calls the timeout. Wilson remembers being surprised.

"I was like, 'Thank god.' I'd never call a timeout in that situation," he says.

The timeout allowed Wilson to get Joe Pavelski into the game to take the faceoff and gave Kane and Parise a breather so they could finish out the game.

Pavelski wins the draw but the Canadians clear the puck fairly quickly after that.

Now we're watching with the same intensity as two guys who have no idea how it's going to end. The final 20 seconds play out in front of us without a word. All you hear is the ambient sound of a nervous Canadian crowd cheering, accompanied by cowbells, the sound of sticks on pucks, and an American team frantic to tie it up, which Zach Parise does brilliantly by banging home a loose puck sent to the front of the goal by Kane.

I just start laughing the moment Parise scores. Years later, it still seems so unlikely that it would happen in those final moments, scored with 24.4 seconds left.

"I can't believe that," I say.

Wilson is laughing, too.

"That wasn't a designed play but I had the right guys. Pavelski and Kaner."

"I can't believe that," I say again. "So what do you say now to the guys at this point?"

"I said, 'Let's go win the game.'"

The final seconds tick away and it's off to overtime.

The Americans had quieted an entire country, at least momentarily. Wilson is shown on the screen. He calls referee Bill McCreary over to the American bench. You can actually hear him on the video asking about the rules in overtime.

"Is it 5-on-5 or 4-on-4?"

"4-on-4," McCreary answers.

Wilson confirms that's what the conversation was in front of us.

"We had no idea what was going on," he says. "We hadn't had one 4-on-4 in the tournament."

Wilson and Team USA assistant coaches John Tortorella and Scott Gordon got together during the intermission to determine how they were going to pair up the forwards for 4-on-4 action.

"We laid out the game plan, how we were going to forecheck and defend," Gordon said. "At that point, who knows if the players are even listening?"

The Americans went to the dressing room confident they were going to win. At this point, it felt like destiny. Ryan Whitney remembers making jokes about crushing the hopes of the entire host country. Team USA thought that the Canadian players might be tight in overtime. The pressure was all on them.

"It was, 'We got this,'" Suter said. "We had just scored."

"We thought we had just as good a chance as they did," Parise said.

Overtime starts. Wilson is into it again. He hasn't watched it since it happened and I kind of just want to let him watch.

It's quiet, although he manages to work in another shot at Phil Kessel when Kessel finishes up a shift.

"I can't imagine me having him out there again," he says.

Then it happens. Crosby is skating the puck along the wall. The puck hits referee Bill McCreary in the skate, something I didn't realize at the time but a detail nearly every American involved in the game brings up.

"The puck comes up the wall, hits the ref's skate. I remember the ref, too," Suter said in breaking down the play when we chatted a few weeks before my visit to Wilson's home.

In Wilson's living room, Crosby ends it, the goal we've all seen a million times. Crosby calls out to Jarome Iginla, takes the feed, and beats Miller. Crosby immediately throws his gloves into the air and the celebration begins in the corner.

I exhale. It all happened so quickly, the momentary confidence a fleeting emotion.

"I wasn't mentally prepared for that," I say.

"Run this one back a little bit," Wilson says.

I start to rewind it.

"Okay. There, it hits [McCreary's] skate right there. That's the only time really that Ryan Miller wasn't ready for the shot. He was getting ready to poke check. The guy surprised him."

"God, it happens so fast."

"So close. That's all you think of. You're so close."

• CHAPTER 3 •

MIKE BABCOCK

Gold Medal Game of the 2010 Winter Olympics

I can still remember exactly where I was when Mike Babcock announced he would become the head coach of the Toronto Maple Leafs.

I'd had enough conversations with him and the people around him to form an opinion about where he'd end up after his contract in Detroit ran out in 2015. I thought he'd stay with the Red Wings, where he'd coached since 2005 and a team he'd led to a Stanley Cup in 2008.

Knowing what I know now, his eventual decision seems so obvious.

When we spoke before the move, the conversations often circled back to the respect he had for the Red Wings organization. He had a great working relationship with GM Ken Holland. He respected and appreciated owner Mike Ilitch, who passed away in 2017.

Babcock and I spoke one afternoon while he was at the airport in Amsterdam on a layover en route to the World Championships that spring in Prague, Czech Republic.

"It's going to be relationship, plan, opportunity," he said, listing the factors he was weighing. "Then you have to go back to your wife and family."

He said his relationship with Holland and the Red Wings ownership was as good as it possibly could be.

"I sure wouldn't rule out Detroit," he concluded. "I'm in a process. I'm going to finish the process."

Later, one of his closest friends confirmed that was the same thing he was sharing with those close to him.

"I honestly don't believe he knew until the very end," said Mike Bean, who played hockey with Babcock at McGill University in Montreal. "He loved Detroit. Absolutely loved Detroit. He loved his relationship with the general manager. He had good friends, his kids had made good friends. They were in a good comfort zone."

Now, years later, I realize that, to Babcock, a comfort zone isn't necessarily a good thing. To him, greatness rarely emerges from within one's comfort zone.

I was standing in my bedroom at home, checking e-mail, when Babcock's comfort zone was blown to pieces.

An e-mail from my ESPN colleague and friend Pierre LeBrun announced the news. Babcock was going to coach the Maple Leafs, lured by an eight-year deal worth $50 million.

Babcock was the first coach I talked to about participating in this book, and I wondered how this career change would impact the plan.

I approached him once at Joe Louis Arena with a half-baked plan for a book, and he sent me out of his office tasked with coming up with a better one. He wrote down the names of the coaches he thought needed to be in the book to make it something worth doing.

The message wasn't explicit but it was understood: don't bother him until there was a clear vision of exactly what was needed from him.

So when I returned to his office a second time, we were ready to get serious.

He invited me in and we sat down at his desk on opposite sides.

He immediately started opening mail. Babcock is a multitasker, not a guy who sits and does one thing at a time. He's always moving. He ripped open a giant manila envelope sent by a fan and pulled out a glossy photo of him coaching during the Winter Classic. In the photo, Babcock is wearing a black fedora and what looks like a Red Wings varsity jacket. He pulled out a Sharpie and signed it.

We started talking about leadership, because ultimately, to him, that's what this book should be about. If Babcock's not teaching and you're not learning, he feels it's a waste of time.

I'm passionate about the topic, too. In fact, some of my favorite conversations are ones I've had with Babcock about leadership. We both read books on it. We talked about influences, and legendary Red Wings coach Scotty Bowman's influence on Babcock is clear. Bowman is a lifelong learner. He has to be better today than he was yesterday. The same is true of Babcock.

I mentioned how much I'd enjoyed a podcast called Startup, because it provided a behind-the-scenes look at building a business from the ground up.

He grabbed a pen and wrote it down. He does that anytime somebody makes a recommendation. Anybody. He wants to learn from every conversation he's having at every moment. It's all about growing as a leader.

"Leadership is a journey. My potential five years ago and my potential now are totally different," he said. "Leadership, to me, is a lifestyle. I don't believe any bullshitter ever motivated anybody. That's a thing of the past. You have to be transparent. You have to be authentic. It's not what you say, it's what you do. But it's every day. That's the hardest part of the job and the best part of the job."

It's a job he's passionate about, a profession he's passionate about. He cares deeply about fellow members of the coaching fraternity. He's proud that a growing number of his assistants are now head coaches. The Babcock coaching tree is full of branches and bearing more fruit than ever. In my mind, he's the best coach in the game.

So when I saw that he was headed to Toronto, panic set in. His life was about to change dramatically. Requests for his time were about to go through the roof. It's one thing to be the coach of the Red Wings, quite another to be the guy charged with turning around the franchise at the center of the Canadian hockey universe.

It would have been understandable if he asked to back out of watching a game with me. The coaches in these pages invested a lot of time—an entire morning or an afternoon to watch an old hockey game—often during the time of year where they finally get a breather from hockey.

Now, a guy central to the story had accepted a job with a franchise where access to him was going to be rationed out in small doses, usually contained to press conferences.

There was a reluctance to ask if he'd still do it, mostly because I was scared of the answer.

When he had committed to helping with this project, he shared the names and phone numbers of his close friends and influences in his life.

I needed to call these guys but I also knew if I started calling a bunch of his close friends, he would get wind of it.

So I took a deep breath and wrote him a text, telling him I was about to start calling his close friends, so if he got a bunch of texts from people saying a writer was calling them, it was for this book.

I hit send and waited.

My phone buzzed.

My probably long-winded and overly wordy text was met with a short response.

"All good," he responded.

All good.

It was a positive sign.

Even better was a follow-up conversation, pinning down an exact time for the viewing.

We settled it. Wednesday morning at 10:30 at his Michigan lake house. I would have gone anywhere in North America to do this interview. Turns out, he was 40 minutes away from where I was sitting.

* * *

I left early.

I had a copy of the 2010 Winter Olympic gold medal game loaded completely on my laptop. I even checked ahead to make sure he had a wireless network, lessons learned from the Dan Bylsma interview.

I was prepared. Everything was going great.

That is, until I was driving on I-96 toward Brighton and recognized a large white water tower, one I passed a million times on my way to East Lansing from Detroit as a college student at Michigan State University.

An alarm went off in my head. I'd blown right by the exit to Babcock's house.

I got off the highway, turned left onto an overpass, and started hauling the other direction. All of the cushion I'd left myself for a guy who expects promptness was gone.

I ended up on an unpaved road and I had no other choice but to trust the GPS, so I plowed on.

I turned left into what was supposed to be his driveway, and thankfully Babcock's summer home with a hint of blue that complements the lake behind it came into view.

The stress of finding the right place was gone when I saw a giant Ford pickup truck in front of the house and a hockey goal on the grass. There was also a large organic garden on the right next to bow-and-arrow targets. It was definitely Mike Babcock's place.

Babcock is on the phone when I arrive. He'd already been water skiing that morning and the two binders on his kitchen table suggested he'd also been working. One binder was for the Toronto Maple Leafs and the other was for Team Canada, playing in the World Cup of Hockey in a couple months. Babcock, of course, would win that tournament with Canada, as he always does during international tournaments.

His wife, Maureen, walks over to say hello while he talks on the phone.

I explain what I was there to do. We were going to watch the gold medal Olympic game together.

"Which one?" she asks.

Of course. He's got more than one.

I compliment their home, and very sincerely. It's beautiful inside. The view of the lake is even better.

"We had a home in Northville. When we went to Toronto we bought this as a lake place. It's worked out," she says. "It's a good, peaceful place around the city."

Entering Babcock's office, his desk is to the left, as is a large, flat-screen Apple monitor. The office is masculine, with dark wood shelving and paneling. The shelves are filled with trophies—some won in hockey, others killed in the wild. There are lots of books. There's a framed picture of a golden retriever.

In the middle of the wall is a large flat-screen television. This is where we'll watch the game.

"So, what are we doing?" Babcock asks.

"We're going to watch the Olympic game."

Again, I forget to specify which one. Maybe it's because to me, there's only one. I was at the 2010 gold medal game in Vancouver. As an American, it was the single best hockey event I've ever witnessed. The crowds were unreal. The hockey was played at the highest level I've ever witnessed. The games between Canada and the United States were tight, competitive, and had seemingly every real sports fan in both countries watching.

In the U.S., the 2010 gold medal game had an average viewership of 27.6 million people. If everyone who watched that game moved to Canada, you'd nearly double the population.

"Have you watched it since? How often do you watch it?" I ask.

The walls of Mike Babcock's home office are lined with reminders of an incredible career.

"I haven't watched it. I don't think. Which game?"

"2010."

"I haven't watched them."

Babcock takes another call. It's Maple Leafs GM Lou Lamoriello. I would tell you what the conversation centered around if I didn't think both Babcock and Lamoriello would kill me.

He hangs up. He's immediately ready to get going.

The start of the game is paused so we can talk about leadership philosophy. Before this meeting, Babcock mentioned the name of Pierre-Paul Allard, a man who has been influential on him and his coaching.

When they met about a decade ago, Allard was a top executive at a California technology company called Avaya. This is what makes

Babcock so unique among his coaching colleagues. So many of his current influences come from outside the game.

"I'm a thief," Babcock explains. "I steal from everybody. I read all the time. I'm trying to meet people all the time to learn."

Babcock met Allard while hunting sheep.

Now, I'm no hunting expert but I can't help but wonder how high the degree of difficulty is to hunt sheep.

"It's impossible. I'm talking those big horn things. It's a 10-day hike to the middle of nowhere and you're freezing your ass off," Babcock says. "I'm above the Arctic Circle and the wind was blowing 900 miles per hour."

The weather was so cold, they were forced to hang out in a cook tent playing cards for hours and hours.

"When you're 10 days in the same base camp, you get pretty close with people," Allard said when we chatted. "The first thing that hits you when you meet Mike is how inquisitive he is. He will ask you or anybody constant questions on what you think."

As Allard got to know Babcock and started watching him closely as a coach, he was struck by his intensity. He told Babcock that he was a much nicer person than he appeared to be on the bench. But Allard admired his temperament. He saw somebody who had a strategy in place and set out to execute it. There was no panic, no overreacting to the game or the referees. He saw that calm reflected in the teams he coached.

"The other thing that's really cool is he is very much a strategist. That's where we hit it off. I view myself the same way," Allard said. "My success in business has been driven by the capacity to execute to a strategy and hold fast, be patient, and execute."

The first time they met, Allard remembers the conversation moving to the Red Wings defense. Babcock was concerned about its strength and devised a plan that leaned even more on Pavel Datsyuk and the forwards in his system.

"Strategically, he's aligning his players, the speed and skill and matching them correctly, and then he executes to a plan," Allard said. "He's very methodical. He follows his game play and strategy."

During another conversation between the two, Allard used the phrase "change agent." In Silicon Valley, Allard found it beneficial to surround himself with change agents—people who constantly look to change elements of their business even before problems occur.

The phrase stuck with Babcock. It came up often during the conversations between the two. How does it work? How does it apply within the game of hockey? Who are the change agents around me?

It's an interesting question, because the hockey world isn't necessarily one that embraces change. Quite the opposite. Things are done in hockey because they've always been done that way. Change isn't just looked at as different, it's looked at as dangerous.

The hockey world is funny though, too. If someone takes a risk and does something differently, there's a race to copy him.

Babcock was looking outside of his sport to find the next thing to copy.

"He applied what he was hearing. He tried to bring people into the organization who would work through with the players how you adapt and change as you get older, as your skill sets change and the game changes," Allard said. "It was very cool how he would internalize these things we would apply to just a standard business and bring them into the world of hockey."

Babcock embraces change because he believes what works now isn't going to work tomorrow. This isn't true just in hockey. It's true in most occupations.

A few months before we sat down to watch the game, Babcock was a keynote speaker for a venture capitalist group. A group of CEOs came in and presented during the afternoon and Babcock was part of a team there to help tighten their pitches.

"These are brilliant guys with brilliant ideas and people are giving them feedback," Babcock said. "I got to be around them all day."

By the time it was his turn to speak, Babcock had changed his speech, applying everything he had learned that afternoon while sitting in on those sessions.

He does this stuff all the time.

"It gives you ideas that spur more ideas and spur thought," Babcock said. "You never know where you're getting your best idea. It could be from your rookie player, it could be from your power skating instructor, it could be from the guy who cooks breakfast. You have to be open-minded."

That's how you create change. You steal ideas from CEOs. You steal ideas from other coaches. You steal ideas from the person who serves up the coffee at Tim Hortons.

No matter what field they're from, Babcock enjoys being around people who are the best at what they do.

"The best of the best are so passionate about what they do, and that passion allows them to grind harder and longer than the next guy," he said. "That's the difference between good and great."

Babcock loves those who put in the work every day. On his teams, he demands it. While he was stealing ideas from Allard, this was a trait that Allard stole right back.

He admired how willing Babcock was to jettison players if they didn't possess the work ethic he thinks is necessary to achieve greatness.

During the roster selection for one of the Olympics, Allard asked him about specific players who were consistently left out of the Team Canada discussion. He didn't name names but these were superstars in the league, the best players on their individual teams.

There were two players in particular that Allard asked Babcock about.

"He said, 'These two guys, they could never make the team. They don't have a work ethic that's strong enough. They would never even play with the Red Wings,'" Allard recalled. "That's why a lot of players on the

Toronto Maple Leafs left right away. Their work ethic was not where a Mike Babcock would set it and there's no exceptions."

This is a philosophy Babcock shares with many CEOs. He knows that most of them have employees in their organization sucking the life out of it but many prefer to ignore the issue. It's a tough decision. There are lives at stake, families.

"As soon as you know they're in the way of progress, you move them," Babcock said. "Period. No matter what the cost."

I still haven't hit play on the 2010 Olympic gold medal game. It's sitting there frozen on the big screen.

There's one more thing I want to ask him about before diving into the game.

"Someone was telling me a story, I think it was Mike Bean," I begin.

Before I can get to the story, Babcock takes the conversation in another direction. Bean is one of his close friends from his college days at McGill.

"Beaner is a good man," Babcock says. "He's smart. He's a patent lawyer. Did he tell you how I told him to quit his job?"

It happened during a summer vacation with a group of families from McGill, this one near Petoskey, Michigan, not too far from where the Red Wings hold their training camp. The group rented a house right on the water. They brought in a chef to cook meals. They had wives and kids and boats. It was a great setup.

One morning, a group of them went for a run, sweating off some of the fun from the night before. By Babcock's estimate, only two of the friends were happy with their current jobs.

Bean had been a lawyer with a national law firm for 16 years. He'd been a partner there for 11. He made good money. He had financial security. He had a family to provide for. He also felt like the company was getting too corporate. He had a stirring inside him that something needed to change.

That's all Babcock needed to hear. He encouraged his friend to quit. He told him to get happy. If his current job wasn't his passion, get out.

"You get in the company, you're the vice president, you have shares, you've got a good pension, but you're locked in," Babcock says. "You don't like what you do. Can you imagine not liking what you do? How can you be great when you don't like it?"

So Bean did it. He quit. He worked out a deal with his firm where both could e-mail his clients and make a pitch for their services. Enough came with Bean that he was able to make a relatively smooth transition.

"It's been great," Bean said. "You kind of have to have an inner faith that you're going to keep plugging away, and you sort of rely on hard work and faith it's going to work out. Even if it's the wrong decision, it's still the right decision. The easiest way to go is to continue on."

There's no risk in easy. There's no thrill in comfort or complacency. It's why Babcock avoids these things at all costs. To him, it's impossible to be great and comfortable.

"It's the risk. That's life. That's where the fun is at," he says.

He has a theory. Everyone says that their college years are some of the best of their lives.

I met my wife in college. I developed lifelong friends in college. I had an absolute blast at Michigan State.

But that's not the point he's driving home. Yes, those were fun times, but the reason he thinks we look back at college as such a thrilling time is because of the uncertainty that is inevitable at that stage in life.

College students are constantly learning. They're trying to create their lives on the fly. They don't know what is going to happen next.

That's what our subconscious yearns for years later. We get into our thirties, our forties, our fifties, with solid jobs and families and pensions and minivans and school tuition, and we slowly try to eliminate as much risk out of our lives as possible.

I know I've done it. A wife, three kids, a golden retriever. I can't think like a 21-year old Michigan State junior.

But that's exactly how Babcock believes we should be thinking.

"You've got to take that into the rest of your life. That's when you're at your best," he says. "I'm a big believer that if they made you change your career every 10 years, you'd be better. You get in a rut. Even coaches, they get fired, they re-invent themselves. They come back. Why wait until you get fired? Why not re-invent yourself every summer? Why not?"

"Because it's hard."

"It takes work but it's fun. What are the best games to play in? They're the 50/50 games. Not the 80/20 games. You're nervous. The adrenaline is going. The more that's on the line, the more fun it is, when you're confident and confident in what you do. Why wouldn't you want to be in those situations? That's where the fun is. That's why they have so much fun at college."

It's hard work. It's stressful. It's also exhilarating.

"Then, it gets to be a grind," Babcock says.

He never says that coaching the Red Wings became a grind. Maybe it never did. But in this moment, the challenge of coaching the Maple Leafs is clearly exhilarating.

Babcock grabs his phone and starts scrolling through a group text that includes his coaching staff in Toronto. He started this particular string of messages at 5:00 AM the previous day.

It's the middle of the summer and he's up early brainstorming slogan ideas for the Maple Leafs in the coming season.

"Last year we had 'Every Day Matters.' I wanted them to know that you come here every day. Every day. Every day. Every day," he says.

He's scrolling and sharing some of the ideas for the coming season's slogan. There are buzzwords like "pride" and "program" and "process" and "growth." Some he dismissed, others he dives into deeper for more brainstorming.

"That's how I do things, because you get ideas," Babcock says.

I could talk about this stuff with him the entire day. I also realize we haven't even started watching the game, it's a gorgeous summer day, and I'm pushing the limits of how much time I should be spending with him.

"Let's get the game going," I say.

"Okay."

I reach onto my laptop and hit play.

* * *

The video we're watching is the raw footage from the Olympic Broadcasting Service. There's no commentary. No play by play. Just the raw sounds of the day, the way we both remember.

The first shot inside the arena is of the fans. So much red and white. Nearly all of them are wearing Canadian Olympic team sweaters. They're holding Canadian flags. One holds a banner that says PROUD TO BE CANADIAN.

"I haven't seen any of this stuff," Babcock says, watching. "I don't remember any of this."

Highlights flash of the path each team took to get there, including a clip of the Americans beating the Canadians earlier in the tournament, the only loss for a long time for this Canadian men's hockey team.

The two captains, Team USA's Jamie Langenbrunner and Canada's Scott Niedermayer, exchange small banners at center ice and shake hands with the game's officials. Then there's a shot of Babcock in full-on Babcock mode. There's a look of intensity on his face. He pulls a card out of the inside of his pocket. Points it at somebody. Gives some instruction. He's into it.

"McGill tie," he says, noting his choice of neckwear.

"McGill tie. What's its record?"

"Two Olympic gold medals."

Mike Babcock's path to the Team Canada bench started at a low moment. The Red Wings had just lost to the Pittsburgh Penguins in the

2009 Stanley Cup Final in Joe Louis Arena. Somewhere in the building, the Penguins were still celebrating when Canada GM Steve Yzerman pulled Babcock aside after an 11:00 PM meeting.

"I'd like to see you in my office," Yzerman said.

The meeting was brief. Yzerman told Babcock he wanted him to coach Team Canada in Vancouver. Babcock accepted and said it was an honor to be picked.

He walked out to his pickup truck, where the gravity of the assignment hit him.

He'd be coaching Canada's team in Canada's game in Canada. This would be the most important international hockey tournament for this generation of Canadian hockey players.

He sat for a moment in his truck.

"I said, 'Oh my god, what have I got myself into?'" Babcock recalls. "I thought the same thing when I got the job at Red Deer College, when I got the job in Moose Jaw. Then you get on with getting prepared to do what you're supposed to do. That's just the thrill."

Living in Detroit helped spare him the distractions that come with being the national coach of the Canadian team. He didn't have to feel the daily pressure because he was on the other side of the border.

When he was named the coach of Team Canada, Babcock met with his family. He told them he expected to win but there were no guarantees. If, for some reason, they lost, he'd still be the same guy. He'd still be their dad. It wouldn't change anything at home.

"We're going to get abused, but I'm still your dad," Babcock remembers telling his kids. "Maybe my career changes. Maybe. I don't know that. Because you don't get to coach a second one if you don't win the first one."

The game begins on the screen in front of us.

Immediately, Canada's Mike Richards comes flying in with an attempted hit on Ryan Suter. Babcock loves it.

He starts taking notes.

"There's a hinge to start the game," he says. "Speed through the middle. There it is. There's the clip. We got them right there, first shift."

Babcock is marking it down in front of him to be used in another coaching lesson down the road, never content to do just one thing at a time.

"Once Suter got the puck, he had nowhere to go. He knew he was getting hit. Ritchie didn't hit him but he buzzed the tower."

Richards had worked his way up from one of the last guys on the roster to one of the three Canadian forwards on the ice to open the gold medal game.

Babcock smiles when talking about Richards. Before they officially announced the Canadian roster, Babcock called Richards to let him know that he was going to be the extra forward on the team.

Richards' response? He laughed. He had no intention of being the extra anything.

"He laughed. I loved it," Babcock says. "In other words, 'No, I'm not.' It's great. I love that kind of stuff, eh? That was his way of saying, 'Fuck you.' He laughed right there on the phone."

We're 26 seconds into the game when Sidney Crosby gets his first shift, taking a faceoff a few feet in front of Babcock.

Crosby had become a story in this tournament because he wasn't meeting some people's expectations on the offensive end. There was speculation on the outside that Babcock was having trouble finding him linemates. As we watch Crosby is now with two veteran forwards in Eric Staal and Jarome Iginla. It appeared to be a nice fit.

But Crosby didn't always look effective in this tournament. When things sputtered early on, Babcock sat down with him to get his input.

"What was that conversation like?" I ask, after Crosby wraps up his shift.

"I just said to him, 'Who can help you?' I wasn't finding him the right people to play with. Then, a lot of times, a player knows that's the last straw, too. If he gets input, it's all on him. He has to get going."

"Is that part of the motivation to have that conversation?"

"Part of it. Part of it is to figure out if maybe there's something I'm missing."

Babcock sees another thing he likes, an active defense, and takes another note. Another clip to highlight down the road.

Watching him prepare for another international tournament, the World Cup in a few months, it's amazing to realize that he was fired from one of his first jobs in coaching, let go by Moose Jaw following the 1992–93 season.

It was a tough blow for a young coach still trying to find his confidence. He had a new baby, a young marriage. He also had a job offer that would provide security and comfort but would mean leaving coaching to work at a management consultant firm. An opening for a coach at the University of Lethbridge offered him an out, a shot to keep following his passion instead of taking a job in business. He stuck with his passion, and by 1994 he had led that team to a national championship.

"There's momentary doubt for everybody but you have to fight through it," he says. "When you get to make a presentation, when you get up to do anything you're not sure of, there's a bit of doubt that sets in. But you feel like it's just going to happen. I believe in my mind and in my heart—that's just how I am. I'm just going to make it happen. Period. I don't know why I'm like that. Why would you leave the Red Wings to go to the Maple Leafs? Why? The money in the end was hardly going to be any different. What's the difference? Why wouldn't you go to San Jose? Because it's the challenge. The excitement. I don't know. You just think you're going to get it done. That's how I am."

Not everybody is like that. Maybe it comes from overcoming an early firing to have success. Maybe it comes from working with such focus and consistency that the end result so often ends up looking exactly how you imagined it.

Maybe he was born with it.

Babcock's mom and dad were each a huge presence in his life. His mom was the communicator. Babcock's friends would come over to his house and end up talking to her the whole time.

"His mom was very open and encouraged honesty, directness, and truth to oneself," his good friend Mike Bean said. "His confidence comes from his family. It was his background. It was the way he was led to think about things, the way he was led to have confidence in himself."

He also moved around a lot as a kid.

"Tons," Babcock says.

I was the opposite. The house I was brought home to as a newborn was the same house I came home to during college holiday breaks. On the first day of kindergarten, I met a kid named Mark. He was my college roommate for four years. He lived across the street from a kid named Teddy. He was the best man in my wedding. I now live a stone's throw from where we all grew up.

I don't know if that stability has made me any less of a risk-taker but it has definitely set my default decisions about life to ones that produce stability.

When I'm around Babcock, I start to wonder what a shake-up would look like.

"What impact did moving around so much have on shaping you as a person?" I ask.

"You're real tight with your family because every day you went to school, you didn't have friends on the first day," he says. "You had to support your family. You're meeting new people and knowing you can survive anywhere. It's being involved in lots of situations, so you knew there were no issues. I think that led to confidence. But what part of what happens to you is it?"

Great question. There are experiences and also influences from the people around you.

"What part is your mum's influence? Your dad's influence? Teachers, the coaches, the college—what part?" he continues. "I don't know what part. What you try to do as a prudent parent is put your kids in a demanding sports environment, help them get better and find things they are good at so they gain confidence."

We're hardly watching the game at this point. At least, I'm not. Every once in a while, Babcock makes a note.

"What a play by Niedermayer, ooooh."

To develop confidence, Babcock believes, you have to be caught doing things well. A good parent will find ways to catch their children doing things well. It builds a circle of success.

The influence from Babcock's father, a mining engineer, is everywhere. It's in the coach's office, where animal skulls sit next to books and family photos. His father loved the outdoors. They camped. They fished. Babcock was hunting moose at the age of three.

But perhaps the biggest influence on Babcock was his father's work ethic. His dad was up early every day to work in the mines. Babcock is the same way. He wants to be the first one to the rink. He's definitely going to beat the players there.

"Every day. And I'm just going to do it until it's done," Babcock says. "I'm going to find a better way to do it tomorrow. The measure of me is the people around me and how well they're doing. Period. No ifs, ands, or buts. You don't get sick. You don't get hurt. You don't get nothing."

"That's a high standard."

"In my house, it was so simple. You do it right or you were reminded."

It started with his dad.

"That's just how he was. Some people would say, 'Oh, what a burden.' It wasn't a burden. You just knew."

Right at that moment, Canada scores the first goal of the game.

The checking line that Babcock loved so much strikes first. Mike Richards fires a shot on American goalie Ryan Miller, who makes the initial save. Jonathan Toews, of course, bangs home the rebound. This was the start of Toews establishing himself as one of the greatest big-moment players of his generation. He'd win the Conn Smythe Trophy a few months later after leading the Blackhawks to their first Stanley Cup in decades.

"There we go," Babcock says as Canada scores. "Turnover."

That's what Babcock notices. We're watching the goal, but he sees the defensive play that made it happen.

Immediately, Babcock shares what he's thinking on the bench. There's no moment for celebration, because he's thinking of the players he wants to take the next shift. His choice says a lot about the players he trusts most, especially since the Toews line was just on the ice.

He turns to Ryan Getzlaf, who is playing on a line with Brenden Morrow and Corey Perry.

"This is important. I've got Getz out next. The next shift after you score or give up a goal, you want to have a good shift," Babcock says.

The camera cuts to Toews on the bench. Babcock loves Toews. Whenever he talks about Team Canada and its leadership group, he mentions Toews in the same sentence as Sidney Crosby and Shea Weber. Always.

"What I like is when you're a good person and you do it right every day," he says. "His will is much greater than his skill. His determination has defined him as a player. He has three Cups and two gold medals. He has that because he does it right all the time. He can't help himself. He's a talent and all that, but he does it right."

I skip to the second period and stop at a point where Babcock is clearly upset on the screen. Eric Staal had just gotten called for a penalty.

"I didn't like the penalty," he says.

We keep moving. Canada kills the American power play and the crowd is into it. Every shot comes with a huge reaction.

With the fans already charged from the penalty kill, the Canadians are flying up the ice with Getzlaf driving down the left side of the zone. He flips a puck in toward Miller, who has Patrick Marleau driving in on him right down the middle. Corey Perry isn't too far behind. The puck never makes it to Miller but deflects out to Perry, who has a couple steps on Joe Pavelski. Perry buries it. Canada is up 2–0.

Babcock starts writing intensely on the notepad in front of him.

"So, you see how it's a broken play?" he says. "Your structure has you in the right spot. Right here. A guy drives wide, second guy through the middle. He threw it in. See how the middle driver, see how he came through?"

That was Marleau. Once the winger got to Miller, he kept on skating to the left of the goal and spun toward the action. He turned just in time to see Perry score the goal.

"It's a broken play but a structured play. That's how randomness makes it hard for the goalie. This didn't hit the goalie and become a rebound—it bounced somewhere. It was random, so the goalie was deep. I always say, on the power play, drive it off their d-men. Just pound it off their d-men. It's coming to our guy in the middle."

So now we're at the point where we're skipping forward to watch goals. We've covered a lot of ground. It's also gorgeous outside, and I know I can't take Babcock's time for granted.

I jump to the American goal that cut the Canadian lead in half. Patrick Kane flicks a wrister toward Luongo and Ryan Kesler tips it just enough to send it past the Canadian goalie.

"Go back. That's great," Babcock says.

Not great in that the Americans scored but great in that he gets another coaching moment out of it. He starts taking notes. His observations are coming so fast, I'm not sure what he's talking about or what to even ask for clarification about.

"Line change drill. Someone stay on? One. Rink wide. Did someone go rink wide? Two in the middle. Backed up. Stop. There he is right there. We did a good job. Really good job. This guy with speed. One, playing two. Good. Dove in. Right now."

Babcock snaps his fingers.

I'll admit, I'm lost. Is he snapping at me?

"Take it back," he says.

He wants me to rewind it, right?

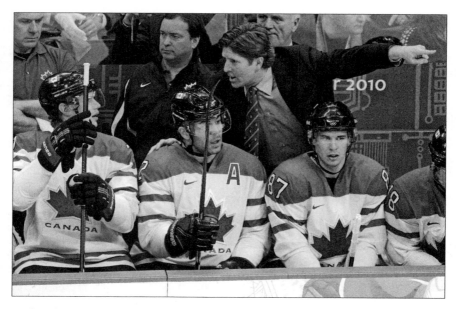

Babcock won his first Olympic gold medal in 2010, guiding Team Canada past the Americans in an unforgettable overtime thriller. (AP Images)

"Both guys move to the outside guy. Morrow should just bump him and don't let him go to the middle and it's done."

He seems satisfied that he's solved the problem. He takes another note. We're done here.

"When do they make it 2–2?"

It's only one of the most memorable goals I've ever seen in my life.

With Ryan Miller pulled, Zach Parise scored one of the most memorable goals in Team USA hockey history. Or at least it is to me. Maybe because the Americans lost, it's slipped away into history.

But man, I will never forget that moment with 24.4 seconds remaining in the game when Parise pulled Team USA even with Canada on its home soil.

As an American hockey writer, I thought I was watching history.

"Let's go to it. Let's go. Zoom ahead more. Let's go until they get the goalie out," Babcock says.

We skip ahead. The Americans are pressuring with just over a minute left when Roberto Luongo pounces on a puck, to an arena filled with chants of "Loooooouuuuu."

Patrick Kane is chewing on his mouth guard. He looks at the scoreboard to check the clock.

There's a shot of the Canadian executives: Steve Yzerman is staring straight ahead, Doug Armstrong is resting on one hand. He's barely moving.

There's a shot of Team USA GM Brian Burke and, remarkably, his tie is still tied. Ron Wilson has called a timeout and both coaches are addressing their players.

The Ramones are playing on the arena speakers.

Future Ducks teammates Ryan Getzlaf and Ryan Kesler meet in the faceoff circle. At this point, Babcock is leaning hard on Getzlaf on faceoffs.

Canada's Shea Weber gets the puck in the corner behind Luongo. He sends it up the ice and it's deflected out of play.

"You're okay at this point, 54.8 seconds left," I say.

"I'd have Drew Doughty out there now."

"Instead of Shea, or with Shea?"

"Instead of Shea. I'd have Bergeron taking this draw."

Timeout is called.

"Ron Wilson said he was surprised you called this timeout."

"I don't know. If you don't call a timeout you're wrong. If you call a timeout you're wrong."

"Who are you sending out there?"

"I have Weber. I still have Niedermayer going to get the puck, which I don't like."

There's an overhead shot of Canadian fans outside the arena in the streets of Vancouver getting ready to celebrate.

With 43.7 seconds left, Brian Rafalski quickly retrieves the puck and sends it up to Joe Pavelski, who gets it to Patrick Kane, who makes a nice little pass back to gain the zone. Pavelski fires a long shot that Luongo gloves but drops back to the ice.

Team USA is buzzing now. Babcock tells me to pause it.

"I don't want Getzy down there. I don't know why we're racing down there. Niedermayer and Weber are both leaving the net, see that? It's because they were on the wrong side off the faceoff. There it is right there. Great clip for me. This is the biggest mistake for me, where Weber and Niedermayer are. It happened twice."

Canada's gold medal hopes are about to take a huge hit, yet Babcock finds a coachable moment.

"What should they have done?" I ask.

"Niedermayer should be on this side. Weber should be on that side. Never leave the back post. [Toews] should be down by the back post."

Parise, as he does every time you watch this moment, scores. The horn blows and Luongo slowly gets up while Parise celebrates in the corner.

"The great thing was there was only 24 seconds left," Babcock says.

The Canadian players file one by one past Babcock on the bench and into the dressing room as regulation ends with the game tied.

It's funny. When you talk to both sides of this epic game, the players all felt like they were going to win. The Americans thought they had the momentum. They wanted to keep playing the game immediately.

The Canadians used the opportunity to regroup.

"To a man, we got back and had a good feeling that if we stayed with what we were doing, we'd find a way," Eric Staal said.

The first thing Babcock did was meet with his coaches. They had to figure out which groups they wanted to send out for the 4-on-4 overtime. They went over their faceoff plan and their forecheck.

Then, with seven minutes before overtime was to begin, Babcock went out and addressed the players.

"Look around the room," he said to his team. "One of you is going to be a hero for the rest of your life. This is going to be over within five or six minutes. Let's play fast. Let's go get them."

And with that, he left.

"Can you tell which players might win it, just by looking in their eyes?" I ask.

"You know, some guys are getting on. Some guys are not," he says. "I thought Niedermayer might be the guy. Crosby might be the guy."

Team Canada files out of the dressing room. "Don't Stop Believin'" is playing as the camera pans a sea of red, with the occasional American flag waving in the middle of it.

"Look at this atmosphere," Babcock says.

"I know. It was crazy."

"How do you get better than that?"

"This is it. They'll never top this."

I really believe that. It's the best sporting event I've ever attended.

"What's great for TV and you guys is that the American team is in it," Babcock says. "Sochi was as big for us in a lot of ways, but because the American team wasn't in it, it's not as big."

Kesler and Toews take the opening faceoff. Babcock matches the Toews line because Kesler is skating with Patrick Kane. He's trying to get one Blackhawks star to help shut down the other.

We start watching and it gets quiet. This is an intense game. It's hard not to sit back and appreciate it.

"Web can skate, eh?" he says, as Weber flies up the ice. "Good job by Suter. Good job by Doughty."

"You love him."

"He's fucking incredible."

Babcock spots Richards. Everybody is getting ice time. Brent Seabrook might be the only one who isn't and he's busy getting the door for everyone on the bench.

"I went with 10 guys," Babcock says. "You've got to make everybody important. That's what I told the coaches right away. That's one of the things we've done at these events. You have to make them important."

Aside from the odd moment, Canada is controlling play. It didn't take five or six minutes as Babcock predicted to his players before overtime started but they followed his orders. They kept coming.

There's one good look for the Americans following a Niedermayer turnover. Joe Pavelski gets his stick on a pass meant for Shea Weber, then spins and fires a shot toward Luongo with 12:35 left. It's a great chance that I'd forgotten about. Luongo makes the save and sticks the puck over to Niedermayer, who then leads a rush up the ice.

He finds Sidney Crosby.

"This is the shift," I say.

Crosby flies down the center of the ice, where Suter and Rafalski collapse on him. He gets off a harmless shot that Ryan Miller sends into the corner.

Crosby and Rafalski go to gather the loose puck.

"I think it hits the linesman's skate," Babcock said. Both he and Team USA coach Ron Wilson remember that clearly. It gives Crosby enough separation to send the puck over to Jarome Iginla as he makes a break for Miller.

There's no play by play on our broadcast, just the natural sound of the game. Crosby's voice comes across the speakers in a fleeting moment.

"Iggy!"

"You can hear Sid call for it," I say. I'd heard in interviews that he did. I'd never actually heard his voice until now.

Iginla makes the pass. Crosby beats Miller. It's over. Crosby throws his gloves into the air and gets mobbed. I look to Babcock for his reaction.

He's shuffling up his papers from all his note-taking.

"It wasn't even close," he says.

I think he's talking about the overtime session. Maybe he means the entire game.

Babcock watches his players celebrate. They come flying off the bench to join Crosby in the corner. Ryan Miller is just staring straight ahead with a blank look on his face.

On the screen, Babcock gives assistant coach Jacques Lemaire a big hug. Then he shakes his hand wildly. They're excited.

"It's exhilaration," Babcock says. "Who gets to be an Olympic champion?"

Not some kid who grew up in the wilds of the Northwest Territory. Not some coach fired in Moose Jaw. Those guys don't get Olympic gold medals, do they?

The players are celebrating in front of him.

"These are great players. Pronger. Niedermayer. Great players. Hall of Fame players," he says. "You coach them but they coach you, too. They share with you and you learn from them. If you can talk to them, they can teach you a ton. Someone is teaching us something all the time. It's incredible."

The fans are going absolutely crazy. It was a party that would last well until the next morning.

I remember filing a game story that night, going to a place called the Library Square Public House for a couple of beers with writers I'd spent the last 17 days with. The party was incredible. People were draped in Canadian flags. There were picnic tables outside and Canadian hockey fans were dancing on top of them.

On the subway ride home in the wee hours, an impromptu rendition of "O, Canada" broke out among the riders on the train.

Ken Hitchcock, one of Canada's assistant coaches, got up early for a flight at 4:00 AM because he was worried the airport was going to be jammed getting out of town. The streets were still full.

"People are going crazy, and you're going home," Hitchcock said. "It was a really strange feeling. It was like, none of us wanted to leave Molson House, where everybody was. When you left, it was 'Holy smokes, we're going back to work.'"

On the screen in Babcock's office, the camera alternates between celebrating Canadian hockey players and the crushed Americans.

Then the players line up. Canadians on one side, Americans on the other. Each player slowly works his way through the handshake line. Afterward, Babcock is near the Canadian bench and his players come over to shake his hand.

"You went there, you did what you were supposed to do, and you won," Babcock says. "Once you've done it, it changes you. So you just go there and you say, 'We're going to get it done.'"

I stand up, ask if I can take a few pictures.

On his bookshelf there's a small black box with a gold medal resting inside. It has the Hockey Canada logo and the words GOLD 2010 emblazoned on it.

"It's too bad it's not the nice one, the other one. I think my other one is up…"

"There's a better one than this one?"

"The second one is much nicer."

He gives me a tour. As we work our way around his house, there are framed hockey photos everywhere. There's an autographed photo of Bobby Orr's iconic picture, the Hall of Famer flying through the air.

"Here's my guy, Bobby Orr. That's always been my guy," Babcock says.

We walk into a room with a beautiful pool table. On top is a ping-pong table. On the wall nearby is a large black frame holding three old Red Wings jerseys.

The jerseys are red and inside the numbers are the signatures of three of the best to ever play for Detroit: Ted Lindsay, Alex Delvecchio, and Gordie Howe. The signatures are gorgeous, each legend adding the year they were inducted into the Hall of Fame. There are black-and-white photos underneath each player.

"Holy cow, where'd you get that?" I ask.

"I had it made. I got them all to sign it and I had it made."

Near the top of the wall are framed pictures of some of Babcock's best teams. There's an empty spot on the wall.

"I have a spot for the World Cup," he says.

He's so confident the Canadians are going to win, he has a place on his wall for the framed team celebration photo. Of course, two months later, they reward his faith.

I look over and see a picture of a team I don't recognize. It's the usual team championship photo, celebrating players piled around a trophy holding up their index fingers.

It's the 1994 Lethbridge Pronghorns. There's Babcock, sitting on the ice to the left, a mop of red hair on his head.

This was the first one, the championship that catapulted him to greater successes. This was the job he took instead of getting into business consulting.

"That's the best one by far," Babcock says.

We step out back and it's a stunning Michigan summer day. The lawn is perfectly manicured. There's a crystal-clear spring-fed lake, with the water skiing course he navigated that morning.

Even the purchase of this home is a lesson in Babcock's resiliency and willingness to grind out successes. He identified this lake as the one he wanted to spend his summers on, and for five years he tried to buy a home on it. He went door to door to see if people would sell.

Mike Babcock, one of the greatest coaches of all time, going door to door. It's just how he operates.

"Finally, these people sold," he says.

I start to pack up, sliding my laptop into my backpack. We're done here but even then the conversation keeps on going about leadership, personal improvement. There's one last swap of book recommendations.

He's reading *The Champion's Mind*, a book that examines how great athletes think, train, and thrive.

I'd just finished a book called *Linchpin*, by Seth Godin. It's filled with strategies to make you more valuable to your employer. I think he'd like it.

"You have to find a way to become invaluable to your organization, where they can't survive without you," I explain in selling the book.

Not that Mike Babcock needs career advice.

"That's what I tell the players to do," he says. "You've got to create value for yourself. Figure out a way to create value. Are you the best penalty killer? Are you the best faceoff guy? Figure out a way to do it and go do it for yourself."

CHAPTER 4

BOB HARTLEY

Game 7 of the 2001 Stanley Cup Final

I bought an RV. A 35-foot Winnebago.

It's just about the craziest purchase I've ever made.

When it comes to big purchases, I'm as conservative and responsible as you can get. I hate debt. Our newest family car is nine years old. We don't own anything with less than 100,000 miles on it.

That went out the window on the day we made this purchase.

The life of a hockey writer means that the entire spring is usually spent on the road covering the Stanley Cup playoffs. This particular spring, I spent more time in St. Louis at the Marriott Grand on Washington Avenue than my own home. I'm not proud of it, it's just reality. You miss Little League games and plays and parent-teacher conferences and birthday parties and pretty much anything that happens from April until the NHL draft is over in late June.

The payoff is usually a summer with the family.

My wife and I looked at this summer, the one in which I'm trying to squeeze numerous film sessions across North America into a two-month window, and realized it was going to be just as crazy as the spring.

So coming off a busy spring and a fall that would include a month on the road because of the World Cup, we decided to do something different.

If I couldn't stay home with the family, the family was coming with me.

I came up with a plan. We'd buy the RV, drive it all summer, and then rent it out when we weren't using it. That way, I could justify the big loan we were about to take out.

That spring, defenseman Brent Burns and the San Jose Sharks made a long playoff run, and Burns and I had conversations about how much he loved taking his family out in his RV.

I saw Burns later in Las Vegas, in town because he was nominated for the Norris Trophy at the NHL's annual awards show. When he came out to chat with the media, I told him my admittedly sketchy summer RV plan. Sometimes, when you're completely irresponsible, you just want some validation from someone you know will provide it. Burns is that guy.

A few minutes later, my phone buzzed. It was a text from Burns.

"Hey, let me know if you want to come out to the RV," he wrote.

"You've got it here?"

"Ya, we drove here."

Of course he did.

"I'm outside under the Encore sign."

Brent Burns had plugged his big rig into the Wynn Encore sign on the Las Vegas strip. What a legend.

I had to see it. I grabbed my backpack, worked my way through the casino, and walked past the valet guys toward the giant Encore sign. Sure enough, what looked like a large tour bus was parked with its sides popped out and a power cord snaking its way to the sign.

That there, Clark, was an RV.

It was a thing of beauty.

While Burns gave me a tour, his kids came in. They were just about the same age as my youngest and couldn't have been cuter. They pulled out an atlas and showed me the different places their mom and dad had taken them. I was sold. I missed my kids. I wanted family adventures.

I sent the picture to my wife and she was all in.

We spotted the Winnebago we'd end up buying on the corner of an autoshop in Traverse City, Michigan, on the way to see some Fourth of July fireworks. There she was, in all her 35-foot beauty. Two popouts on the sides. A nice kitchen and a bathroom with a shower. Two televisions. Once we started looking around, we were hooked. She had more miles than we wanted but for $19,000 you've got to make some concessions.

Two weeks later, we were the proud owners of a 2004 Winnebago Sightseer.

Was it an impulse buy? Absolutely. Did we regret it three months later? Probably.

But Bob Hartley, the veteran NHL coach of the Colorado Avalanche, Atlanta Thrashers, and Calgary Flames, agreed to meet me in mid-July near Hershey, Pennsylvania, and everyone was coming with me.

I wish I could say it went smoothly. I really wish I could. But driving this big rig, with my entire family and a golden retriever on board, was terrifying.

It started going south shortly after leaving Michigan. First, we nearly got wedged between two giant concrete walls outside a tollbooth. An employee came sprinting out of her booth when it looked like we wouldn't fit.

The interstate was also full of potholes and our new camper wasn't exactly absorbing them. Little did I realize while flying down the road in the center lane that a giant piece of metal underneath the camper was slowly shaking loose with each bump.

We stopped at the next tollbooth and pulled over to investigate what was making the loud screetching noise. Underneath the RV, a rusted sheet of metal protecting the right front headlights from rocks, rain, and snow was hanging on for dear life, the bulk of it dragging on the highway.

We realized then that we brought a ton of food, a bunch of movies, and a few board games—but no tools in case something went wrong. It was almost 10:00 at night, the kids were wiped out, and I was undernearth the RV, twisting this giant piece of metal, hoping to break it off. Instead, I knocked a wire loose, one that powered a light on the side of the vehicle.

At this point, my hands were bleeding. We had no idea what we were doing. We were getting a little scared.

I shoved the metal sheet into the undercarriage of the RV and we decided to call it a night, pulling into the nearest campground.

My wife and I retired to the back of the RV with a box of crackers and a giant vat of red wine. We drank until we fell asleep.

The next morning was a new day. By the time we hit the mountains of Pennsylvania and started going through the tunnels, we were having a good time. We were ready to move into this thing full time, even downloading podcasts about how to pull it off.

We pulled into the Hersheypark campground, ready for an adventure.

I was ready for Uncle Bob.

* * *

Bob Hartley won his Stanley Cup in 2001, guiding the Avalanche to a victory over the New Jersey Devils. I've got a copy of Game 7 from that series on my laptop and we've agreed to watch it during a break at his annual youth hockey camp in York, Pennsylvania.

Hartley and I have a bit of history. He was the head coach in Atlanta when I had my first job as a beat writer. I showed up to cover his team as an ambitious but green journalist and he helped break me into the game of hockey. I was the only person on the beat every single day, so we saw a lot of each other. For a coach and the journalist covering the team, that can be both good and bad.

I didn't stay in Atlanta much longer after he was fired as the coach, accepting a job as *The Sporting News'* national hockey writer. One of my

Bob Hartley took a break from his annual youth hockey camp to relive Game 7 of the 2001 Stanley Cup Final.

mentors at the newspaper, columnist Jeff Schultz, threw a going-away BBQ at his house and invited Hartley.

Bob showed up with a bottle of Dom Perignon to mark the occasion. My wife and I drank it with my brother and his wife the night we sold our house in Atlanta before moving home to Detroit.

At the BBQ, Hartley sat patiently while my two-year-old son put stickers all over his arm, covering his watch that was probably worth more than my car.

I knew then that we'd be okay after our times together as reporter and coach.

For our film session, I rented a car to make the 40-minute drive from the campground to Hartley's hockey camp. The rink was buzzing with activity, running like a well-oiled machine.

It takes all of 30 seconds to hear his voice.

"General!" he shouts, spotting me carrying a backpack and notepad. Hartley is a nickname guy. Everyone gets one and he started calling me

"The General" within hours of our first meeting. Maybe because my last name is close to Custer? I honestly don't know.

He's in Calgary gear from head to toe: black track pants, a black-and-red Flames jacket. He's got hockey skates on and a whistle around his neck. His salt-and-pepper hair is more salt than pepper compared to our days in Atlanta, but otherwise he looks exactly the same.

He's standing in front of a photography backdrop. Flames center Sean Monahan is on his left, winger Johnny Gaudreau is on his right. There's a long line of kids from the hockey camp waiting to get their picture taken with the trio.

You'd never know he'd been fired by the Flames just a couple months earlier.

One by one, they bang out the photos before Monahan and Gaudreau sit down to sign a bunch of autographs. There are hundreds of kids.

"Gaudreau and Monahan, eh?" I say to Hartley as he walks by.

"The newbies, they've got to pay their rent," he says.

Hartley has been doing this camp in the area for 21 years and this year there are more than 500 kids in attendance. Teaching has been a passion of his for decades. We'd get into that shortly.

This isn't Hartley lending his name to a camp and parachuting in. He's into it. He's out on the ice giving constant instruction. If he sees a kid doing something he doesn't like, he provides discipline. He's proud that he's already taken away three or four cell phones that day. He sleeps on a cot upstairs.

As we sit down to watch the 2001 Stanley Cup clincher for Hartley and the Avalanche, he gets a call from a parent who is a little concerned that his son is going to quit before the end of the camp.

Hartley won't have it.

"He will not quit, if I have your support," Hartley tells the dad. "The worst thing we can teach the kids is to quit. I don't think there's a bone in his body not hurting right now. For me, I say it's a hockey camp but it's also a life experience."

The conversation goes on for a couple more minutes, with Hartley assuring the parent he will be there every step of the way to help the kid through it. It captures Hartley quite well. He pushes really, really hard but in the end this kid is going to be better for it. Hartley's players usually are.

Finished with the phone call, he cracks open a Coke Zero. His drink of choice used to be Diet Coke, now it's Coke Zero. As long as I've known him, I've never seen him have a sip of alcohol. His lack of a taste for beer makes him a rarity in the world of hockey, where that seems to be a prerequisite.

As a kid, he'd bring his father a beer, sometimes pouring it into a glass too quickly. His dad would have him drink the foam and he didn't like the taste. It removed any interest he may have had in beer early on in his life.

As he got older, he noticed that nothing good resulted from excessive drinking. In his small town, he saw people dying from alcohol-related problems. He played in a men's baseball league as a teenager and would sleep on ballfields and in cars in order to attend the tournaments on weekends. He'd see the older players show up for morning games and puke their guts out after a night of drinking.

"I was so proud that I was in the lineup, I didn't want to take a beer with the fear I would strike out or miss a fly ball and the coach would stop me," Hartley says.

As he worked his way through the minor leagues as a hockey coach, he'd see the perils of drinking from players who couldn't stop.

At one point in the American Hockey League, a player showed up to camp with a broken leg. He got mixed up with the Hell's Angels and they had broken it.

"In a fight?" I ask.

"In 'dealings.'"

"Geez."

"He came to me and I said, 'What happened?' He said, 'I broke my leg working out.' I knew the kid, so I made a few phone calls. I grabbed him in the office the next day. I said, 'You know what? Don't lie to me. I might be your best ally.' He started to cry and said, 'I'm so scared.' I said, 'Now, we will take care of you.' Today, the guy is a good businessman. Once in a while, he calls me to thank me."

We move to a small office at the rink. Before the action begins, I ask him to tell me how he wound up in Colorado after Marc Crawford left the organization and created a coaching vacancy.

As Hartley tells it, he was hanging out at home with friends on a Sunday afternoon when his wife came over with the phone in her hands. Francois Giguere, the general manager of the Avalanche, was on the line. He wanted to talk in private.

Giguere asked Hartley to get on a 7:30 PM flight from Harrisburg that would eventually take him to Colorado.

"Bring your best suit," Giguere said.

A storm was starting to roll in and Hartley was in his swimsuit with a house full of people. He apologized, then made it to the airport in time for the flight from Harrisburg to Pittsburgh. The plane then sat on the tarmac for three hours. The sky had now turned pitch black from the clouds coming in.

Finally, the plane took off, but the storms had turned the Pittsburgh airport into a disaster. There were stacks of luggage everywhere. Hartley had never seen anything like it.

Around 2:00 AM, Hartley finally got his ticket from Pittsburgh to Colorado for the next morning. He took a cab to his hotel and told the same cab driver to pick him up in a couple of hours to take him back to the airport.

When he returned to the Pittsburgh airport, with a ticket to Colorado and a possible new job waiting for him, he was told his ticket was no good, that the flight to Denver was full.

"Are you a hockey fan?" Hartley asked the gate agent.

"Yeah, I'm a big Penguins fan."

"Look at me," Hartley told the agent. "I'm telling you, you need to get me on this flight. Get me with the pilots. Get me with the baggage.

Get me anywhere. I need to get on that flight. I'm the coach of the Hershey Bears in the American League and I'm going to get a job with the Colorado Avalanche. You give me your business card, the first time we get to Pittsburgh, I will have two tickets for you. I'm not bullshitting you, I need to get on this plane."

The guy started typing. Moments later, a ticket printed out. Months later, the guy would get his Penguins tickets.

When Hartley arrived in Denver, a driver was waiting for him, holding up a card with a fake last name so nobody in the airport would know that Hartley was in town to talk about the coaching job. The Avs were that secretive.

They negotiated a deal and Hartley was set to take over one of the most talented teams of that era in the NHL, a team built around Joe Sakic, Patrick Roy, and Peter Forsberg.

Along with a team that was loaded with star power came pressure.

"It's not every day you can start your coaching career on a team that can win a Stanley Cup. For me, it's way more challenging. I transform pressure into challenges. Challenges are way more positive," Hartley says.

He stops talking now because he knows the Avalanche are about to score in the game we're watching.

He has every moment of this game memorized and, on cue, Alex Tanguay scores to put the Avalanche up 1–0 on the Devils.

"You knew it was coming," I say.

"If you look, I had changed my lines for Game 7. I had put Danny Hinote on the first line. From fourth line to first line with Alex Tanguay and Joe Sakic, because of this guy," Hartley says.

"This guy" is Scott Stevens, the Hall of Fame defenseman who was giving the Avalanche fits all series.

"This guy had been a wrecking crew in the playoffs," Hartley says. "Hinote's job was to go and hit Brian Rafalski as many times as possible. To draw Stevens' attention to him. Look right there, look at the nice little pick he did. Look. Look at the shot."

As Tanguay skates along the wall, Hinote gets in the way of both Stevens and Rafalski, giving Tanguay just enough space to get to the front of the net and get off a good shot.

Hartley always keeps a stack of business cards with him when he's making up lines for his next game. They are either his own cards or somebody else's. On the back of the business cards, he writes the names of his players.

The night before Game 7, Hartley shuffled the card with Hinote's name on it like he was moving the Jack of Hearts in a game of solitaire. He was looking for a solution to the Scott Stevens problem.

"Obviously, Stevens was on the ice every time that Joe [Sakic] was on the ice," he says. "So I was trying to get a little bit more room for Milan Hejduk on another line. At the same time, to get a little speed and a little nastiness with Tanguay and Sakic. I knew Danny would forecheck like the devil. That was his job."

Hartley wanted Hinote to throw pucks in Rafalski's corner and then try to flatten him. Force Rafalski to play tough minutes.

"Bob knew what he was doing," Hinote said when we chatted by phone about that moment. "He came to me that morning and said, 'You're starting tonight with Joe and Tangs.' I'm 22 and I'm trying to go home and have a nap. No chance."

Hinote saw the logic in Hartley's lineup, and soon after saw the leadership skills of Sakic. Maybe sensing some nerves in the young forward, Sakic chatted with Hinote before the game and told him to just play the way he always played. Be physical on the forecheck. Don't try and do something he didn't normally do just because he was now playing on the top line.

"It was a dump and chase that led to the first goal and I got an assist. I went in and hit Scott Stevens, puck came loose, Tangs grabbed it, and I set a little pick. It was exactly what Bob Hartley had drawn up in his head. It worked out...He put himself on the line [with that lineup]," Hinote said.

Putting a grinder on the top line is the kind of move that would be loudly second-guessed if the Avalanche had lost this game. Instead, Hartley's game plan paid off with a 1–0 lead.

The television screen cuts to a shot of Avalanche defenseman Ray Bourque, who'd been traded to Colorado from Boston the previous season. He couldn't be happier. He has both arms raised in the air, his stick raised high. He wears a huge smile as he skates toward the bench to hug Hinote and Tanguay. His family is shown on the screen celebrating.

This was Bourque's last chance at a Stanley Cup after a legendary career as a Bruin, and his team was now up early in a game where every goal was absolutely huge.

This game didn't mean everything just to the city of Denver. The Avalanche had been adopted by the fans in Boston, too.

The Avalanche had lost Game 5 at home. They were too eager, too unfocused. From the view behind the bench, it looked as though they tried to win the whole game in the first period. The loss meant they were headed to New Jersey for Game 6, where the Devils could win the Stanley Cup on home ice.

On the mornings after games, Hartley would meet with his players to give them an opportunity to talk.

The day after that Game 5 loss in Colorado, nobody said a word. Hartley circled the room and it was dead quiet.

Suddenly, Ray Bourque stood up.

"He had tears in his eyes," Hartley recalls. "He said, 'Boys, I will let you decide how many games I have left to play in the NHL and if I'm going to win a Cup.' Tears were running down his face and he just sat down."

The Avalanche practice that followed was one of the most intense Hartley had seen.

He pulled over his assistant coaches and let him know what he had realized.

"There's no way they're going to beat us," Hartley said.

When the Avs' team bus arrived in New Jersey for Game 6, Hartley saw the truck in front of them with the Stanley Cup in its case. Patrick Roy always sat behind Hartley on the first team bus. Hartley leaned back to him and pointed out the case. He knew Roy knew what was inside.

"Fucking Cup is not going to get out of the box," Roy said.

Mostly because of Roy and an incredible first period in Game 6, the Stanley Cup stayed encased for another night. This series was great because it featured two of the best goalies of all time in New Jersey's Martin Brodeur and Patrick Roy going toe-to-toe. Even in the moment, that was something Hartley could enjoy.

"I'll be old and I'll be able to tell my friends I watched one of the biggest matches in goaltenders between Patrick and Marty Brodeur. What do you want more than this? They had a battle that was just unbelievable," Hartley says. "Patrick never wanted to beat the New Jersey Devils or the Detroit Red Wings. He wanted to beat the other goalie. Patrick would see this as a one-on-one matchup."

Years later, when Roy got into coaching, he'd phone Hartley for advice, advice the coach was happy to share. At his core, Hartley is a teacher. You see it in how he's constantly teaching lessons in his camp. You see it in how much instruction there is on the ice during a Hartley-led practice.

When he was in high school, his summer job was working with mentally challenged children. For three or four years, he spent his time teaching the kids ball hockey and other sports as the sports director.

It was about this age he started traveling to help out at hockey camps, where he taught the basics of hockey. When he coached in the NHL, he brought that mentality with him.

Hartley starts rattling off the names of young players he helped develop. Chris Drury, Milan Hejduk, Alex Tanguay, right on down to the guys at the camp that day—Sean Monahan and Johnny Gaudreau.

He doesn't know where the teaching mentality came from, only that it fit his passion. He enjoys working with the kids on the ice in Hershey as much as the millionaires on the ice in the NHL.

He spent summers growing up helping out at hockey camps, and he traveled anywhere to do it—Las Vegas, Los Angeles, Montreal, Quebec City, Ottawa. Anywhere a hockey camp needed a hand, Hartley was happy to help.

"I just loved it. Go, go, go," Hartley says. "To me, minor hockey is the roots of the game. That's where it starts. For me, it keeps me sharp in my coaching. If I think that details are important at the NHL level, imagine how important it is for little kids."

Before we sat down to watch this Game 7, Hartley and I grabbed lunch together, along with Sean Monahan and Alex Pruitt, a writer from *Sports Illustrated* who stopped by to do a story on Hartley's camp. The meal captured how Hartley's teaching doesn't stop when he leaves the ice.

First of all, we were eating at the same school cafeteria as the 200 campers breaking for lunch. Monahan, who would sign a contract a couple of months later worth $45 million, was looking through his salad bar options that were little more than shredded iceberg lettuce and some cheese. There was a bin of plastic sporks on the left.

Everyone was in the same boat in this camp. Millionaires and kids alike.

We sat down at a table and Hartley reminded everyone of the "Catholic school" rule: no hats at the table.

He cares about this stuff. He cares about respect and being a better person on and off the ice, even if it seems old-fashioned.

Back in front of the laptop, I ask him why that's important for a hockey coach, how that relates to winning and losing in the NHL. He doesn't have an answer, other than to say he cares about the guys. Trying to explain it further, his thoughts drift to two of his former players in Atlanta, Dany Heatley and Daniel Snyder.

In 2003, Heatley was driving his Ferrari with Snyder in the passenger seat. Heatley lost control of the car and both players were thrown from the vehicle. Snyder fell into a coma and died six days later. Heatley pled guilty to second-degree vehiclular homicide.

"Every day, I was going from one hospital to the other," Hartley says. "My wife, Micheline, would make cakes, make cookies. I would stop at P.F. Chang's or Macaroni Grill and buy a bunch of meals so that the families wouldn't have to eat hospital food all the time. I remember the night Danny died, I was going to the Braves game against the Cubs in the playoffs…"

Just as he's getting into the story, the Avalanche score for the second time. It's Alex Tanguay again.

"Rewind this," Hartley says.

It's Tanguay's second goal, but this one is all Joe Sakic. He breaks in on Brodeur and fires a shot, and the rebound goes right to Tanguay.

"We called the play right away. I knew they would change. I'm pulling Hinote again and we're stretching Tanguay right off the glass. We stretch. It's a 2-on-1 because he's coming from the bench," Hartley says.

The game continues and Hartley gets back to his story about Snyder.

At the Braves game, he received a phone call from Snyder's mom, LuAnn, with good news. The doctors were now suddenly more optimistic.

In the fifth inning, Hartley got another call from LuAnn.

"'He's dead,'" Hartley says, repeating her words. "You know? Just like that."

There's a penalty in the game in front of us.

"We're going to score on this."

Hartley moves on to a story about Flames forward Michael Ferland, whom he helped deal with alcohol addiction.

"I told Ferly, 'I already saw one of my players buried, I don't need a second. We're here to help you.'"

On the screen, Joe Sakic scores. It's now 3–0. Hartley doesn't miss a beat.

"Ferly started to break up. Cried like a baby. He came around my desk, gave me a hug, and said, 'Please, help me. I don't know what to do.'"

Hartley also has a reputation around the league of being really hard to play for. There are plenty of players who will always be grateful for the opportunity he gave them or the way he helped them sort out their lives. But there are others who were happy to see him go when he left jobs.

"Bob was harder on the young guys," said Dave Reid, a forward on this Avalanche team. "Bob's practices were very long. Nothing was left unchecked. There was a lot of detail that Bob put into preparation. He was very hands-on."

I broached the subject with him.

"You know you have a reputation as a guy who is hard to play for," I point out.

"I don't agree with this. I think I'm very easy," Hartley says. "Ask Mark Giordano. Ask the guys who work. For me, that's one thing I demand. I demand hard work. I've won six championships in the five leagues that I've coached. You don't win by luck. You don't win by saying, 'Okay, we're going to get on a good streak.' It's a process. That process demands commitment. I don't like cheaters. I don't like lazy guys."

Hartley tries to make the most out of every minute. In the gym, in video sessions, in practice. He's teaching lessons off the ice. Catholic rules and all that.

The moment he showed up in Atlanta, he joked that the country club life that may have existed before he arrived was over.

"I'm very honest. I don't bullshit," he says. "If it's black, it's black. If it's white, it's white. Some people like this, some other people don't like this. I'm not going to lie to no one just to please someone. If I'm happy, I say it. If I'm unhappy, I say it. I believe that's part of the job. I know one thing—I make people better."

As if on cue, an image of Eric Messier appears on the screen. Hartley motions toward the laptop as if he's looking at Exhibit A to make his point.

On a rainy Sunday in the summer of 1995, Hartley was watching television with his son Steve. A commercial came on for the local roller hockey team, featuring cheerleaders, players, and a strange road runner mascot. Bored at home, Steve suggested they attend the roller hockey game being played that day.

At the game, Hartley noticed a player named Eric Messier. He later called Messier and convinced him to attend hockey camp. Here he is, years later, about to win a Stanley Cup.

In Messier, Stephane Yelle, and Shjon Podein, Hartley had a third line he thought was just as good as Detroit's famed "Grind Line" of Kirk Maltby, Kris Draper, and Darren McCarty.

"If not better," Hartley says of his checking line. "You put them on the ice, the other team never got a shot. They blocked shots. Mess knew the game well and played so smart."

Hartley has always had his guys. Guys who wouldn't be in the league if it weren't for him. Guys who sometimes never get back in once Hartley is no longer their coach.

It's the guys who are overlooked at times that he loves. The ones who are extremely loyal. They've never had anything handed to them; they earned every promotion they got, every shift they got.

In some ways, they're a reflection of their coach. In the NHL, there are coaching and management cliques. There are the Hockey Canada guys. There are the coaches from Quebec. There are the USA Hockey guys.

As is the case in any industry, the cliques tend to hire people they are comfortable with, those they know well.

Hartley isn't part of a clique. He didn't play in the NHL, so there are no former teammates around to hire him. He's a French-speaking coach from Ontario who worked his way up to the Colorado Avalanche job, winning championships at every level. His Stanley Cup with the Avs earned him a shot in Atlanta, where he was the only coach in franchise history to take the Thrashers to the playoffs.

Even so, it wasn't until his friend Jay Feaster became the general manager in Calgary that he got another shot in the NHL. That's just how it goes.

So yeah, it's no surprise he loves players like Messier, a guy he found in a roller hockey league. Their paths to the NHL were both unlikely.

Hartley started out as a goalie coach for a Junior A team in his hometown of Hawkesbury. During the day, he worked in the local windshield factory. He liked that job. He liked the guys who worked next to him on the line, sanding the sharp edges of large pieces of glass. He had a wife and two kids and was making $45,000 a year at a job close to his home. He was set. There was no reason to mess up that stability.

When the Montreal Canadiens won the Cup in 1986, he visited the Stanley Cup at the shopping mall 30 minutes away in Lachute. He harbored no dreams that he might one day win it.

"No. I'm a factory worker for the rest of my life," Hartley says. "The story of a factory worker is, once you buy a lunch pail, you die with that lunch pail. There's no shame in this. I have the utmost respect for factory workers."

Hartley might have been content in the factory but Hawkesbury Hawks team president Jacques Tranchemontagne had another idea. Tranchemontagne knew Hartley well from coaching him as a baseball player growing up. Hartley impressed him and the players with his teaching skills as the goalie coach, often jumping in to help the forwards and defensemen.

The Hawkesbury team didn't win an exhibition game. Then they lost every game to start the season. It prompted a meeting with Tranchemontagne, who wanted Hartley to become the head coach.

But Hartley liked his life the way it was. He deflected the offer.

"He didn't want to do it. He's a family man," Tranchemontagne said.

Hawkesbury was losing money. Things were so bad that the bus company that ferried the team to and from games didn't want to continue to do so because the Hawks owed it so much money.

Eventually, Hartley agreed to be the head coach but didn't make any long-term commitments.

The Avalanche's Stanley Cup victory in 2001 was the first for the franchise, defenseman Ray Bourque, and their coach, Bob Hartley. (AP Images)

"I told him, 'I'll give you $250 until Christmas and $250 the rest of the year,'" Tranchemontagne said. "He said, 'Okay but I need two new suits.'"

Hartley began coaching while keeping his full-time job at the factory.

"Bob finished working at 3:00 PM and at 3:15 he was at the rink and stayed until midnight," Tranchemontagne said. "He's a work addict."

Hawkesbury made the playoffs but was about to get swept out of the first round when Hartley called his wife on the morning of Game 4. Hartley told her it might be his last game as a head coach, and that the next time he'd be on the bench was when his two-year-old son Steve started playing minor hockey.

"You might win," she said.

"Maybe," he answered. "But if we lose, I'm done."

Of course, they won.

With a minute to go, Hawkesbury scored a goal that changed the trajectory of Hartley's life.

"I can still see the puck go in. That goal was like I got an injection of the coach's drug," Hartley says.

Hawkesbury was knocked out the next game but Hartley was hooked.

"I sat with my wife. We have a mortgage, we have two young kids, the Hawks are not profitable in those days. We had zero money," Hartley says. "My wife, she had it in her blood. She said, 'Go for it. If that's what you want to do, I'll support you.'"

He gave his notice at the plant even though his friends tried to talk him out of it. To them, this was just about the most irresponsible thing a guy with a mortgage and two kids could do. Even if he was re-hired after the coaching gig didn't work out, he would have lost his seniority in the union. He was tight with the plant manager. He was the recreational director of the plant. All of that would be gone.

But once he got that injection of the coach's drug, that was it. It had ignited his passion.

"I said, 'One day, I'll bring the Stanley Cup to the plant,'" Hartley said. "Right then, they thought I was really crazy."

* * *

On the small laptop screen in front of us, Hartley is now in the final hockey period of his life without a Stanley Cup. During the second intermission, Hartley would have his last meeting with his players until the Stanley Cup parade. They just didn't realize it at that point.

Before speaking to his players, he was pulled aside by head equipment manager Wayne Flemming, a guy they all called Smokey. Smokey was getting a bad vibe from the dressing room. Even though they were up 3–1, the players were tense.

Hartley always came in to chat with six minutes left in the intermission.

"Let's make a deal," Hartley remembers telling his players. "We're up 3–1. Let's play the best third period we can play. Never mind the Stanley Cup. They need to win the third period to keep this game going. Us, we can tie the period or win the period. Let's play a 20-minute game. Never mind what's at stake. The Cup is going to be there. The Cup is waiting. Don't play this third period to win the Cup."

The chat worked.

Now, the game is in its final couple of minutes. Hartley is playing Joe Sakic as much as possible. He's completely comfortable sending out Messier's line.

"The clock is going way too slow. Trust me," Hartley says.

Nobody in the crowd or on the bench is sitting. Hartley's voice is going hoarse from shouting out the line combinations. He puts Milan Hejduk and Alex Tanguay back together, because Hejduk is as effective as anyone he's ever coached at getting the puck out of the defensive zone. He's making sure nobody is on their backhand, so pucks are getting out of the zone as efficiently as possible. He has first and second options on faceoffs, thanks to the depth of this group. Every detail is covered. It was all falling into place.

The crowd is deafening. The only challenge remaining is making sure Ray Bourque is on the ice for the final moments.

Finally, broadcaster Gary Thorne's voice comes across the speakers: "Ten seconds left to go!…The Colorado Avalanche have won the Stanley Cup! Raymond Bourque, the dream has come true!"

Bourque made hats for the players before the playoffs with 16W printed on them, a reference to the 16 wins needed to win the Stanley Cup.

Now, Bourque and the Avs had won No. 16. It set up one of the most famous scenes in NHL history.

As is tradition, the Stanley Cup is first handed to the captain. NHL commissioner Gary Bettman has the microphone and hints at what's to come.

"There's one player who has waited a long time to hoist this," Bettman says to huge cheers. "Joe Sakic, come get the Cup so he and the rest of your teammates can hoist it."

Sakic grabs the Cup, and he and Bettman hold it together long enough for a photo. Then, in a moment that shows how much class he has, Sakic doesn't even lift it over his head in celebration. He turns to his right and immediately hands it to Bourque.

"I knew I was going to do something," Sakic said when we chatted about this moment. "I didn't know exactly what…Once I got the Cup from Gary, I saw Ray there—actually I saw him right before—and I handed it to him. I knew I'd get it back. It was awesome."

Bourque holds it high, hoisting it up and down. He gives it a long kiss, then raises it again. He tries to give it back to Sakic, but is denied. He's told to go for a skate, which he does.

It's one of the great moments in sports history. Bettman might have had the best seat in the house for it.

"For Raymond to finally reach this point after his long and distinguished career, you could see how much it meant to him. You could also see how much Joe understood it meant to him," Bettman said.

Watching the scene between Sakic and Bourque unfold, Hartley sums it up perfectly: "Best pass in hockey history."

It was made possible in part because of the efforts of a coach who was once reluctant to give up his morning shift in the windshield plant. At a private party celebrating the Cup, his old boss Tranchemontagne and a few friends from back home presented him with a wood carving of the Stanley Cup. It's a piece of art that has the names of players on all the championship teams he's coached, from Hawkesbury to Laval to Hershey and now Colorado.

Watching him interact with the kids at his camp, you would never know he'd reached the pinnacle of the sport with some of the best players of their era. He was just a guy who loved teaching and loved the game even more.

"I loved him," Sakic said. "He was a great coach. He held everyone accountable."

"The guy never changed from making $30,000 to a million," Tranchemontagne said. "He's coaching for the love of the game."

He's pretty darn good at it, too. That night in Colorado was just another example.

With that classic game over, I pack up the laptop and we say our good-byes.

After all, Uncle Bob has got kids on the ice waiting for him.

CHAPTER 5

TODD MCLELLAN

Gold Medal Game of the 2015 World Championships

I'll admit it: I was willing to stretch the rules for Todd McLellan.

I wanted this book to be full of Stanley Cup winners or coaches who played for Olympic gold.

Todd McLellan didn't fit that criteria. At least, not yet. He's going to get one or the other before the end of his career. He's too good of a coach not to.

Besides being one of the best coaches in the game, he's also a guy who has a firm grasp on what it takes to be a leader and a coach in the game today.

He took over as the head coach of the Edmonton Oilers in 2015, and with that job came the responsibility of coaching the NHL's next superstar in Connor McDavid. It has the potential to be a perfect fit.

So when he led Team Canada to gold at the World Championships in 2015, helping Sidney Crosby join the Triple Gold club, I had a game to highlight. I'll concede right now that unless you're a die-hard Canadian or hockey fan, that championship game doesn't rank among the all-time greats. You may not even know who Canada played in the final (it was Russia) or where the tournament was even held that year (they were in Prague, Czech Republic).

But McLellan is someone I wanted in this book, a coach who represents the next generation of great leaders, guys who can relate to today's young players. So when he agreed to watch that game against Russia, I jumped at the chance.

As it turns out, McLellan spends his summer in Kelowna, British Columbia, a part of the world that is a slice of heaven. That was just a bonus.

I knew nothing about Kelowna but started to suspect how nice it is on the drive in from Vancouver.

The route was simply stunning. It's a winding path through the mountains just north of the state of Washington. The only drive in my life I've made that is similar is the stretch from San Francisco to Lake Tahoe.

I was staying at a resort in Kelowna, right on Okanagan Lake. It took me five minutes after checking in to realize that half of the hockey world hides out there in the summer. If Canadian players from Ontario scatter into cottage country during the off-season, the players from this side of the continent are all right here.

I got to my room and realized I hadn't heard from McLellan since I'd arrived on this side of the world. I called and left a voicemail. I wasn't nervous but it would have been a long way to travel if he'd completely forgotten he'd agreed to sit down with me. And again, I would've totally understood if he had. Watching an old hockey game with a writer wouldn't be on my short list of things to do if I were him.

At 7:49 PM, my phone rang. It was Todd; he'd been on his boat all day and missed the calls.

"What time do you wake up?" he asked.

"I'm on East Coast time, so I'll be up early," I said.

"Perfect. I'll pick you up at 7:30 AM in my boat."

That was the first time I'd ever made plans to be picked up in a boat, but it definitely gives one a glimpse into how McLellan operates. Somebody makes it this far out to see him and he's going to do it right.

We agreed to meet the next morning at the boat gas pump near my hotel.

* * *

It's the morning of our meeting and I can't find the gas pump.

The concierge at the hotel has no idea where it is. I ask the bartender—not pausing to wonder why there's a bartender working at 7:20 in the morning—and she suggests that the nearest gas pump for a boat is at the Eldorado Hotel, some 20 minutes away.

I walk outside onto a boardwalk near the lake. I pass a couple of seaplanes but no gas pump. I send McLellan a text—the last thing I want to be is late for a guy going out of his way to find me. He calls immediately.

"Start walking toward the big bridge on the promenade. I'll meet you in a minute," he says.

I start walking on what I think is a promenade. Honestly, I'm not sure what a promenade is.

Suddenly I spot Todd walking slowly toward me. He's barefoot, wearing a swimsuit and a blue T-shirt. He's wearing sunglasses, his gray hair cut short in a buzz cut. He's got the relaxed look of a man on vacation.

We shake hands and climb into his ski boat, which is parked in a nearby marina. It's awesome. It's blue, white, and gray, with a bar across the back to pull water skiers or surfers. It's got a completely digital dashboard and country music is playing on the radio. The engine roars when he starts it up.

"Better than picking you up in the car?" he asks.

"Best treatment yet."

"Hey, I haven't gotten you there yet. If you're swimming, you're in trouble."

He pulls away from the marina and starts giving me a tour. We're working our way toward the big bridge I crossed the night before to get to the hotel. He shares a story about coming to this lake as a kid on vacation or for hockey tournaments. The bridge used to float on pontoons, he says. That doesn't sound right to me. Or safe. But I'm no engineer.

"There's downtown Kelowna. Great golfing over here. Wine. The lake. The first three weeks of July were so hot," McLellan says. "You surf?"

"Oh, no."

"You may have to learn how. I'll put you on the board."

McLellan's boat is designed specifically to create a wake for surfing. It fills up with water to weigh down the back end, and if you're athletically skilled and coordinated enough, two people can surf on the wake at the same time, following right behind the boat without any attached rope.

His two sons do it all the time. One is headed to college to play hockey. The other is a dynamite golfer.

I'm a writer who barely likes to take his shirt off in front of his own family. There's no way I'm trying to surf for the first time in front of the McLellan family.

"You get out there and do that?" I ask.

"Oh yeah, we were out all day yesterday. The kids are either on the jet skis or the boat."

We're now on the other side of the bridge. He points to an area where Dany Heatley has a home. Milan Lucic used to live in a house to our left.

The boat finds another gear. We're moving now.

"The best part of the day is the morning," McLellan says. "The paddle boaters, the kayakers aren't out yet. You have the lake to yourself. That's the Hotel Eldorado over there. There's a canyon, you can see it in the back there. The railroad used to go up and around the canyon and keep going. Now, you can ride your bike there."

This is all I want to do. Hang out on the lake. Maybe have a beer.

"Look at the hot air balloons going up over there. [Arizona Coyotes defenseman] Luke Schenn just built a place in the bay."

"It really reminds me of Lake Tahoe," I say. "This is unreal. I may have picked the best day of the year to do this. I'm sorry."

"This is almost every day."

We start closing in on his dock. The boat slows down. He cuts the engine and we're both grabbing rope to hook the boat to the dock.

The house is gorgeous. Walking toward the McLellan home from the lake, there's a lush green lawn that leads you up to a patio with a large outdoor television. This is where we'll watch the game, making me feel slightly less guilty about keeping Todd inside on a beautiful morning.

But first, we go into the kitchen to meet his family.

Sitting at the counter are Todd's oldest son Tyson and his girlfriend, Reagan. The two met while Tyson was playing hockey in Iowa, where he played for the Waterloo Black Hawks of the USHL.

Tyson was with his dad in the Czech Republic when McLellan guided Team Canada to gold. He sat in the coaches' box during the games and helped out. On the night Canada won gold, the two took a photo together on the ice, confetti all around them. McLellan is wearing a gold medal around his neck and has his arm around his son.

I spent about 10 days in the Czech Republic during the tournament. After starting out in Ostrava to see future Buffalo Sabre Jack Eichel play for Team USA, I drove across the country in a rental car to catch a game between Sweden and Canada in Prague. That game ended up being Canada's only real scare of the tournament.

Sweden jumped out to an early lead. Canada was down 3–0 almost immediately.

"It was like they had six guys on the ice," Canada defenseman Jake Muzzin said later of the Swedes.

This was my first exposure to a Canadian team that was supposed to be a powerhouse. Needless to say, it wasn't impressive.

Jay Woodcroft was an assistant on that team, as he is on just about any team McLellan coaches. He'd explain later that Canada had just come off an emotional win over the Czech Republic. The game against

Sweden was at an odd time of day, and the boys had a hard time getting things going.

Woodcroft said the message McLellan sent during the first intermission was pointed. This game was the Swedes' entire tournament from a seeding standpoint and they were playing like it. Canada wasn't matching their desperation.

"That was the turning point of the whole tournament," Woodcroft said. "In between periods was one of the finest coaching performances I've seen from Todd in my 10 years being around him. He was authoritative, challenging. He was unafraid to make the changes that were necessary. That ability to express his dissatisfaction—concisely and with authority—and his ability to make adjustments sets him apart in terms of coaches in the world."

McLellan put Jordan Eberle and Taylor Hall on a line centered by Sidney Crosby, among other changes. The tweaks worked.

Canadian defenseman Patrick Wiercioch tied it in the third period. Tyler Ennis later broke the tie, and Tyler Seguin added insurance at the end.

McLellan and I chatted in a hallway after that game. He had recently been fired by the Sharks and was in talks to join the Oilers, although that second bit of information he kept to himself at the time. We made a plan to meet for coffee the next morning to talk about his future.

Canada was staying at a hotel near the arena. We met in the lobby and walked to a nearby café, grabbed some coffee, and sat outside on metal chairs. It was a beautiful morning and McLellan was in a reflective mood, between jobs while trying to lead Canada to a gold medal. It was a thankless task, really. If he won gold, he did what he was supposed to do. If he didn't, it'd be a black mark on his résumé shortly after parting ways with San Jose.

He stressed that his focus was on leading Canada, but he was definitely interested in knowing what the latest speculation was on the coaching vacancies around the NHL. We talked about the different openings, with

Getting picked up in a boat by Edmonton Oilers coach Todd McLellan is really the only way to travel.

Mike Babcock being the big free agent. He casually mentioned that Peter DeBoer would do a great job in San Jose if the Sharks offered him the job. (They did offer him the job. He did do a great job.)

We chatted a little longer about what he'd seen from the Oilers players, since there were rumors Edmonton could be his next stop. Then, we wandered back to the hotel.

There were no signs that the burden of coaching the Canadian team was bothering him, nor did the idea that he may not know where he'd be coaching when the tournament was done.

Instead, his focus was on the task at hand. It's how the best coaches operate. Let others worry about the big picture; he was trying to build off the win over Sweden the night before.

Back in the kitchen of his summer home, hanging out with his family, I'm reminded of that experience. The trip to Prague. Those conversations with McLellan. The stunning beauty of the city. I'd go back in a heartbeat if I could.

"I was blown away by Prague," I say to McLellan.

"Was that your first time over there?"

"Yeah, the Americans were in Ostrava. I went there first, then went over to Prague to see Canada. You guys were doing it right."

"That was the one thing I thought was excellent, how they set up the hotel. It was like an Olympic village. Every other team that played in our pool stayed there. You going to show Craig after this what surfing is? Maybe he'll try it?"

Oh god, here we go.

"I don't know," I answer. "I've never even water skied."

"Everyone I've seen do it has gotten up," Reagan adds.

I change the subject. We start talking about college. Todd's wife, Debbie, enters the room and there are more introductions. The family couldn't be nicer, absolutely salt of the earth. I mean, besides the million-dollar summer home we're currently standing in.

With the small talk over, we wander back outside to the patio to set up.

The game appears on the screen but before we dive into it, I want to talk to McLellan about what makes him such an effective coach.

He's a planner but more importantly he's good at clearly articulating what he expects from his players and why it's necessary for success. He's got a booming voice that makes his practices fun to watch because you know exactly what he's saying. Much of his focus is on getting players to understand why he's asking them to do what he's asking them to do.

"That's the trick to coaching," he says. "Regardless of what our abilities are, we can find drills, we can find patterns to skate, and show the players how to do it. It's getting the players to understand why they're doing it. What's the reward for doing it?"

McLellan played during a time when players didn't ask why. But he had the benefit of having his father, Bill, as a hockey coach early on in his development. When Todd got into coaching, his dad became one of his scouts. When Bill and I chatted later over the phone, he was scouting for Medicine Hat.

"Todd's always been very attentive," Bill said. "He just didn't go to the rink and skate. He wanted to know what was going on. He always wanted to know why we were doing it. He wasn't one of these kids who wanted to skate and have fun. He was so inquisitive."

McLellan learned from his dad as well as from a coach named Doug McKay. McLellan's last year as a player came in Europe. He was on the verge of getting married, so Debbie went home to plan the wedding. McLellan's team fired its Dutch coach and brought in McKay, who needed a place to stay. Luckily, McLellan needed a roommate and a match was made.

"We started planning practice. We started planning tactics. That's where I started to ask, 'Why?'" McLellan says.

What he learned most from McKay was the difference between playing and coaching. A player could practice and then go home. The coaching staff, if it was any good, was constantly working and preparing for the next game.

McLellan was offered another contract to play in the Dutch league but realized there was no future in that. He was getting married and he had to find a job in North America. His friends in hockey all became cops or firemen. His family had a history with the Royal Canadian Mounted Police. None of it appealed to McLellan.

He opened up the *Saskatoon StarPhoenix* newspaper and saw an opening for the head coaching position of the North Battleford junior team. He sent in his résumé, nailed the interview, then got the phone call that would change the course of his life.

"I hung up the phone, looked over at Debbie, and said, 'I got the job in North Battleford.' She said, 'Good.' I said, 'Not really. Now what? I don't know what I'm doing.'"

McLellan concedes that it would never happen like that today. Junior teams in Canada aren't looking for head coaches in the classifieds. Heck, the classifieds barely even exist anymore.

But he was willing to take the risk and learn as he went along.

"I didn't get the 'why' part yet," he says. "It was just drills, pattern skating, yelling and screaming between periods—not really having a purpose behind things."

He and his young assistant coach Blaine Gusdal were learning on the fly. There can be something completely invigorating about diving in head-first and learning your way out of something.

"I look back and it was still one of the most rewarding experiences I ever had as a coach," Gusdal told me later. "We did everything together. We would sit in this cramped little coaches' office; we didn't have much of a dressing room the first couple years. We would sit and draw up plays and draw up systems."

Even then, Gusdal saw something different in McLellan.

"He was brilliant at 25. That first year, we took it on the chin but we changed the culture of the team. We went from last place to second place in the division. He was the coach of the year in the second year. It was a complete 180 of the team."

The success came quickly for McLellan in junior hockey and it caught the eye of Minnesota Wild general manager Doug Risebrough, who brought him into the organization to be the head coach of its IHL and then AHL team. When he was first hired, McLellan and Risebrough had dinner together, and on the way back to the car they had a conversation McLellan remembers well.

"Now my job is to slow everything down for you," Risebrough said.

"What do you mean by that?" McLellan asked.

"You're going to be in a hurry. You think you can coach in the NHL right now. You have to take the steps," Risebrough said.

Years later, Risebrough remembers those conversations with McLellan. He saw a talented coach who seemed destined for success. But he'd also seen versions of coaches like McLellan whose careers were sidetracked because they took the wrong job in an effort to advance their careers too quickly.

"Those guys, they're going to get there no matter what. They're going to get there because their ability and their success is going to stand out," Risebrough said. "Just don't push it. If you get in the wrong situation at the wrong time, if it doesn't work, the outside world will see the coach as being a major factor."

Taking the wrong job can change the image of an up-and-coming coach in a hurry. It can happen to anyone, in any profession. Be careful taking a job that looks like a promotion if the job isn't the right one with the right organization.

In 2003, McLellan led his AHL team to a Calder Cup, and Risebrough's suspicions about McLellan's ability to coach paid off. His patience was being rewarded.

In the Minnesota organization, McLellan got a close-up look at how Wild head coach Jacques Lemaire operated. He was immediately able to identify what has stuck with him the most about Lemaire's approach.

"Clarity," McLellan says. "Jacques could take a difficult task and, with a French accent and broken English, explain it clearly. 'I want your stick here. This is what's going to happen.'"

He told me a story that captured Lemaire's ability to teach with clarity.

The Wild were working on one-on-one drills when Lemaire picked 6-foot Christian Matte to take on 6-foot-6 defenseman Andy Sutton in the corner.

"Christian is working him over and Andy is just standing there," McLellan says. "Jacques blows the whistle. 'Christian, what are you doing?' 'I'm playing one-on-one.' He goes, 'No, you're wasting energy.'"

Lemaire told him instead what he wanted him to do.

"Just relax," Lemaire said. "Sutton is like a big truck driver. He's backing up but eventually he has to turn the wheel. When he turns the wheel, I want you to go right here with the stick. Stick on puck."

They did the drill again. Sutton backed up but the moment he exposed the puck, Matte knocked it loose. All the effort in the world from Matte in the corner wasn't going to do him an ounce of good if he wasn't doing the right thing.

"Rather than doing the drill and wasting energy, Jacques took that moment and simply explained what he wanted from a small player. Jacques understood not everyone plays the same way," McLellan says.

The incident stuck with McLellan.

He moved on to the Detroit organization, where daily drives to practice with Mike Babcock helped shape him even more.

Every step of the process was integral to preparing him to be a future NHL coach.

In Minnesota, Risebrough told him that there were distinct stages to a successful career. First was establishing a passion. To be great, coaching had to be an obsession. The second was working on your craft, focusing on daily improvement. Then it was setting goals and climbing the ladder. The final stage was reaching the point where you can start to turn down opportunities that don't align with how you want to live your life.

McLellan was most certainly at the final stage when he parted ways with San Jose. He had a team in Edmonton aggressively pursuing him, even when Babcock was also out there as a potential hire.

"That guy had so many options," said McLellan's longtime friend Kelly Chase. "The Edmonton Oilers didn't go after Mike Babcock. They went after Todd McLellan and said, 'You're our guy. We don't have to interview anybody else.' He wanted someone to be loyal to him."

He got that in the Oilers, shortly after his impressive showing in the World Championships.

* * *

"Alright, let's get this thing going," I say to McLellan, leaning over to my laptop to press play on the gold medal game between Canada and Russia.

We watch on the outdoor television, the lake to our left. Soon the screen fills with a shot of Canada's Matt Duchene sitting on the bench as the arena starts to fill with fans, a look of intense focus on his face.

Highlights of Canada steamrolling its way through the previous games in the tournament flash on the screen after that. Jordan Eberle banging the rebound of his own shot past a Swiss goalie. Brent Burns burying a shot past a poor goalie from Belarus on a one-timer.

A few minutes later an interview with McLellan plays. He's wearing a look of intensity on his face, a gray suit, a blue shirt, and a tie. His message during the interview is that his team is looking to embrace the opportunity in front of it. For players usually in the middle of the Stanley Cup playoffs, this is one of the rare chances at World Championship gold. For Sidney Crosby, it's even more meaningful, because a win makes him a rare member of the Triple Gold club—winner of Olympic gold, World Championship gold, and a Stanley Cup.

As the video plays, McLellan says that some of the Russian team's antics added fuel to the Canadians' fire.

"One of the things we had was motivation from the Russian group," McLellan says. "For example, they would go out for 20-minute warm-ups and we would go out for 16-minute warm-ups. We would stay on the NHL program. They were out there four minutes before we got out onto the ice. When we walked onto the ice, they all lined up on the blue line to stare us down."

"To intimidate you?"

"Yup. Our players didn't even realize it. They're looking around like, 'What are these guys doing?' In old-time hockey, that could have gotten ugly. There would have been pucks going the other way."

McLellan and the players noticed another thing that rubbed them the wrong way before the game began.

"They had gold water bottles on their bench. The players saw it. We were driven. I think that helped us at the beginning of the game. They poked the bear a little bit," he says.

This was another in a long line of big games between Alex Ovechkin and Sidney Crosby. If Canada could contain Ovechkin in this game, it would go a long way toward winning gold.

A picture of Ovechkin taking a shot in warm-ups is on the screen.

"What's the game plan to stop Alex Ovechkin in a game like this?" I ask.

"We didn't want him on the power play. That was one way. Playing fast—their team, they were skilled but I don't know if they played at the pace we played at. It helped us. It took Ovi out of the game. He's a great player but you can't do it by yourself."

McLellan doesn't mince words; he knows he had a great team in this tournament. He had Crosby and Brent Burns and Tyler Seguin, Taylor Hall, Claude Giroux, Jordan Eberle, Jason Spezza, Nathan MacKinnon, Matt Duchene—it was ridiculous. The plan was to take advantage of that speed and blow teams off the ice.

They also had the perfect goalie to play that style in Mike Smith, who could retrieve the puck and send it back up the ice before the other team knew what hit it. It was like having three defensemen.

"You look at our lineup, it was a pretty special group," Smith said. "We had a lot of fun, we jelled together. I know nobody talks about the World Championships much, but it was a real special team. It was a really cool moment in my career."

In tournaments like these, McLellan has learned to simplify his approach. He wants his teams to play with speed and to put a lot of shots on goal. Don't overpass, don't look for the prettiest play. Shoot the puck, get it back, and shoot the puck again.

The challenge is communicating that in a way that everybody understands. The hockey world has a lot of different phrases that often mean the same thing. The terminology in a Mike Babcock meeting is different than the terminology in a Dan Bylsma meeting or Joel Quenneville meeting.

This is where McLellan excels. He makes sure that no player leaves a meeting unprepared.

"Even as a staff, I might be talking about working above the puck—that'll mean something to me and Mike Babcock—but if you get a new coach in there, he's going, 'What the hell does "working above the puck" mean?' Some say 'backcheck,' some say 'track.' There are a number of different languages, and hockey can be a different language altogether. Nobody puts a hand up in a group and says, 'I don't get it.'"

"These guys are expected to know it."

"Or you go in between periods and say, 'You've got to work harder.' You can't just tell them generalities. You have to give them a *way* to work harder. 'We're not disciplined.' What does that mean? Are we slashing all the time? Are we out of position? Are we not changing on time? Is our shift length too long? Are we arguing amongst each other? It means something different to everybody. The hockey world uses a bunch of words that aren't even really defined."

Amen.

The game gets out to a flying pace immediately, with Canada pressuring early and strong play by Russian goalie Sergei Bobrovsky up to the early challenge. Sidney Crosby makes a great pass to Jordan Eberle for an early scoring chance. The conversation shifts to one about Crosby.

The morning after the Penguins were eliminated from the playoffs that spring, Team Canada GM Jim Nill received a text from Crosby's agent, Pat Brisson.

"I called him and once they knew the schedule and explained everything, right away, Sid was on board," Nill said. "Right away."

"I just wanted to keep playing," Crosby explained, laughing, when I asked him about it in Prague. "It's tough losing...I just wanted to keep playing and hopefully come here to find a way to put a positive note at the end of the year."

McLellan has learned how to coach great players, including Sidney Crosby at the 2015 World Championships. (AP Images)

He was getting that opportunity against Russia. And his coach was glad to have him.

"Pittsburgh loses and I get a call and it's, 'Hey, we're going to add a player.' I'm thinking, 'Now?'" McLellan recalls. "We kind of had an agreement, this was going to be our team. I'm thinking, 'Who are we adding?' When they told me, I said, 'I think that'll be okay.'"

At that point, the level of seriousness with this group of Canadian hockey players increased dramatically. The team went from very good to possibly one of the all-time greats.

"It was like winning the lottery," Jake Muzzin said of adding Crosby. "You get the No. 1 player in the world playing for your team, it brings a lot."

"For him to do that, it made our whole group be like, 'Alright boys, we're here to win this,'" goalie Mike Smith said.

We move right on to the second period and, at this point, it's still a game. The Canadians are up 1–0 on a Cody Eakin goal as play starts in the second, but that would change soon enough thanks to the same line that opened the scoring.

All these stars around him, yet it's Tyler Ennis who puts the Canadians up 2–0, wrapping one around Bobrovsky just about two minutes into the second period.

"Goal," McLellan said as Ennis squeezes it by Bobrovsky. "Just too fast. We worked on that transition a lot. Look at how he drove the first guy back. Eakin drives him back, that d-man takes him and can't meet him at the post. The goalie is slow."

McLellan is just about to get up for more coffee when another Canadian scores.

Sidney Crosby. The captain.

Jordan Eberle slides a nice pass to Crosby for a one-timer and it's 3–0. The broadcaster rightly observes, "Canada has started to strangle the life out of this game here."

McLellan agrees.

"That's the nail in the coffin. The game just changes," he says.

"Did you learn anything about Sid as a player seeing him up close?"

"I didn't learn a lot but I got a lot confirmed."

"Like what?"

"Just the type of person he is. The individual. I watched him carry himself around my son Tyson, how he included him after and during the celebration and stuff like that. Talking to him, we talked a lot about Connor [McDavid] and how he would feel. He was excellent."

Right after this tournament, McLellan would take the job in Edmonton and be the first NHL coach for Connor McDavid. At this tournament, he got a head start on how to handle him from Crosby.

"We talked about Sid's entry into the league and how he had a really good support system in place," McLellan says. "Where he lived. How they treated him. He was well-tuned with the media at that point, he'd learned to deal with it. It's still about physically maturing, getting your rest and eating. Not necessarily protection away from the rink but good guidance. Great family. His family was over there. His sister. Connor is the same way. There are similarities between star players."

It was a nice little feed from Eberle that set up the goal by Crosby, sending the puck to a spot on the ice rather than to Crosby's stick. It showed the hockey sense that would make Eberle a forward McDavid would later tell McLellan he enjoyed playing with.

A few minutes later, a turnover by Russia's Ilya Kovalchuk leads to an odd-man rush for Team Canada. Claude Giroux makes an impossible pass to Tyler Seguin for the fourth goal of the game. The Canadian bench is going crazy. McLellan straightens out his jacket, then calmly pulls a sheet of paper from his inside pocket and examines it while his players celebrate.

But at this point he knows. This game is over.

"You have a good feeling. Now, you're starting to think, 'How are you going to keep your foot on the gas?'" he recalls. "When you look at the clock, it's, 'Holy shit, there's still a lot of game left.'"

The outcome of this game is decided halfway through the actual action. There's a belief among some coaches that if you can get a big lead on the Russians, you can suck the will to win right out of them. This group of Russians does nothing to dispel that notion. They're outclassed in every way in this game.

The second period ends.

"Pause it and I'll take you around our place," McLellan says.

We start at the front door. We turn and you can look right through the front door and out the back, where we were watching the game and to the lake in the distance.

The view on this day is stunning. In the far distance is a mountain. The lake is crystal-clear and blue. His long dock extends into the water, with a couple of jet skis and the boat we drove in on floating above the surface.

Having this view as you walked right into the house was all by design; credit to the guy who built the place.

"He owned a lumber mill and he was really about wood. He wanted to be able to drive in the driveway and see right through to the lake. So he started with that," McLellan says.

The doors and walls to the patio slide open, blurring the line between indoors and outdoors. He has me open the door and it's the heaviest door I've ever felt.

To the right of the front door is a towering fireplace, flanked on either side by white shelves holding a few large pieces of pottery and glassware.

"That's marble. He needed a crane to bring pieces in," he says.

"That's awesome. Look at that view."

"I have a little office here, haven't really set up."

There are framed pictures on the floor, still wrapped in plastic.

There's one picture of a smiling Team Canada coaching staff from the World Championships, gold medals draped around their necks. McLellan is in the middle, Jay Woodcroft and Peter DeBoer are on his right. Woodcroft would join him in leaving San Jose to go to Edmonton. DeBoer would replace him in San Jose.

To McLellan's left is Misha Donskov and Bill Peters. Under the photo is an engraved metal plaque that reads THANK YOU FOR YOUR LEADERSHIP, GUIDANCE AND FRIENDSHIP.

"This is one of my favorite ones, with the coaches after," he says.

We wander to the other side of the house, where the kids are staying. The walls are a whitewashed wood.

"West Coast Beech," McLellan says.

We look back out toward the lake and there's a little beach area.

"I would never want to leave this," I say.

"You have to go back to work at some point."

So we get back to work.

* * *

We start the third period. Canada is up 4–0 and the suspense that is usually present in these classic games is gone. That's just fine, because it's a beautiful summer day and gives us time to chat.

Todd's son Tyson joins us on the outdoor furniture, taking in the final minutes. We're now just hockey fans talking about the stuff you might talk about over beers in the summer.

Like how much an offer sheet for Connor McDavid would cost.

"We'd just match it," McLellan says. But now he's curious. "Who can offer sheet him?"

We try to figure it out. It's fun. So is the talk of the celebration after this championship game. Hockey Canada set up a room back at the team hotel so friends and families could have a place to celebrate in Prague with some privacy. The party was still going at 5:00 AM.

"I was supposed to go downtown with Tyler Seguin and I wasn't allowed," Tyson says.

"There's a reason," his dad shoots back.

"That's good parenting," I say, backing up Todd on this one.

"Tyler is a good kid. A little misunderstood. He's full of life."

"He was one of the nicest guys there," Tyson says.

"We're to blame for some of the stuff that happens to these young guys. Not we. The game," McLellan says.

He changes the subject to Jake Muzzin and how underrated he is. Steady, good defender who can provide offense.

For what it's worth, the feeling is mutual. Muzzin loved playing for McLellan.

"He was honest. It wasn't a joke. It wasn't easy," Muzzin said of McLellan's approach. "He had a game plan and made sure we stuck to it—video, everything. It was very professional. Good coach."

The game is winding down and McLellan makes a point of trying to get Sidney Crosby on the ice at the end, since he's about to join the Triple Gold club.

The final horn sounds, and McLellan officially has his World Championship gold. He's now forever part of one of the most talented and successful teams Canada has ever sent to this tournament.

The Canadian players are hopping up and down on the ice in celebration. The camera cuts to a disappointed Ilya Kovalchuk, his head pressed against his stick. Alex Ovechkin is leaning on the Russian bench, watching the Canadians celebrate.

One by one, the Russian players are awarded their silver medals. Then the Canadians take their turn, bowing down slightly to have the gold medals placed around their necks.

Once the medals are handed out, Rene Fasel, president of the International Ice Hockey Federation, hands Sidney Crosby the championship trophy. Crosby raises it over his head with a yell and then skates over and hands it to Jason Spezza.

Confetti is pumped into the air along with fireworks. Claude Giroux gets the trophy and pretends to drink out of it.

The Canadian national anthem begins and the players belt out the lyrics. The Canadian fans who made the trip to Prague do too. There are a lot of them in the stands.

"I never realized until I got there how passionately people follow that tournament," McLellan says.

On cue, the screen shows two fans in white Team Canada jerseys, singing loudly. One has his red hat pressed over his heart.

The flags are slowly raised to the rafters. Russia's is on the left. The Stars and Stripes are on the right, courtesy of Team USA's third-place finish.

In the middle is the red Maple Leaf. Canada has won another championship in as dominating a manner as you can do it, without a single loss on the schedule.

"O, Canada, we stand on guard for theeeee…"

We hear the final notes of the anthem as a close up of Sidney Crosby fades in. He's smiling and singing loudly.

As an American, I'm a little jealous but mostly impressed. Gold in Vancouver. Gold in Sochi. Gold in these World Championships. Gold in the World Cup. It's a generation of Canadian hockey players, and their coaches, for the ages.

CHAPTER 6

MIKE SULLIVAN AND JOHN TORTORELLA

Game 6 of the 2016 Stanley Cup Final /
Game 7 of the 2004 Stanley Cup Final

I wish I could say that I'd spent years arranging the perfect time and place to sit down with Mike Sullivan and John Tortorella on the same summer day and watch hockey with them.

Because it's a heck of an idea. It's just that it didn't come from me—it came from Tortorella.

We were on the phone hashing out a date to watch Game 7 of the 2004 Stanley Cup Final, where his Tampa Bay Lightning beat the Calgary Flames. Tortorella said he had an opening while he was in St. Paul, Minnesota, working with his Team USA coaching staff, which included Penguins head coach Mike Sullivan, before the World Cup.

The USA Hockey staff had a meeting early on a Thursday morning to talk about the World Cup, and then most of the coaches were traveling home that afternoon. Tortorella had a conference room already reserved, so he suggested we watch two games back to back.

Of course, I was sold. I pitched the idea to Sullivan and he loved it, too.

It was the opportunity of a lifetime—watching hockey with two best friends who just happen to be terrific NHL coaches, with Sullivan coming off a Stanley Cup championship just a couple months earlier, the first of his two with Pittsburgh.

On the morning of the meeting, while I was waiting in the lobby of the historic Saint Paul Hotel, the doors to the conference room opened. Out came American coaches Jack Capuano, Phil Housley, and Scott Gordon, along with Tortorella and Sullivan. Their meeting was over. Torotrella walks over and says hello. Our meeting can begin.

I still couldn't believe my luck.

I walk into the conference room and the remains of the USA Hockey meeting are everywhere. At the front of the room is a white board, with a hockey play diagrammed in black marker. There is a long conference table covered with a tablecloth, a couple newspapers and empty water glasses scattered around. In the front of the room, a large television is waiting for the two games we'd be watching.

The first game, with all three of us watching, would be Sullivan's 2016 Stanley Cup clincher—Game 6 in San Jose. The Penguins won 3–1 to finish off the Sharks and win their first Stanley Cup since 2009, the second for Sidney Crosby.

Sullivan is seated in a large leather chair immediately to my right. He's wearing a red polo shirt and navy pants. Directly across the table, Tortorella is seated and wearing a navy Under Armor T-shirt. Brian Burke, the Calgary Flames' president and a longtime NHL GM, is also present.

I get the game hooked up and the broadcast kicks in.

"What is this one?" Sullivan asks.

"The game you won the Stanley Cup."

"Oh. Okay."

"Have you watched it yet?"

"Not in its entirety."

The story of how Sullivan arrived at that moment with the Penguins is one of perseverance and taking advantage of an incredible opportunity. He was also the perfect coach at the perfect time.

On December 12, the Penguins fired Mike Johnston and promoted Sullivan from their AHL team to be the head coach. The hints began even before then.

"A couple of weeks leading up to it, I was talking to him on a fairly regular basis as to what he knew about our team," said Penguins GM Jim Rutherford, who made the decision. "How close was he following it? What does he think the plusses and minuses are? We were talking on a pretty regular basis."

When Rutherford asked Sullivan what he thought was wrong with the Penguins, the word Rutherford remembers Sullivan mentioning most frequently was "juice." The Penguins, for whatever reason, were lacking it.

"He uses the word juice all the time," Rutherford said. "He said there's more there to get out of them."

That eventually became Sullivan's job.

"I phoned him and said, 'Pack your bags. Be here by morning,'" Rutherford said. "When he got that phone call, he was ready for it."

No surprise—he'd only been preparing for that call for a decade. That's how long it had been since his last NHL head coaching job, in Boston. His path was a lesson in faith and how relentless work can get you back to the place you believe you belong.

What makes Sullivan's story great is that he suspected coaching the Penguins would be his last shot. He'd already been fired from one NHL head coaching job after two seasons. An assistant coach for Tortorella in New York and Vancouver, the duo had been fired together in both places in high-profile coaching regime changes.

The guy who had been coaching and teaching, even during his days as a college hockey player, felt that failure as the head coach in Pittsburgh would be a career killer.

After getting the job, he called his dad to share the news…and his concerns.

"He said, 'I don't know what's going to happen. If I take the team and I don't do well, I'm going to be fired. I'll never get a job again,'" George Sullivan said. "He said, 'There's a fear of trying to pull all those egos together.'"

Managing egos is the flip side of having a team loaded with stars. Sidney Crosby, Evgeni Malkin, Kris Letang, Phil Kessel, Marc-Andre Fleury—all great players but all players who have egos of varying sizes. You don't get to be one of the best in the world without one.

"It was a lot riding on this for me, personally," Sullivan says. "If I don't have success, how many opportunities am I going to be afforded? So I knew that if I didn't have success with this group that I might not get another opportunity to be a head coach."

Fair or not, Sullivan had been lumped together with Tortorella through the years as close friends and constant companions behind the bench. When Tortorella failed, Sullivan often paid the price, too.

There were times Sullivan came close to his own breakthrough. When Kings GM Dean Lombardi was looking to hire a coach in Los Angeles, he came close to hiring Sullivan for a job that eventually went to Terry Murray.

Tortorella and Sullivan both interviewed once for an opening with the New York Islanders. Tortorella said he got cold feet because of suspicions surrounding ownership, so he called GM Garth Snow to withdraw from consideration.

"I knew Sully was coming in, and I told Snow the day I interviewed, 'That's the guy you have to hire,'" Tortorella says.

The Islanders hired Scott Gordon instead.

Both Tortorella and Sullivan once interviewed for an opening in Atlanta.

"Johnny Anderson got the job. I didn't want the job. I wanted Sully to get the job," Tortorella says.

Sullivan had a lot of close calls but never another real chance after getting fired in Boston.

"I couldn't believe people bypassed that guy," Tortorella says. "He's just dynamite."

Partly because of the missed opportunities, Sullivan and Tortorella consciously decided to stop working together after doing so in Tampa Bay, New York, and Vancouver.

As Sullivan's crowning moment is just starting on the screen in front of us, this is where the conversation begins.

At the bottom.

In May of 2014, Trevor Linden, the Vancouver Canucks' new president of hockey operations, fired Tortorella and Sullivan in his first big move.

"I knew I was gone," Tortorella says. "In my exit meeting with Trevor, I brought in bullet points on what I thought needed to happen. Trevor and I had a very, very frank conversation. And I left. Trevor called me one day in the summer and said they were going to make a change."

"It was like a week later," Sullivan says, continuing the story. "He called you on the night before and called me the next morning. He was very respectful."

Months later, while walking down the red carpet at the Hockey Hall of Fame on induction night, Linden politely stopped to chat about this moment.

To him, it was simply two hockey guys who had a difference in philosophy.

"I had a tremendous amount of respect for John," Linden said. "We had some very good hockey conversations and discussions about the game and the philosophy behind it. I think there are always relationships, however short, that are unique that you never forget. That was one of those conversations I had with John."

He appreciated how forthright and honest Tortorella was about the situation—even if he didn't agree with it. Tortorella, when he opens up, has that effect on people. He believes so passionately in what he believes that you can't help but respect it.

When the news became official, Sullivan realized what he had to do next—separate himself from Tortorella.

"I knew that if I wanted to reach my aspirations to be a head coach again, I had to get out of his shadow," he says. "It's just the way the league works…"

"You get labeled," Tortorella interjects.

"You get kind of pigeon-holed as an assistant coach or 'Torts' guy.' I think that probably happened to me."

Sullivan's instincts told him he needed to go back to the American Hockey League as a head coach. Ultimately, that's what he did.

"Can I pop in here?" Tortorella says. "I think it's really cool, it's really something for other coaches to watch and learn from. Remember, his next year, he was player development coach in Chicago. He stayed in it, ends up winning; the organization wins the Stanley Cup. I know he's not fulfilled, he's not coaching. He's not in the fire. He stepped into that and then went to the minors."

Brian Burke is quietly looking over papers at the conference table a few seats down.

Tortorella looks at him as he continues.

"I have a general manager sitting over here—I think some general managers missed the boat on [Sullivan] a number of times," he says. "I thought the Rangers did when they fired me. It seemed like when I got fired, he came along with me. They didn't look too hard. They didn't look hard enough. It's a great learning experience, what he did. You've got to park your ego. He's played in the league. Head coach in the league, been in the league forever as a coach. I've heard young coaches say, 'I don't even want to be an assistant coach. I want to be a head coach.' It's a great lesson for coaches to watch what he did. Now, he has a Stanley Cup ring."

Sullivan made three smart moves that ultimately led him to his success in Pittsburgh. He divorced himself from Tortorella after he sensed the perception was becoming that he was nothing more than Tortorella's assistant. He then went to a successful organization in Chicago to get an inside glimpse at how one of the league's most powerful franchises operates, taking a job that wasn't part of the coaching staff to make it happen. Then, he re-established himself as a head coach by moving down a level to take the AHL job in Wilkes-Barre. To take a step forward in one's career, sometimes one has to take a step backward.

Just a couple of good friends getting together to watch hockey: Mike Sullivan (left) and John Tortorella (right).

Sullivan could have been an NHL assistant until the end of time but took risks to keep his dream of another head coaching job in the NHL alive. He adopted an approach that mirrors his father's—that life and athletics are a marathon.

"I always said to myself, I'm not going to be able to control certain aspects of the business," Sullivan says. "I'm going to have to be willing to do what it takes to get where I want to go. Did it happen as fast as I wanted it to? No. There were some days I wasn't sure I was going to get a chance again."

Sullivan also tried to use the downtime between jobs to become a more informed coach. The day-to-day demands that come with coaching don't provide a lot of opportunity to take on massive projects. Suddenly, when they were between jobs, both Sullivan and Tortorella had that time. They used it to dive into analytics.

The two friends tracked every even-strength goal scored in the league, to see if they could detect any trends.

That might catch some observers by surprise, because Tortorella has a reputation of being an old-school coach. And yet, he was open-minded enough to see if his deep-rooted beliefs would be confirmed when he started tracking the raw data.

Sullivan is progressive in his approach, so the project was a natural extension of that.

In hockey, especially in coaching, analytics is always a bit of a hot-button topic. When I ask about this massive project, Sullivan defers for the moment to Tortorella.

"I think some of the analytics in our game that are spoken about so much right now, to me, it's ass backward," he says. "They don't make any sense. I don't think it is the proper way to assess a player or assess the team and how they're playing. I also think there's some really good analytics."

So this project, on some level, became an attempt at coming up with better data.

"There was a lot of minutiae with it. There were a lot of things we tracked," Tortorella says.

They'd note how each goal was scored. Did it come off the rush? Did it come off defensive-zone coverage? They categorized each and every goal. They split up teams and tried to decipher what information was relevant and what wasn't.

"You're trying to cut the fat off the meat. I don't think we're even close yet as a league," Sullivan says.

One of Tortorella's teams to break down was the Boston Bruins, and he went in with a preconception of how he thought a majority of the goals a team coached by Claude Julien would be scored. He anticipated that most of them would be the result of the Bruins working the corners.

He ended up being amazed at how many goals the Bruins scored off the rush. His intuition as an opposing coach didn't match the data he was accumulating. It's just about the perfect defense of why analytics can be a useful tool if you've got the right data.

"It was a really good process," Tortorella says. "This game is such a spontaneous game, it's really hard to spit out numbers as we do with the Corsi and Fenwick 30 minutes after the game."

"And context is so important when you're talking about analytics," Sullivan adds. "For example, we play Kris Letang a lot behind Crosby's line. That's going to have an impact on their possession numbers because of the types of players they're playing against, or how we deploy them within our strategy. We try to use the analytics we do have and we try to apply context to them. Does that make sense?"

"Yeah," I say. I mention that I didn't necessarily want this to turn into an analytics debate with noted skeptic Brian Burke in the room. Burke looks up and doesn't miss a beat.

"You guys can hand me an air sickness bag at any time," he says.

We laugh.

"What it did do was clarify your own convictions," Sullivan adds.

"You can get caught up in it and say, 'Am I doing something wrong? Do I have to get up to speed?'" Tortorella says. "I think Sully is known as and is very progressive…I'm not against it, I just want it to be an edge."

"I think it's all good," Sullivan says. "We're all going through a necessary process that we're all trying to figure out. We're just not there yet. Maybe some of the other sports that lend themselves to statistical analysis—they're a little bit further. In baseball, either you hit the ball or you don't hit the ball. You either catch it or don't catch it. In our game, it's gray. What's a scoring chance? Who is responsible? That depends on how you play. It depends on who you ask. There's a lot of subjectivity."

Sullivan stops, his eyes on the screen. He knows a goal is coming.

Pittsburgh's second power play unit is on the ice. Penguins defenseman Brian Dumoulin raises his stick to shoot, and Sharks penalty killer Melker Karlsson goes into a shot blocking position, turning his back momentarily to Dumoulin. The Penguins defenseman takes advantage by resetting, finding a shooting lane, and firing a puck that beats Sharks goalie Martin Jones.

The Penguins are up 1–0 in a critical game. Crosby and the first power play unit never leave the bench.

"I remember putting them on the ice because I thought Sid was exhausted. So we went with our second unit and they went out and scored. Our bench got about a foot taller. It was great," Sullivan says.

Play resumes and Sullivan points out the players on the ice at this point. It's his fourth line following that Penguins goal, centered by veteran Matt Cullen.

It's a sign of the faith he had in the depth of this team.

"This line was invaluable for helping our team win. They didn't light it up on the scoresheet. A guy like Tommy Kuhnhackl is a young player, he's a hard player to play against. He's really good on the wall. He does a lot of those things you can't necessarily quantify," he says.

Sullivan loves this fourth line. He loves the pride they took in playing their role, which was huge in moments like this. The Penguins had taken the lead and they were out there to make sure the Sharks didn't get one right back.

It's a workmanlike shift and a reflection of the way the Penguins had evolved under Sullivan. It was all business. They reflected their coach, as teams often do.

"I could see his personality in them," says Tortorella, who watched the Penguins' playoff run closely. "Remember, we played against this team a lot when we were in New York. I just watched that team change how it carried itself. It changed when he came."

Before Sullivan arrived, the Penguins had the reputation of sometimes getting rattled when things weren't going their way. They were an emotional wave pool. I ask Tortorella what the Penguins started to look like when they started to reflect Sullivan more closely.

"They were very businesslike. Through the playoffs, especially their top players, they were businesslike. I'm not trying to run down that organization but I know...when they were in the playoffs a few years prior to that, they self-imploded at certain times," he says.

Tortorella points to Game 5 of the Stanley Cup Final in Pittsburgh as the moment that best displayed the Penguins' maturity.

The weather on the day of the game was gorgeous. Like most of the media, I was staying at the Marriott right next to the arena. Walking down the hill toward the entrance, the streets were absolutely jammed with people. Long before the game was set to begin, fans in black and yellow, many with signs and blown-up thundersticks, were already chanting, singing, and celebrating. There was championship anticipation in the air.

The Penguins lost that Game 5 at home. They played great but the Sharks prevailed in large part because San Jose goalie Martin Jones was a wall. The streets after the loss were eerily quiet. Roads that were once packed with thousands of fans were completely deserted.

A dumpster full of deflated thundersticks and crumpled-up signs was overflowing. One dejected fan staggered up the hill, wearing a Kris Letang shirt jersey, a beer held loosely in his hand, his arm dangling by his side.

It was almost post-apocalyptic.

I'd seen this group of Penguins blow a series in which they had a commanding lead before. Coming back from their loss in Game 5 would be the ultimate test to see if they were truly different under Sullivan.

The next morning, Sullivan called Tortorella, a call Tortorella was expecting. Sullivan was distraught because the Penguins had a chance to win it all, played great, but couldn't get it done. The series was headed back to San Jose, where anything could happen.

He was worried about the Sharks' momentum. He was worried about how his Penguins would respond after crushing the hopes of tens of thousands of their fans.

Tortorella shared how the conversation between the two friends began that next day:

"Hey, what's going on?" Tortorella had asked.

"What do you think is fucking going on?" replied Sullivan.

"Sully, you're going to win there," Tortorella said.

From the outside, the Penguins looked too fast for the Sharks. For better or for worse, the Sharks weren't splitting up their top line to give the Penguins something else to think about. It was going to take more than a fluke goal to turn this series. Most of the media felt Pittsburgh would be victorious in the end, but the Penguins were in the middle of the storm and had to deal with the stress.

Tortorella shared his advice with Sullivan during that phone conversation.

"When you get on that plane today, you'd better have your chest puffed out and be as confident as you can be," he said. "They're taking cues off you today. Is it going to be panic by the coaches? Or is it going to be, 'Fuck it. Let's just go down there and get it done. We know we're better. We know we played better.'"

Tortorella closed the conversation with Sullivan by predicting the series was going to end in San Jose. He had no doubt.

"It wasn't even close," Tortorella said. "The score was close but it wasn't really close."

If there was any doubt the Penguins had adopted the businesslike approach of their coach, it was erased early on in Game 6. They came out and took an early lead and kept on going from there.

It's not an attitude that a coach can build in one meeting or even one stretch of play. For Sullivan, his efforts to change the psyche of the Penguins started the moment he was promoted to the head coaching job.

He started with complete and brutal honesty. He gathered the players and told them that nobody had more respect for what they had accomplished than he did. He looked around the room and saw a team loaded with talent. All-time talent.

"Our challenge right now is to figure out how to become a great *team*, because great *players* don't win championships," Sullivan told his players.

He was taking over a team loaded with expectations. The Penguins won the Stanley Cup in 2009 with a young Sidney Crosby and Evgeni Malkin. It was viewed as the start of a dynasty.

It never occurred to anybody that this group would be one and done. Then injuries crushed the Penguins. Crosby missed parts of two seasons while recovering from concussions. Even when they were all healthy, something was off.

In meeting with the players, Sullivan tried to get to the root of the problem. He appealed to their pride but also a maturity level he knew they now had, one that might not have existed in previous years.

He wanted the team's identity to revolve around speed and skill. Then he clearly showed how each player on the roster would contribute to that identity, even if every player didn't have those attributes in equal servings.

He also wanted resilience to be a word that guided them.

"Can I add one?" Tortorella interjects. "Accountability."

It's every new coach's favorite word. Tortorella knows this.

"We always talk about it. It's an easy word to talk about. It's hard to fucking get. Especially from an outsider, especially with that group there. It looked like there was some entitlement, and that's a hard group to get together and come in when he did."

Tortorella isn't the first to suggest that there were times it looked like Crosby, Malkin, Letang, and Phil Kessel felt they were entitled to success rather than earning it the hard way.

But Sullivan is quick to defend his players. What he learned immediately was that these guys were highly skilled and great people. He caught them at a time when they were ready to listen.

"This group gets misunderstood over the years," Sullivan says. "I think their intentions were honorable as far as trying to win. But they faced trials and tribulations along the way that we had to figure out how to overcome."

Sullivan had someone on the Penguins coaching staff research the team's record during a certain time period when it was trailing after two periods.

"They had zero wins," Sullivan said. "I asked the group, 'Can we explain this?' They didn't have an answer. It's a tough one. My point in showing it to them wasn't to humiliate them or browbeat them in any way. It was an honest assessment of what our mindset was. What I tried to do was challenge the group and say, 'This has to change.'"

To change it, he needed a complete buy-in from his captain, Sidney Crosby.

Sullivan knew well from coaching against the Penguins for years that there was more than enough talent in the room to beat any team on any night. He told the players that their biggest opponent was sitting in that dressing room listening to him speak.

He found a group very receptive to the message, including Crosby.

"His maturity level and his approach and the way he responded to some of the challenges we put in front of them—they were honest, straightforward challenges," Sullivan said. "He responded the right way in every circumstance."

Sullivan met with Crosby privately. He articulated what his game plan would be in terms of how he wanted the Penguins to play. He just wanted the focus to be on hockey. Nothing else. Just hockey.

He put it on Crosby.

"I said, 'We need you to lead the charge for us.' He was on board. I asked him for his input and his feedback because these guys are grown men. They're mature guys. They've been in the league a long time. We value their input. Sid is a real insightful guy."

"What was something he told you?" I ask.

"One of the things that we talked about was simplifying our game and playing more north/south and trying to take advantage of our speed. He wanted to play that way and wanted to play that speed game. That was something that when we first took that team over we felt we had to be better at. He was very much on board."

Six minutes have passed during the second period of Game 6 as we watch and chat. The Penguins are holding a 1–0 lead when San Jose gets back into the game.

Sharks defenseman Brent Burns gets control of the puck and finds Logan Couture streaking down the left side of the ice. Couture flicks a wrister past Pittsburgh goalie Matt Murray and suddenly the game is tied.

Couture raises his arms in the air and is mobbed by teammates. Smoke is shot down from the rafters as the building erupts in cheers.

"That Shark Tank was loud," Sullivan says, watching. "Wow."

Then comes the shift that Sullivan calls the biggest of the playoffs for the Penguins. The building is still buzzing from Couture's goal when Crosby's line hits the ice.

Moments after leaving the bench, Crosby rifles a one-timer with 12:47 left in the second period that Jones saves. Letang corrals the rebound, turns to his backhand, and skates toward the slot. He backhands another shot, and there's a battle in front of Jones before the puck is sent into the corner. Sharks center Joe Pavelski looks like he's going to secure the rebound but is pressured from behind by Crosby. The pressure forces a pass up the boards that the Penguins keep in the zone. At this point, 25 seconds of offensive pressure have elapsed since Crosby's initial shot.

The puck works its way around the boards, behind Jones and now to the other side of the ice where Crosby is there once again, engaged in a battle to keep it in the offensive zone. Somehow, Crosby, Patric Hornqvist, and Conor Sheary work the puck to a waiting Letang.

Letang fakes a shot and then skates in on the attack. He sends a pass to the front of the net for Hornqvist, who is tied up and can't connect. Crosby, again, jumps on the loose puck and quickly skates behind the net

After spending much of his career as an assistant coach, Sullivan won the Stanley Cup as head coach of the Penguins in 2016. (AP Images)

as Letang finds an opening in front of Jones, raising his stick slightly in anticipation of a pass.

Crosby finds him and Letang fires a shot. It beats Jones and the Penguins are up 2–1.

It was 33 seconds from Crosby's shot to Letang's, 33 seconds of completely relentless pressure. If you're looking for resiliency from the Penguins, that shift displayed it. Crosby wasn't going to be denied.

"This shift here was the biggest shift of the playoffs," Sullivan says. "Sid and Tanger elevate their game at a key time. Watch this play."

The replay shows the angle from behind the net, Letang and Crosby puck handling with expertise and precision.

"It wasn't just the goal, it was the 50 seconds leading up to it," Tortorella says. "The goal against didn't affect them at all. They just went back to work, and prior to the goal, they're in their zone just buzzing them. It's usually the other team that gets the momentum off the goal. It absolutely reversed on the next shift. It wasn't a 15-second goal. It was a 50-second goal."

"To me," says Sullivan, "that's the culmination. Sid and Letang, I thought they were just tremendous in the playoffs. Their numbers are not indicative of the impact and the influence they had on the games and the respective series. That for me, that shift is a snapshot of their leadership."

"They were men," adds Tortorella. "Okay. He can't say it. I will. That wasn't always there. They'd go flailing if they got scored against before. Instead, they just went about their business."

Another factor Sullivan points out is that his stars realized the urgency to win now. According to the players, it wasn't until after the team went on a 14–2 run to end the regular season—plus getting a healthy Malkin back in the lineup for the playoffs—that they truly realized the opportunity in front of them.

Players like Crosby and Letang and Chris Kunitz, who had been a part of previous disappointments and of teams that didn't always have their best weapons available at the most important times, told their teammates that things were falling into place for the Penguins at just the right time.

"It's crazy when you hear that from Crosby and Letang and Kunitz," said Patric Hornqvist. "They've been through this story once before. They really saw something special in this group."

Not only did they see it, they let the group know it. They let the younger players and those who weren't a part of previous teams know that these opportunities couldn't be wasted.

It especially hit home after they cruised past the New York Rangers in the first round, playing well, with a deep and mostly healthy team.

"They said, 'C'mon guys. We have something special here. You never know if you're going to be in the second round of the playoffs ever again,'" Hornqvist said.

The team we thought might pile up Stanley Cup rings after 2009 had learned perspective the hard way over the years.

Time has also helped mature Kris Letang. Still, one of Sullivan's ongoing tasks during the playoffs was to make sure Letang's emotions remained where the team needed them to be.

Having coached against Letang, Sullivan knew the opposing game plan well: hit him every chance you get and try to knock him off his game. Teams know that if they can get to Letang, the Penguins aren't nearly as good.

"And they're right," Sullivan says.

Letang is deeply competitive and, at times, he gets so revved up it ends up hurting himself and the team.

"He's a brave kid. He's the type of guy, when he goes back for the puck, he always wants to make the play. He'll hold on to pucks for a long time, waiting for something to open up," Sullivan says.

Sullivan encouraged him to occasionally take the simple play and stay out of harm's way, avoiding a few of the extra hits that come with trying to win every battle.

"His resolve was being challenged in every series. The Washington series was probably the most indicative of that. They tried to pound us. He was the No. 1 target," Sullivan says.

Sullivan also put it on the coaching staff to make sure the team's tactics were protecting the players and putting them in position to succeed as much as possible. That's where Sullivan really excelled in the eyes of his old friend and Rangers team executive Jim Schoenfeld, who coached Sullivan as a player in Phoenix. Schoenfeld watched as Sullivan made subtle tweaks to the way the Penguins played in the playoffs, depending on the opponent.

"In our series, they changed the power play breakout during the series," Schoenfeld said. "They did a lot of indirect passes and tried to outnumber us in the neutral zone. He had a bag of great variety and he knew when and how to use it. That takes intuition. That takes in-game evaluation. They outnumbered their opponents most places on the ice. In the defensive zone, they always had support. There were things that were constant. There were a lot of nuances."

If a team like the Capitals tried to pound the Penguins on the forecheck, the Penguins would simplify their breakout to relieve the pressure quickly.

"We might have to rim the puck on the wall and chip it and make a space play and make a footrace," Sullivan says. "So we can use their aggression against them by making sure we get back to pucks quickly."

In the next round, the Lightning tried to take the wall away from the Penguins after noticing their tendencies against the Capitals. When that happened, the Penguins tweaked their breakout and looked to come up the middle more often.

"There's always that cat-and-mouse game with coaching staffs, more I think in a series than in the season," Sullivan says. "It's kind of read and react. It happens a lot on special teams. It happens sometimes on the breakout. Most of the adjustments are on special teams. Whether teams are doing a certain breakout, power play breakout. It's not just a one-coach thing. It's a coaching staff thing."

"What's the key when you're standing in front of the group at the board?" I ask.

"You can't have too many changes. He's great at that," Sullivan answers, nodding at Tortorella. "That may be something I took from him. If you have too many, the message gets lost. You have to be crystal clear on how you articulate to your players. When I was in college—Jack Parker was my coach—he always had a line he would say to us: 'Let me explain this not so you can understand it but so that you can't possibly misunderstand it.'"

We laugh.

Parker, naturally, loved coaching Sullivan. When he recruited him to play at Boston University, he knew Sullivan would eventually be a captain. He saw a young player who wasn't starry-eyed. He saw a young player who knew exactly what he wanted out of the college hockey experience, knew the importance of a work ethic and living up to high expectations.

Early in his career, the coaching staff at BU had concerns about his lack of speed. By the time Sullivan left, he was one of the fastest skaters in the league.

"He was the captain of the team senior year and one of the most influential guys we've ever had on the team," Parker said when we chatted.

Parker also believed kids don't care how much hockey a staff knows until they know how much the coaches care. In Sullivan, Parker sees a coach who is so genuine in his motives that NHL players quickly realize everything he's doing is geared toward the team's success.

"There's not a phony bone in Mike Sullivan's body. There's not a political bone in Mike Sullivan's body," Parker said. "That's what his great asset is—the fact that he knows how to talk to people to get them on the right page."

There's no better example of that than the production and cooperation Sullivan got out of Phil Kessel.

Ron Wilson's experience with Kessel in Toronto wasn't unusual. He can be a frustrating player for coaches but Sullivan knew he needed him on board for the Penguins to have any real success.

Early on in their tenure, Sullivan and his staff settled on the idea of trying Kessel on a line with center Nick Bonino. They thought it would give the Penguins balance on all three lines, featuring Crosby on one, Malkin on another, and Kessel on the third. They didn't see much downside, since the Penguins weren't exactly tearing it up when Sullivan took over.

So Sullivan invited Kessel into his office and shared the idea. They talked about creating balance in an attempt to get Kessel on the ice against the opposing team's third defensive pair. At the time, Kessel was playing with Malkin but that line wasn't generating as much offense as Sullivan thought it could.

"Phil at that time didn't have a lot of interest," Sullivan says. "He understood our logic. I'm not sure he agreed with it. To his credit, he said, 'Whatever you want.' But I do think that for players to be at their best, they have to believe. At the time, he was a good soldier. He did it but I don't think he really believed."

Then came a game against the Columbus Blue Jackets that changed everything. John Tortorella's Columbus Blue Jackets.

"The goon squad over there was trying to pound us," Sullivan says.

In that March 11 game in Columbus, Kessel started the game on a line with Carl Hagelin and Malkin, but Malkin crashed into the boards awkwardly and was injured. He would miss the rest of the regular season.

Sullivan plugged Bonino in his place and the creation of the now legendary HBK line was truly born. The Penguins won that game in Columbus and 13 of the final 15 games of the season.

That line was a big reason why. Kessel had 16 points in the final 16 games of the season. He was an offensive force in the playoffs, where he had 22 points in 24 games, including 10 goals. Had it not been for Crosby, Kessel would have been the playoff MVP.

"You came to the ice every game and you felt like you were going to be a difference maker. You knew your line was going to create at least three or four Grade A chances," Hagelin said of his line.

And now, as the game we're watching stretches into the third period, they're closing in on winning a Stanley Cup.

The coaches and players know the Cup is in the building. Behind the scenes, Penguins who aren't in the lineup, including an injured Trevor Daley, are starting to get their gear on so they can skate with their teammates on the ice.

Sullivan admits any doubts started to disappear around this point. As the clock ticked away in that final period, Sullivan no longer feared a bad bounce. He saw a dominant Penguins team playing in front of him and his gut said he'd be a Stanley Cup champion that night.

"You just get the sense behind the bench, you know? 'We're going to win,'" he says. "I can feel it on the bench. I can see it in their body language. I can sense it. That was the feeling I had. I just felt like we had complete control and our guys, they could see it. They could taste it. They could smell it."

He saw it in the chatter among the players as they hopped over the boards. He saw it in how disciplined their shift lengths were in that period. It was like clockwork.

"At that point they would have done anything to keep it out of our net," Sullivan says. "We only gave up, I think, two shots against, and it was just rolling one line after the next. Push the pace as much as we could. Make them play 200 feet."

There's 2:37 remaining in the game when a graphic pops up on the screen showing the shot totals. The Sharks had managed just one shot on goal in the entire period, even though their season is hanging in the balance.

When that graphic is shown, Tortorella marvels at the Penguins' dominance.

"San Jose has never been in it. This series was never close," Tortorella says.

Even so, Sullivan keeps coaching in the final two minutes. Protecting a one-goal lead, Sullivan replaces Phil Kessel with Eric Fehr on the HBK line.

"It puts two centermen on the ice if there is an icing, but he's also more willing to block a shot and play on the wall and do some things," Sullivan says.

It's just a glimpse into how Sullivan has found the right balance with Kessel.

"Phil accepted it. He was great," Sullivan says. "A guy like Eric Fehr, he knows that this is part of his contribution. It makes him feel good about himself. Phil accepted it and I think it was these types of little circumstances that helped us become a team."

NBC's Doc Emrick's voice fills the room. His volume and urgency is a little louder as the final moments move closer:

"Sent back out to Hornqvist! Hornqvist with the net empty. He scores!"

Hornqvist's goal seals it but it's the moment right before that makes it. Sidney Crosby blocks a shot from the point, then calmly gathers the puck and sends it over to Hornqvist for the final goal.

Penguins owner and legend Mario Lemieux is shown on the screen. He raises his arms in celebration after Hornqvist's goal. He hugs his wife, Nathalie.

Sullivan again sends out the HBK line with Fehr playing in Kessel's spot. Sharks forward Joonas Donskoi manages a shot on Matt Murray. It is the Sharks' second shot of the period. It comes with 49 seconds left in Game 6.

The puck finds its way to Logan Couture at the point, and he winds up and fires a massive shot. Fehr steps right in front of it, blocks it harmlessly to the corner, and the puck is sent down the ice.

"That's why Eric Fehr is on the ice and not Phil," Sullivan says. "What I loved about Phil is he really accepted it."

When Sullivan first took over in Pittsburgh, one of things he focused on was removing all the distractions that always seemed to cloud the

Penguins. The phrase he used repeatedly was, "Just play." Coaches often use mottos or phrases as a reminder that cuts to exactly what they want their teams to do. In the case of the Penguins, Sullivan felt that if they could remove the outside noise, the pressure, the expectations, and just focus on the game, they would be in great shape.

"Just play," Hornqvist said. "We know we have the chemistry and the players and all the right tools. He always talked about the noise. Don't worry about the noise. Play hockey and do the right thing out there."

With 30.2 seconds left, the screen fills with a close-up shot of a gray shirt. In all caps on the top are two words: JUST PLAY. Underneath are four white strips, meant to look like white tape. The Penguins wrote a W for each win and made a check mark for each series victory.

"There's our T-shirts," Sullivan says, smiling at the memory.

The clock winds down and the game ends. The Penguins are, again, Stanley Cup champions. The players pour onto the ice and pile on top of goalie Matt Murray. The extra players emerge from the tunnel and join the celebration.

There's Trevor Daley, out with a broken ankle, celebrating with the group. He was the first to get the Stanley Cup after Crosby.

"Trevor's mom is in the hospital. She passes away about a week later. He's out on the ice with a broken ankle. He can barely get around," Sullivan says.

"Yeah, he said he was in pain, but it was worth it."

"Well worth it."

There's a shot of Kessel on the screen. He has a giant beard and his hair is stringy with sweat. For years, he'd been the target of criticism both externally and internally.

Now, he was a Stanley Cup champion.

"Look at Phil," Sullivan says. "I was really happy for him. These guys, they went through a lot. Early in the season, the criticism Crosby went through. Phil has always gone through it. There were so many people doubting these guys. To overcome that was huge for them."

The celebration is off and running. Eventually it moves into the visitors' dressing room in San Jose. Sullivan was with his coaches in their office, while the players celebrated in the locker room with the Stanley Cup.

He took his tie off and was summoned into the dressing room to join the party.

Crosby and his teammates soaked Sullivan with champagne. His dress shirt was drenched.

He asked Penguins equipment guy Dana Heinze for a replacement shirt and Heinze came back with one of the gray Just Play shirts.

Crosby spotted his coach wearing the shirt, the four white strips on the back blank. Crosby grabbed a black Sharpie and started filling in Ws and check marks.

Sixteen Ws in all.

In that moment, Sullivan was completely separated from Tortorella. He was no longer Tortorella's understudy or the career assistant. He was the Stanley Cup–winning head coach of the Pittsburgh Penguins. He was the guy who re-ignited Crosby, the best player of his generation.

That's how he'll be remembered after this victory.

Tortorella was happy for his friend, but even more, he realized he learned a ton watching how Sullivan operated during this playoff run. He watched every game. He had conversations only the two of them will know about.

The relationship between Sullivan and Tortorella is definitely one of teacher and student—it's just that the same guy isn't always in the same role.

"I learned more from him in the eight years together than he learned from me. He won't admit that, but I did," Tortorella says. "He's been really good for me. I miss the fuck out of him. He's going to be good for a long time."

* * *

At the conclusion of the Penguins' win over the Sharks, we quickly switch games. Sullivan has a flight to catch, so I'm trying to get as much viewing time with him as possible before he leaves.

It's still Tortorella, Sullivan, and myself in a conference room at the Saint Paul Hotel. We've finally waited Brian Burke out, who left for lunch. Papers are scattered on the table. Tortorella, from what I detected during the previous game, is ready to open up.

It's very much something Sullivan wanted when we chatted by phone in the days leading up to this film session.

"I've had this struggle with him for years," Sullivan said. "He's a real guarded guy. All people see is the hard shell on the outside. They don't see the real person and how caring he is for people, the things he does for people behind the scenes. He's a stubborn Italian. He gets beat up a lot. He's one of the more misunderstood people in sports."

We're watching Game 7 of the 2004 Stanley Cup Final between Tortorella's Lightning and Darryl Sutter's Calgary Flames. The game is in Florida and the ABC broadcast begins with an overhead shot of Tampa Bay's Brad Richards taking a faceoff against Craig Conroy.

The video is a little blurry. It's not in high definition. It's the last game before the 2004–05 lockout that changed the NHL forever, with new rules favoring speed and skill. It's like watching a game from another era, unearthed from a time capsule beneath the arena.

Tortorella shakes his head when the game begins.

"It's a long time ago. It's a great lesson—you just never know when you're going to get back there. It's so fucking hard," he says.

"It's so hard," Sullivan agrees.

"We didn't even know what we were doing. We were just playing."

Success came fairly fast for Tortorella at the NHL level but he most definitely paid his dues to get there.

Rick Dudley, the former NHL player, coach, and executive who always had an eye for talent, gave Tortorella his big break. One of Dudley's closest friends was a guy named Frank Perkins, who coached the

Virginia Lancers in the old Atlantic Coast Hockey League. Tortorella was a hardworking winger putting up 30-goal seasons on that team, and he had made an impression on the intense coach.

In 1986, Dudley got a job offer to coach the Flint Spirits in the International Hockey League and brought Perkins along with him as an assistant.

Then, one Tuesday afternoon in February, Perkins passed away in his living room.

"His heart stopped," Dudley said. "It was so difficult. Frank was my best friend. It might have been the worst day of my life."

At his funeral, Dudley remembers running into Tortorella, who was by then the head coach in Virginia. He remembered how highly Perkins spoke of Tortorella and it made a big impression on Dudley. During their brief exchange at the funeral, Dudley remembers really liking him.

When sizing up coaches, Dudley asks three questions: Are they willing to put in the work? Will they put the success of the organization before their own personal ambitions? Are they non-political?

That last one is a big one. It's a phrase that was used to describe Mike Sullivan. Tortorella, as it turns out, is so non-political it probably works against him, something we'd dive into over the next couple of hours.

It's an important characteristic for Dudley.

"People who are political, they're looking to get to the next rung," Dudley said. "I make them understand that collective success is individual success...We cared about the players. If you're political, players figure it out eventually. They know you don't care about them as much as you do yourself."

Tortorella met the criteria perfectly, so Dudley made his pitch. He wasn't going to get rich coaching in New Haven but if they had success together, Dudley would remain loyal to him.

Tortorella and his wife, Christine, were living in a double-wide trailer at the time. She was pregnant with their second child, and Tortorella was earning $6,000 a year to coach in Virginia. He was offered $18,000 to coach in New Haven.

Meanwhile, Christine was offered a job in Florida that would have paid her $80,000 a year and set the young family up for a much more comfortable life.

But Tortorella didn't want comfort. He wanted to chase his passion.

"I said, 'Christine, I want to do this,'" Tortorella says.

It wasn't just the money that was sacrificed. Christine had to handle the move to New Haven with her parents. She had to take on a heavy load at home because Dudley is relentless in his work and preparation and demands the same from his staff.

"I learned how much preparation went into it," Tortorella says. "Duds thought out of the box. He always was trying to improve himself as a coach and trying to get any edge possible for his team. It was a lot of work with him. A lot of work."

When Dudley was hired to coach the Buffalo Sabres, he brought Tortorella with him. Eventually, the two reunited again in Tampa Bay.

About five minutes have elapsed as we talk about the path Tortorella took to get to this Game 7. A young Brad Richards is shown on the screen in front of us, chewing on his mouthguard. A stat is flashed on the screen: the Lightning were 31–0–2 when he scored a goal that year. He was a huge part of their success, along with guys like Vincent Lecavalier and Martin St. Louis.

"Look at Richie, it looks like he's 10 years old," Tortorella says.

Then we all break into smiles as an extended shot of Tortorella appears on the screen. He's wearing a dark suit, a maroon dress shirt, and a tie. His dark hair is long and his beard almost matches, save for a touch of gray.

"Oh fuck," Tortorella says as he looks at his younger self. (It's a word he uses a lot. For the sake of brevity, most have been removed here.)

The smile on Tortorella's face is quickly replaced by a wince. Right on cue, Sullivan gives his best impersonation of what Tortorella is thinking behind the bench at that moment.

"Fuuuuuuuuuuuck!" Sullivan yells. Everyone in the room laughs.

And with that, Sullivan has to call a cab and get going.

He stands up and the two old friends exchange a few thoughts on training camp. Sullivan has a couple breakout schemes he wants to share with Tortorella before the World Cup begins.

Sullivan opens the door and says one last good-bye to his friend.

"Say hello to the family," Sullivan says to Tortorella.

"You do the same."

The door closes and Tortorella makes clear the admiration he has for his friend.

"Great fucking coach. Better person," Tortorella says. "I couldn't have been more thrilled for anything—other than me having an opportunity to win a Stanley Cup—than that guy winning it. So good."

But we're no longer here to talk about Sullivan. Tortorella knows it. He looks up and he's ready to do this.

"Go," he says.

I don't want to mess around. I want to get into the principles that drive Tortorella. Is he as unwavering as his reputation makes him out to be? Why does everybody who plays for him have to block so many shots? Why is he so misunderstood, if he is truly misunderstood at all?

"I think there is a perception that it's my way or the highway. It's so untrue," he says. "But I do have convictions. I do have a thought on what it is to be a pro."

"What are the principles you won't change? What are those convictions?"

"The biggest conviction for me is that your family is the most important thing in your life. Whether you are married with kids or you're the son of your mom and dad. Your family is the most important thing. That's unwavering. That takes everything."

As he talks, he's banging his fingers on the table in front of him. Emphasizing the words that are most important to him.

"Then, it's how you practice. I think we get lost a little bit. We always worry about the games but you become how you practice. I think your work habits, as far as practice and your effort within the games, that has to be at a care level every night, and that's where I am demanding. That's where sometimes I may wear players out."

The season the Lightning won the Stanley Cup, there was a game in December where Brad Richards made the mistake of not blocking a shot. This is a guy who had 79 points in 82 games that season. He scored 26 goals.

Surely, Brad Richards can step out of the way of an occasional shot, no?

In Boston, the day before Christmas break, Richards tested the theory.

"You know where this is going," Richards said on the phone while retelling the story.

Tortorella let him have it.

"He said, 'If I ever see this again, you'll be in the stands the rest of the year,'" Richards said. "He went pretty hard at me. It didn't make for a great Christmas break."

Richards also pointed out that he had just four goals in 31 games at that point. He'd go on to score 22 goals in the 51 games after Christmas.

So much of Tortorella's energy is focused on the mental part of hockey. He's always looking for the right buttons to press in order to get players to play their best while remaining committed to the team's success.

It took years before he got the Lightning's mental toughness to the point it was when they won the Stanley Cup clincher we're watching. In fact, by the time the Lightning were playing in this Game 7, he'd been mostly hands-off for months. He had done all of his coaching and preparation for this game in the years that preceded it.

"How do you develop a player who is not mentally tough into a mentally tough player?" I ask.

"That's a great question. I believe there are different levels that you can get players to. I do play, what I call, mindfuck games," he says. "I sometimes develop and manipulate conflict to test the player, but you have to be really careful. You can really damage a player and that may be

Tortorella's coaching style has made him a lightning rod for criticism over the years, but it also brought him a Stanley Cup with the Tampa Bay Lightning in 2004. (AP Images)

irretrievable if you go too far. I still believe in trying to push players to a point where they say, 'You know, I never thought I could get to this spot.' That's my job."

To Tortorella, it's easy for a coach to take the team handed to him and try to win hockey games. The harder job is to try and push each individual player to new limits, to take them out of their comfort zones and get a performance out of them they didn't realize they had in them.

It's dangerous territory to tread as an NHL coach, especially when we're talking about millionaire players who are often treated with kid gloves by everybody else.

"I've made mistakes along the way and I'll make more along the way. I believe in that part of the game. I don't think it's an Xs and Os game anymore. It's a mindset game. It's what you're willing to give. It's what you're willing to sacrifice," he says.

This gets at the heart of how Tortorella coaches, how he treats his players, and how he tries to maximize their potential. So much of it is mental.

We're far enough removed from the game in front of us that I turn to those players for examples of what this leadership strategy looks like in real life.

I start with the star of this game.

Ruslan Fedotenko scored two of the biggest goals of his life in this Game 7, single-handedly providing the offense needed to beat the Flames. He was a 25-year-old kid from Kiev when he won this Stanley Cup. In this playoff run alone, he scored 12 goals.

With the benefit of time, Fedotenko now has perspective on what it was like to play for someone who pushed him to his limits.

"Torts is a different person as a coach," Fedotenko said. "Off the ice, he doesn't let people know he has the biggest heart. He'd do anything for you."

On the ice?

"He's a hard ass. Some players respond to an F-U. He wants to get in that contest and get people going…I have a hard time responding that way. I take it more personally."

Fedotenko said Tortorella was the best Xs and Os coach he's ever played for. He appreciated that you always knew exactly where you stood with him.

But when he was called out in front of teammates or yelled at, he honestly didn't know what to do. Responding in kind wasn't in his nature.

"I grew up in the Soviet Union, where you respected your elders. You respect your coach. You never talk back to your parents," he said. "It didn't matter how much Torts pushed me. I wasn't going to give him the satisfaction. He wasn't going to ruin my day. I'm going to go laugh with the other players and make sure he sees me."

According to Fedotenko, Tortorella had a predictable response to that approach.

"He pushes even harder. Not every player responds the same way. I couldn't tell him, 'Fuck you, Torts.' Especially in front of the other players. To me, it was disrespectful."

By the time he played for him in New York, Fedotenko understood his coach's approach. It wasn't personal. Tortorella was trying to bring the best out of each player. He was trying to win. It wasn't for his ego. It was all designed to maximize effort and get the team headed in the right direction, exceeding limits the players might not be able to do alone.

"People forget that all he cares about is winning," Fedotenko said. "He will not sway under the pressure of media or what's the right thing to do. If he believes it, he goes with it."

As I've talked to Tortorella and his players, I thought about how I would respond to being yelled at, being singled out at work in front of my friends and colleagues.

I think I would shut down. I can't imagine a scenario where I would yell back.

Talking to Brad Richards, I realized Tortorella would probably ship me off a team he was coaching. He wouldn't have time for someone who wasn't going to push back. He wants a team full of players who aren't going to back down from anyone, including their head coach.

"He didn't want pushovers," Richards said. "He wanted everyone to do some kind of push back. Whether it was on the ice or challenging him in the office. He wanted to notice that something was getting through to you. Some guys would wake up the next day and run people through the boards to say they got the message. As tough as it was, you knew you were allowed to do that back to him."

The results in Tampa Bay were undeniable.

"He molded a young group of guys and made us hard," Richards said. "He made us professionals."

The biggest battles on this Lightning team, at least publicly, were between Tortorella and Vincent Lecavalier, the young superstar and franchise cornerstone.

Their feud was legendary. To try and get through to his young center, Tortorella used a wide-ranging array of tactics, down to stealing his parking spot—at least, that was one story circulating the hockey world.

"Someone else told me to go there. I wasn't that arrogant to say, 'I'm taking your parking spot.' That never happened," Tortorella says.

When Tortorella arrived, the players were a little too comfortable for his tastes. He saw signs that they were in control of the environment, not the coaching staff.

"Vinny will readily admit that he was doing things the wrong way. He had an entourage around him that was telling him [what to do]," Tortorella says.

So, the battles between Lecavalier and Tortorella began. Some were public, some private.

"What did those look like?" I ask.

"They were bad. They were really bad," he says, pausing for a moment to watch the game in front of him, now showing a replay of Calgary's Martin Gelinas' no goal in Game 6.

Bad enough that Lecavalier wanted out and nearly got his wish.

At one point, Lightning owner Bill Davidson came to Tampa Bay to sit down with CEO Tom Wilson, president Ron Campbell, GM Rick Dudley, assistant GM Jay Feaster, and Tortorella.

Ownership gave Dudley the green light to trade Lecavalier under certain conditions. Not long after that, Dudley had a couple of deals on the table, including a package from the Toronto Maple Leafs that included defenseman Tomas Kaberle and winger Jonas Hoglund, according to one Tampa source.

Lecavalier's agent, Kent Hughes, said he received a call from Dudley saying a deal was done. Dudley says it never quite got that far.

"No one in Tampa knew what was being discussed," Dudley said.

The internal debate over dealing Lecavalier resulted in a regime change. Dudley resigned as GM and Feaster was promoted to his spot in the middle of the 2001–02 season.

Instead of trying to trade Lecavalier, Feaster wanted to repair the relationship between the player and Tortorella, an effort Feaster said hadn't been made.

"We didn't do anything at all to manage the situation or manage Vinny," Feaster said. "I was dead set that I was not trading him and I was not firing John."

Feaster's solution was to bring Hughes to Tampa Bay for a meeting to try and clear the air.

"I came down and I met with John. I remember it like it was yesterday," Hughes said. "Tortorella said, 'You must think I'm some kind of gorilla.' I said, 'No, but I think there's a problem between the two of you. How do we fix it? How do we get him to see you for who you really are, and for you to see him for who he really is?'"

For Tortorella, the breakthrough began when he stopped having one-on-one meetings with Lecavalier and moved them in front of the team.

"If I'm going to tell Vinny to fuck off, it's going to be right in front of everybody. They're going to see what's going on with him on the ice,"

Tortorella says. "That's what started the ball rolling…He wasn't loved by his teammates, the way he was acting. When I have a Freddy Modin come and say, 'You know what? Now we know he's being treated like you're treating us.'"

By moving the battles where the team could see them, the star players were under added pressure from teammates to play the way they had to, the way Tortorella demanded. Tortorella wanted Lecavalier playing both ends of the ice. He didn't want Lecavalier walking by teammates as they were getting in a postgame workout. He wanted Lecavalier to join in.

"I wanted him to stop thinking about himself and think about the team, because he was so fucking good," Tortorella says.

Things with Lecavalier came to a head during a meeting in Carolina. Lecavalier finally had enough of the yelling and the criticism. He finally pushed back and laid into Tortorella.

"I smiled and said, 'It's about fucking time. I've been kicking the shit out of you for however long and you sit there and take it,'" Tortorella says.

This is how Tortorella thinks. He was so happy that Lecavalier was finally pushing back. Tortorella is banging on the table again as he says it, one for each word.

"I wanted him to fucking care. I wanted him to stop taking my shit and say, 'Fuck you. I'm going to show you.'"

Hughes put it this way: "Vinny gave John some of what he wanted. John gave Vinny some of what he wanted. Ultimately, John gave Vinny a lot more freedom. The way Vinny and Marty St. Louis were playing at the end, when they were tearing the league apart, was not necessarily the way John wanted them playing."

The Lightning started to make headway and those meetings became less frequent.

"They understand the method to the madness," Tortorella says. "It wasn't just him. It was so, so public because of Vinny's stature. It went on with everybody."

After he left Tampa Bay for New York, Tortorella's Rangers would eventually become a destination for former players with whom he clashed in Tampa Bay, including Richards, Dan Boyle, and Fedotenko. Tortorella even heard that Lecavalier wanted to join him in New York.

"It was the only time you won. You gravitated back to that feeling," Richards said about his decision to become a Ranger. "He was a big reason that I signed. I remember talking to him and he said, 'You've got to let '04 go. It's a new team, new era, everything is different.' You're always searching for those years and I saw that coming with the Rangers. I was hoping we could get things going and things didn't work out perfect."

Tortorella never defends himself publicly. When stories emerge of battles with players, he doesn't back down. He's just trying to win. He's not going to apologize for it.

But on this summer afternoon, far from the action of a hockey game or a contentious press conference, Tortorella starts to loosen up a bit. He has an opportunity to explain himself and takes it.

"People don't understand how much I care about my players. No matter what is public out there, what is being said, my actions on the bench—I make my own bed, I get it. But they don't understand what really goes on with my relationships with players," Tortorella says.

One of the things he promises every player is to always tell them the truth. As the coach in Columbus, Tortorella had a misunderstanding with Scott Hartnell at the trade deadline in 2016. Out of respect for Hartnell, he refused to share any more details.

But Hartnell thought his coach misled him and it still bothered Tortorella.

"He came to me a couple weeks later and I was crushed that I had not let him know exactly where he stood," Tortorella says. "I don't want a player going home not knowing where he stands."

The problem is that where a player stands isn't always where he wants to be. Tortorella tells them anyway. And players now are different than they were in 2004.

"It's a hard thing to do and it turns ugly sometimes. A lot of coaches don't want to do it. They really don't. If you lose a player, if you lose your best player and they decide they're out, then where are you?" he says. "That's the fine line. That's the risk you take. If a player doesn't understand what you're doing and what you're trying to do—with me, it's always explained. Sometimes I wish—a number of times—I wish the demeanor in which I explained it was different."

Tortorella believes that if there's a problem between a player and a coach that occurs on a Monday, it has to be addressed on Monday, because chances are, another one is coming on Wednesday. Leaders who let conflicts pile up often run into trouble.

He embraces the conflict. He sees issues as coaching opportunities. Conflict in a Tortorella dressing room is not only welcome, it's necessary. If there is conflict, that means problems are being solved.

So when people like Dudley say there isn't a political bone in Tortorella's body, that's what they mean. He doesn't hold his tongue just to keep people around him happy or pleased.

"I think it's a cop out, being political. It's an easy way to coach," Tortorella says.

"Yeah, but you can maybe keep your job longer."

"I want to do my job the right way. Especially early on, I was fighting with you guys all the time."

I'd never had any run-ins personally with Tortorella. As a young hockey writer, I'd learned the hard way that he never wants to talk about the other team. He had cut me off multiple times over the years when I asked about players he was competing against.

If I sensed he wasn't in the mood to talk after games, I'd keep my mouth shut. I had that luxury. Writers covering him on a daily basis, such as Larry Brooks of the *New York Post*, didn't. They battled through the years, sometimes on camera, especially when Tortorella coached the Rangers.

"It was to the point where I was stupid," Tortorella says. "I know I made a lot of huge mistakes early on that still follow me. But I am never going to worry about what people are saying or what people think about me if I think I'm helping a team."

I point to the television, where his team is closing in on a Stanley Cup.

"I imagine at this point, with this group, you felt like you could say anything you needed to at any point to any these players," I say.

"And more importantly they could say it to me. That's when I knew. The turn of the year, we had our concept down."

There's now 5:30 left remaining in the second period of Game 7 between the Lightning and Flames. Tampa Bay is working the puck down low and it ends up on the stick of Lecavalier along the boards. Lecavalier skates up the wall, and then quickly spins back toward the goal line. He spins again, now working his way back up the wall and toward the center of the ice. It's shaping up to be a series of moves for the ages, a series of moves few players can pull off.

There are now four Flames around him.

Impossibly, he spots Fedotenko in the center of the ice and swings the puck up to him. Already with one goal in this game, Fedotenko takes a moment to control the puck and then fires a shot that beats Miikka Kiprusoff's glove side.

As it's happening, Tortorella stops talking.

"Rewind that," he says. "Watch Vinny on that play. I just want to watch this."

The same player with whom he'd had so many disagreements is now changing the course of franchise history with this Herculean effort. This is the skill that Tortorella saw in Lecavalier. If there's any doubt he loves his players, it's gone when watching the way he's watching Lecavalier at this moment.

"I don't even know how he sees him," he says of the pass to Fedotenko. "He sees him. Look at that play with the skates."

"Through four guys."

"He knows Feds is there, kicks it to his forehand, and makes the play to Feds. How good was that? I've got goosebumps here. I've watched it 100 times and I've still got goosebumps."

As play continues, Tortorella starts to reflect on his time after Tampa Bay. He didn't believe he and his coaching staff should have been fired in New York. He felt differently about his time with the Canucks.

"I think I should have gotten fired out of Vancouver," he says.

"What was the difference?"

"I didn't do a good enough job making an adjustment in our concept with the injuries they had."

To him, things took a turn for the worse when he picked backup goalie Eddie Lack to start over Roberto Luongo in the Canucks' high-profile outdoor game, the Heritage Classic, in early March of 2014.

This decision captures his inability to be political. Luongo had lost five consecutive games before the Olympic break, and Lack played well in the first two games after Sochi. Tortorella believed that Lack gave his team a better chance to win. Simple as that.

Tortorella was aware it could create another goalie controversy for the Canucks, after one had been solved when Cory Schneider was traded to the Devils. Luongo made it very clear that he wanted to start the outdoor game, so Tortorella knew he might be antagonizing his starting goalie. Luongo had won over the Vancouver fans after handling the Schneider situation with grace and class. He'd also won multiple Olympic gold medals and believed he'd earned the right to start the Heritage Classic.

The easy thing would have been to start him. But Tortorella just couldn't do it. In his mind, Lack was playing better.

As Lack took his place in goal before the game, Tortorella couldn't help but notice the response.

"When they announced Lacker as the starting goalie, when they booed him, I said, 'Aw, fuck,'" he recalls.

The Canucks lost. The fans were chanting "We want Lou!" in the second period. Lack didn't play particularly well in a challenging circumstance.

Tortorella went into the press conference and saw a room packed with reporters and cameras. If there was anyone in the media who wanted to take a shot at Tortorella, he had given them the perfect opportunity.

"They're licking their chops," he says. "I said, 'This is an easy one to poke holes in. I get it, guys. Poke your holes. I'm going to answer every question, but I tell you right now—if I had to do it again, with the circumstances I felt was going on with our goalies, I would do the same thing.'"

Later in his career, Luongo and I talked about that moment.

"He doesn't think of anything but winning the game," Luongo said. "I thought he was a great coach to be honest with you. It's just part of who he is and that's fine. I accepted it and it led me to be where I'm at today."

From my distant perspective, I didn't think that was the incident that did Tortorella in. I thought it was the time he went after Bob Hartley in the hallway. I raise that point.

"The Bob Hartley moment. That's embarrassing to me," Tortorella says.

Before a mid-January game against Hartley and his Flames, Tortorella got word that Calgary was going to start the game with its fourth line, one that included noted fighters Kevin Westgarth and Brian McGrattan. The move appeared to be a response to the bad blood created after a previous game between the two teams that included a hit on Canucks defenseman Andrew Alberts, one that ended his career. He's still dealing with the effects of the concussion he suffered.

Before the game, Tortorella apologized in advance to his players for what he was about to do. He told them that if the Flames wanted a fight, that's what they'd get.

"If it gets a little fucking dicey, we're all in," Tortorella said.

Tortorella decided to have defenseman Kevin Bieksa take the opening draw. He also sent out fighter Tom Sestito and rookie Kellan Lain. Starting a rookie is a decision he regrets.

At the drop of the puck, five fights broke out simultaneously. Tortorella was absolutely livid with Hartley.

"Bob Hartley is a good friend of mine. People don't know that. I think he's a really good coach. But he does some really stupid things," Tortorella said. "You can see what's happening. I didn't even watch it because I was too busy yelling at Hartley. I wanted to get his attention. I did not coach that first period because I was so wired up. I let my emotions get the best of me. I couldn't wait for that period to get over. I was off that bench 10 or 15 seconds prior, just before the period was over, because I wanted to get to the hallway."

Alberts was watching the game near the Flames dressing room and could hear the sound of rushed footsteps as Tortorella made his way toward Hartley during intermission.

"We have an in-house feed of the other walkway," Alberts said. "You could see Torts trying to get in the locker room. It was like 'Holy shit. What is going on?'"

Tortorella was held up by a number of players and members of both coaching staffs. Then-Canucks assistant Glen Gulutzan did his best to hold Tortorella back as he tried to get a piece of Hartley.

"The guy that was, and I know I'm getting off subject, but I need…" Tortorella says, pausing for a second. This moment still cuts deep for him. "That Brian McGrattan was unbelievable."

Tortorella is referring to the 6-foot-4 Flames enforcer who was playing the role of peacekeeper.

"That really could have turned ugly. He could have killed me. McGrattan just said, 'Torts, you got to get the fuck out of here.'"

That moment, and not the outdoor game, might have been the beginning of the end for Tortorella in Vancouver.

"That probably had something to do with it," he admits. "They were really conscious of the brand there. Yeah, that's one of the most embarrassing moments. My players loved it. Within the room itself, at the time, they loved it. We win it in the shootout. You hope it galvanized them. I think it did. We just weren't good enough to keep it rolling."

I know Tortorella wants the only focus to be on winning games. That's all he cares about. But time and time again, because of his convictions and his inability to be political even for a moment, he finds himself, not his players, in the spotlight. The last thing he wants, and I believe this, is for everything to become about him. But it's inevitable in moments like these.

"Sometimes I make mistakes because I don't want to be political," he says. "I get stubborn in that I want my guys to know that I'm going to be totally upfront all the time. It's almost trying to be so unselfish that you're selfish. Ninety percent of the time, the way things are handled, honestly, it's really good. But that 10 percent just takes over. It turns into a clusterfuck. It becomes about me. If you knew me, it is the last thing I want."

And he is trying to change. When his Team USA squad was eliminated in the 2016 World Cup after a lackluster loss, reporters covering the event hustled over to the press conference area, expecting fireworks. They prepared themselves for a livid and combative Tortorella. One media member jokingly grabbed one of the bags of popcorn lined up on a nearby table, as if he was getting ready to watch a horror film.

But there were no fireworks. No fights. No storming off. Tortorella was crushed by the loss but remained in control of his emotions. He expressed his disappointment in a way that truly conveyed how he felt for those players and for GM Dean Lombardi, who built that team.

"His disappointment about our lack of success at the World Cup, I think he felt more pain for Dean than for himself," said Scott Gordon, one of the Team USA assistants. "He knew how hard Dean had worked. It bothered him that we didn't have more success."

He's learned that you can still hate to lose without alienating those around you. That said, he's not perfect. During his first year in Columbus, GM Jarmo Kekalainen made it clear there was still room for improvement.

"He said, 'I can't stand being around you. It's tough to be around you when we lose,'" Tortorella recalls Kekalainen saying. "I was kind of shocked when Jarmo told me that. I thought I was really getting better at that."

"I remember when Jarmo hired you. I said to him…"

Tortorella anticipates my question.

"What the fuck are you doing?"

We laugh. I explain that I thought the Blue Jackets were too consciously going in the opposite direction from the personality of their previous coach, Todd Richards. I certainly had my doubts about how Tortorella would work out in Columbus after how things went down in Vancouver.

But similar to the feeling his friend Mike Sullivan had when he took over in Pittsburgh, Tortorella may have realized he wouldn't have many more chances if things went badly with the Blue Jackets. Maybe that's helped in the evolution of his personality.

"I have changed. I really have," he says. "I have tried to back off with my emotions, especially on the bench. That's where it's all public. I'm going to change even more."

He's willing to evolve on some things. He never will on others. Plus, he's closing in on 60 years old as we're talking. At that point, there's probably only so much a person can change. Perhaps that's why he's lumped in at times with other older coaches like Bob Hartley and Mike Keenan, comparisons that bother him. When I mention Hartley's name, he quickly shoots it down.

"I refuse to be compared to Bob Hartley," he says. "I'm not trying to run down Bobby. I think Bob Hartley is a really good coach. I don't look for personal attacks. I'm not looking to be mean, I'm looking to get a problem solved because I have another one coming tomorrow."

He's banging the table with his hands again. This really means a lot to him, this distinction from other coaches.

"I don't want to be compared to Mike Keenan. Mike Keenan doesn't want to be compared to me. I don't think anybody wants to be compared to anybody. I wish people could really understand who I am. But I make my own bed."

"Do you really care what others think?"

"I'm a human being. Of course I do. I'm not going to sit here and lie. If you ever said you don't care about your reputation, what someone is saying about you, you're a liar. You're a human being. I can't let it affect my decision-making."

It gets quiet.

One of the explanations I'd heard from someone who knew Tortorella well was that, on the day of the Hartley incident, his son Nick was being deployed. Nick is a member of the elite U.S. Army 75th Ranger Regiment, and when he's deployed his family often doesn't know where he's headed. I can't even imagine the stress that adds to a parent's life.

Tortorella rejects this reasoning.

"Nothing to do with it. My son is there now, he left two weeks ago. This is his third deployment. It's stressful but it does not affect my decision-making, how I act," he says. "It's constantly on my mind, even during the game. But that Bob Hartley thing, I'll tell you straight up, I put my guys out there to fight. He wanted to brawl, we brawled. I apologized before it happened. I felt I had to fight for my team. At the end of the first period, I was going to fight for my team. That's why I went down the hallway. As Neanderthal as it sounds, and it is, that's my thinking. That's all I was thinking about on the bench."

After the incident, Tortorella and then-Canucks GM Mike Gillis flew to New York for a disciplinary hearing with NHL league executives. In front of NHL commissioner Gary Bettman and some of the most powerful people in hockey, Tortorella had to sit and watch the replay of his actions on a big-screen TV.

Bettman tried to give him an out, suggesting that perhaps he just momentarily lost his cool between periods. Had Tortorella agreed with him, it might have lessened the punishment he'd receive.

But if we've learned anything about Tortorella, it's that he won't shy away from the truth just to make life a little easier.

"I said, 'No, I knew I was doing that in the middle of the first period. I couldn't wait for the period to get over,'" he recalls.

Underneath the table, Gillis hit Tortorella on the leg in an attempt to keep him quiet. In the end, the coach was suspended 15 days and prohibited from contacting his players during that time.

It was his career low point.

His career high point is about to play out on the screen in front of us.

* * *

There's about one minute remaining in the game and Martin St. Louis is behind the net retrieving the puck, trying to hold off a late Calgary charge while protecting a one-goal lead. He gets absolutely flattened by Andrew Ference. Ference's stick gets St. Louis in the face. The back of his head crashes into the boards.

"Rewind this," Tortorella says. "This is where he gets hurt. Ference runs him over behind the net. He goes down to the other end. Here it comes. Just fucking runs him over."

St. Louis is sporting a full beard. He has long hair coming out of the back of his helmet, and now has a stream of blood coming down the center of his face.

"Look at him. Is that terrific? Just his look. I put him back on the ice the next shift. I needed him to play," Tortorella says.

On the screen, a trainer tends to St. Louis, wiping the blood off his face, and you can tell what St. Louis is saying: "I'm fine. It's okay. It's okay."

When the Lightning go on the power play, St. Louis is back on the ice. With 48 seconds left, he fires a one-timer just wide. He's given everything he possibly could give to the Lightning's effort to win a Stanley Cup.

Back home, Tortorella has a picture of St Louis on the trainers' table getting stitched up after winning it all.

The clock ticks away. The keeper of the cup, Phil Pritchard, has the trophy on a table with a blue tablecloth. Wearing his white gloves, he's polishing it as the last 30 seconds wind down.

Finally, the horn sounds and Tampa Bay's Nikolai Khabibulin throws his stick into the air, jumping about as high as a goalie loaded down with equipment can jump. The players leap off the bench to join him.

"Yeah," Tortorella says, watching it unfold. "That was a great group of guys."

We watch some of the celebration. There's a shot of Darryl Sutter, the opposing coach and someone Tortorella has complete respect for. As the two coaches shook hands, Sutter expressed his appreciation for how the Lightning played.

"You wore us down," Sutter told Tortorella. "I didn't think you'd be able to do that."

Tortorella and I have now watched two games together. We're well into the afternoon. I don't want to take up any more of his time.

"Is there anything about this team that we didn't get to?" I ask.

"One thing I take out of it is that sometimes innocence, and the players not understanding the pressure of Game 7 or the Stanley Cup playoffs, is an advantage," he says. "That was definitely an advantage for us. The coach was young, the GM was a no-name. The team was young, sprinkled with a couple veterans. We just played."

They just played.

The NHL locked out its players the following season so this group never got a chance to properly defend its title. Eventually, the top players were dispersed, starting with Khabibulin, Richards—even Lecavalier and St. Louis.

And the coach would go, too. Four years later, Tortorella was fired at the age of 49.

It all seems so long ago.

"I think we're good here," I say, wrapping it up. "The only thing I didn't get to the bottom of—what was the story behind that quote in your high school yearbook?"

In 2013, while Tortorella's Rangers were playing the Boston Bruins, a local radio station dug up Tortorella's high school yearbook from Concord-Carlisle High School in Massachusetts, because that's what local radio stations do during the playoffs.

In all its black-and-white glory, there was a young John Tortorella, with a collar just slightly too big and long hair brushed to the side. Underneath his name were some inside jokes, including the all-caps question at the end of the paragraph that read: "WHERE IS MUSKY?"

I pull out my phone and within seconds, the yearbook picture appears. There's the quote. He starts reading all the inside references.

I need to know. Where is Musky?

"I don't have a clue," Tortorella says. "I don't have a fucking clue what that means. Musky. You can put that in your book."

• CHAPTER 7 •

JOEL QUENNEVILLE

Game 6 of the 2010 Stanley Cup Final

Joel Quenneville was a bit of a long shot to participate in this project.

Quenneville has made an art form of deflecting any attention brought his way while helping make the Chicago Blackhawks a modern dynasty. He has been so effective at appearing to be uninteresting that people sometimes make the mistake of thinking he's not a great coach.

I was sitting in Joe Louis Arena watching a Vancouver Canucks practice when Ray Ferraro, who played with Quenneville in Hartford and for him in St. Louis, got on that subject.

"Mike [Babcock] gets all the credit for being the best coach in hockey. Somehow, the guy with three Stanley Cups flies under the radar. Joel couldn't care less, I'm sure," Ferraro said. "I can guarantee you, when he goes into the Hall of Fame, his speech will be the best. He'll have people laughing. He's just a good, good guy. He's won three Stanley Cups and if you ask people who are the best coaches, they say [Babcock] and they might say Ken Hitchcock. They might say Barry Trotz. Somebody would go, 'Oh, what about Joel?'"

Part of that is because he's been doing it with a great team. Quenneville has won multiple Stanley Cups on a team that is driven by Jonathan

Toews, Patrick Kane, Marian Hossa, Duncan Keith, and Brent Seabrook, just to name a few.

"They have to throw guys overboard every year [because of the salary cap]," Ferraro shot back. "Mike had Pavel Datsyuk and Henrik Zetterberg and Nick Lidstrom. They were good players, remember? That's not to chip away at Mike. Everybody has good players that are even considered in that conversation."

Quenneville's success speaks for itself.

If the best coach in the game isn't Mike Babcock, it's Joel Quenneville. It's why I desperately wanted time with him. I wanted a chance to get beyond the vanilla quotes. I figured that sitting down and watching Game 6 of the 2010 Stanley Cup Final, where the Hawks beat the Philadelphia Flyers in overtime to win their first Cup in 49 years, would give us an opportunity to break through the usual press conference conversation.

Not having Quenneville in this book would be like collecting all the T-206 tobacco cards but leaving out Honus Wagner. It would be a huge hole.

That was my pitch when I pulled aside Blackhawks public relations director Adam Rogowin at the 2016 NHL Draft in Buffalo. I was pinning down dates in the summer to sit down with coaches and desperately wanted to arrange one with Quenneville.

I wasn't necessarily optimistic when our conversation ended and spent the summer focusing on other coaches.

Then in August came the e-mail from Adam I'd been waiting for.

"How does Tuesday or Wednesday of next week work?" he wrote.

Oh baby. It worked perfectly. Quenneville could have asked to do it on Mars and it would have worked perfectly.

It even gave me a few more days to continue collecting my favorite Joel Quenneville stories.

I heard over and over again how much guys loved playing for him. But what does that mean? How does he win players over so consistently?

Kelly Chase, who played for him in St. Louis, was the first to share a Quenneville "bonus story." Once he did, I went looking for more.

Some NHL players have bonuses built into their contracts that are tied to individual or team success. Quenneville liked to be aware of the milestones his players were close to reaching near the end of the season.

"The last games of the season on the road, we always played on the West Coast," Chase said. "He used to send around a pen and paper and you'd write down the bonuses you needed."

One year, Chase needed to be a plus-10 to receive a $25,000 bonus. He had been sitting out games down the stretch, but Quenneville found a way to get him in the lineup by the end. He also put him on the ice when the opposing team pulled their goalie to maximize his chances.

"I got my plus-10," Chase said.

When Tyson Nash played for Quenneville in St. Louis, he was due to receive a bonus if he averaged 10 minutes of ice time per game that season.

The last game of the season was in Detroit and the Blues had already clinched a playoff spot, so Quenneville was free to do whatever it took to get Nash to that number.

"I'll never forget it. Every time I came off the ice, he yelled, 'Get back on the ice!' I played power play, killed penalties. This was the best night of my life," Nash said.

He finished that season averaging 10:03 of ice time. It required him to play 16:16 in the final game of the season to get that bonus.

"He made it happen," Nash said. "I got the bonus. I almost had a heart attack the same night. All those things make up Joel Quenneville. I would fight anyone for that guy."

Perhaps the most legendary Quenneville story is one that still gets brought up when the St. Louis Blues involved get together for a beer. I had heard a couple different versions of the story but Chris Pronger was adamant that his version was accurate. He called from the airport before boarding a plane and shared the story.

"We played our last game of the year in L.A.," Pronger said. "Pavol Demitra needed one point to get a $500,000 bonus and Scott Young needed one goal to get a $300,000 bonus. There were 15 seconds left and the Kings pulled their goalie. Pavol gets the puck. Jaroslav Modry, his countryman, is back there playing defense for the Kings. Young is on the right side. Pavol can literally shoot it into the empty net but Pavol waited for Young. He passes it across to Young, who shoots. It's going in the middle of the net but Modry dives and catches it with his stick. Everyone on the L.A. bench is screaming at Modry: 'What the fuck are you doing? You idiot! It doesn't mean anything!' He's acting like it's Game 7 of the Stanley Cup Final. Everybody is pissed off at Modry."

No goal was scored and no bonuses were reached because Demitra had waited for his teammate and tried to help him rather than scoring on his own. Realizing what had happened, Quenneville took the video to the Blues owners. He told them those were the type of players he wanted, guys who would risk their own money in order to help a teammate get his.

"They didn't have to do anything," Pronger said. "Joel just made them aware. They gave Pavol the bonus."

"That's the right thing to do," I suggested.

"That's easy for you to say. You're not the one cutting a $500,000 check."

It was a great story that shows the kind of selflessness and teamwork Quenneville works to inspire in his players.

This was the Joel Quenneville I would get to see for a few hours on an August morning.

* * *

I'd been to United Center a million times covering the Blackhawks over the years, thanks in large part to the long playoff runs Quenneville has orchestrated as their coach.

This morning definitely felt different. I walked toward Gate 3½, near the statues of Bobby Hull and Stan Mikita, as I had done countless times for playoff games. But now Madison Street was empty. No mobs of fans outside the arena in Kane and Toews jerseys. Nobody asking to buy and sell tickets. Just one guy waiting for me with the door propped open to take me down the stairs, through the hallway, and into the Blackhawks coaches' office, in the inner sanctum of the arena.

The Blackhawks run everything like a well-oiled machine. When I arrive, Chicago's video coach, Matt Meacham, is already there to help make sure the game is loaded on the big screen in the office before Quenneville gets there.

Then Quenneville enters the room wearing black shorts, a blue T-shirt, and black athletic sandals. A little summer tan makes his legendary gray mustache pop even more than usual.

He sits at the head of a long white conference table with all the markings of a hockey rink surface on top of it, ready to go if he wants to diagram plays with a dry erase marker.

On the wall directly in front of him is the screen we'll be watching, flanked by two more white boards for diagramming plays. There are a couple of large framed pictures of Blackhawks players on the left, along with a giant season schedule.

Someone in the room brings up a round of golf they played the previous day and Quenneville perks up. He wants to know how it went. How many beers were put away?

He couldn't be more down to earth if he tried. At this point, he has three Stanley Cup rings as the coach of the Blackhawks, but he's a guy you would immediately feel comfortable playing golf or betting on some horses with, two things he loves doing.

"How's the golf around here?" I ask.

"Outstanding," Quenneville says. "Some of the best on the planet. There's Butler. There's Butterfield. There's Olympian Fields. There's

Medina. There's that place where the guy who has all the money—the guy who got ticker tape going?"

I have no idea what he's talking about. I take a stab at it.

"Bloomberg?"

"No. Same idea. Bloomberg did media. What's his name, that guy?"

"The guy who invented ticker tape? That has to be a couple of generations ago."

"He's got a beautiful layout. The LPGA used to practice out there."

(We don't get to the bottom of it. Later, the best I can guess is Rich Harvest Farms, owned by a guy who invented a method that incorporated separate stock exchange software programs into one.)

But either way, it's a nice jumping-off point to talk about his career, because if Quenneville wasn't behind the bench in the NHL, he'd probably be working in finance.

While playing for the Hartford Whalers toward the end of his career, Quenneville spent his summers working as a retail broker at Legg Mason in Connecticut. He had a small list of clients.

In 1991, he found himself playing in the AHL and knew he was closing in on a fork in the road—join the rest of us in the real world or find his next job in hockey.

"This business, it's not a job," he says. "It's kind of fun. It's a great opportunity."

So he chose to stay in the game, like many of his teammates from those old Hartford teams.

"You can look on every team in the league, there's a Whaler somewhere in the organization," he says.

He's not kidding. I picked a random season from Quenneville's years in Hartford, 1989–90. As we sat in that conference room, Ron Francis was the GM in Carolina. Pat Verbeek was the assistant GM in Tampa Bay. Kevin Dineen was on Quenneville's staff in Chicago. Dave Tippett was the head coach in Arizona. Guys like Scott Young, Dean Evason, Brad Shaw, Randy Cunneyworth, and Ulf Samuelsson are all established coaches. Goalie Mike Liut was a prominent agent, representing Blues star Vladimir Tarasenko, among other clients. Brian Lawton was both an agent and a general manager. Kay Whitmore works for the NHL. Ray Ferraro is working in television but will end up getting hired by a team as soon as he's ready.

It's crazy. For some reason, those Hartford players refused to leave the game.

"Why do you think that is?" I ask.

"I don't know. It was a fun team. We had a great group. Everybody was chummy together. It was a small little town and we turned the organization that wasn't winning into one where we had a parade because we lost in the second round to Montreal."

We both laugh.

"That's how excited everybody was for our team. I think we were a big part of that community. Everybody liked the team. It was a fun place to be."

Nearly every one of those guys are fun to spend time with. Ferraro is a blast. Liut is a fantastic storyteller. Tippett is salt of the earth.

They had fun together. They didn't want to leave.

"Sometimes you see a guy and you think something fits them," Ferraro said, trying to explain the Hartford phenomenon. "Like, I always saw Ronnie Francis managing. I always saw Tip as a coach. Mike Liut being an agent? Perfect. Mike could have been head of the Players Association. Now, Joel? I never put together whether Joel would be a coach. It never occurred to me. But when you step back and think about it—I used to joke, he was one of the best players in the league who couldn't skate, shoot, or pass."

Quenneville succeeded because he had vision. His mind was always thinking about the game. He was a few steps ahead of everybody else. He still is.

"You're on the bench and most coaches call which line is up and which line is next," Ferraro said. "Joel calls out three line combinations. You have to be awake. That's how his brain works."

The summer after he played in Baltimore, Quenneville went to Hall of Famer Roger Nielson's coaching clininc in Windsor. He started getting a taste of what his life might look like behind the bench. Cliff Fletcher hired Quenneville to be a player and assistant coach for the team in St. John's, Newfoundland.

Marc Crawford was the head coach of that team. As he transitioned into coaching, Quenneville found himself hanging less with the players and more with Crawford and the coaches. Little by little, Crawford gave him more responsibility. A pregame speech here, running a meeting there.

"It was a great match between us," Crawford said. "I had more coaching knowledge than he did at that time. He just had a great hockey mind, as we've turned out to learn."

It's his mind, Crawford believes, that sets him apart from other coaches.

"Great players, like Wayne Gretzky and Joe Sakic, they could see the plays develop. Joel has that kind of vision as well. That's what he has that is better than anybody else in the league. His vision and how he manages the bench, how he doesn't miss things. He's the best I've seen. And he's a really fun guy. You've got to have a little bit of that."

Quenneville and I are reminiscing about his time in St. John's when the game begins on the screen in front of us. It starts with a shot of famed Philadelphia anthem singer Lauren Hart, waving to the crowd shortly after finishing her rendition. The crowd in Philadelphia is going crazy. The fans are all wearing orange T-shirts that say UNFINISHED BUSINESS. They handed them out to the media as well. The shirts are huge. For years I've worn it while cutting my lawn.

The Blackhawks are up 3–2 in the series and are one win away from winning their first Stanley Cup since 1961.

Immediately, the moment rushes back for Quenneville.

"I remember the emotion of that building when she would sing," he says, referring to Hart. "You'd get the buzz in our building but you still felt it there, too. Kate Smith would pop up on the screen. It was very cool."

A shot of Chris Pronger appears, a giant in his orange Flyers jersey. There's a scowl on his face and a look in his eyes like he knows something the rest of us don't.

Pronger and Quenneville grew up together in St. Louis—Pronger as a dominant defenseman and Quenneville as a head coach learning the ropes.

"You could tell he was basically hurt," Quenneville says, referring to Pronger's play in this series. "He knew the strategy. He knew his team. He kept everything in the right perspective from the other side. We knew what kind of player he is."

Pronger confirmed that he wasn't close to healthy against the Blackhawks that year.

"I hurt my knee in the Boston series," Pronger said. "Throughout the rest of the playoffs, against Boston, Montreal, and Chicago, I had my knee drained. I had two M&M-sized chunks floating around in there."

As the game begins, two things stand out to Quenneville. The first is that the Blackhawks were coming off a Game 5 he felt was the best game they'd played all year at home. They won 7–4.

The second is that Patrick Sharp and his Blackhawks teammates were able to carry over that play immediately into Game 6.

"We came out flying in this game. Sharpie, it was the best game he probably ever played for the Blackhawks," Quenneville says.

Sharp won three Stanley Cups in Chicago before being traded to Dallas, a casualty of the Blackhawks' salary cap challenges. A couple of months after sitting down with Quenneville, I relayed his old coach's comments to Sharp. He was two hours away from playing a game for the Dallas Stars, not exactly a time players typically like to get nostalgic about the past. But hearing Quenneville's comments brought Sharp back to that place in time. Back to that arena in Philadelphia, where he had one of his proudest moments as a player.

When Joel Quenneville took over the Blackhawks in 2008, the roster was talented but unproven. Nearly a decade later, they're the salary cap era's version of a dynasty.

"He told my father on the ice after that game when we were all celebrating, that was the best he'd ever seen me play," Sharp said. "That's something that I always took with me. At the time, I was a younger player, so caught up with scoring goals and getting points and being the best goal scorer I could be."

That game was different. That playoff run was different.

"I was engaged in every shift. I was going hard to the puck area every time. I was fearlessly going at the puck. That game, and that playoff run as a whole, I was focused on playing like an animal."

The game begins with an overhead shot of Jonathan Toews taking and winning the faceoff against Daniel Briere.

About 30 seconds of play elapse before there's a whistle. The camera zooms in on NBC's Pierre McGuire, standing between the benches. That's who I'm looking at—but not Quenneville. He spots Blackhawks equipment manager Clint Reif, whose death in 2014 shook the entire organization.

"Oh my god, good to see Clint in that picture," Quenneville says.

As he would all game, Quenneville interrupts with quick observations. He can't help but recognize small plays being made by his guys in front of us.

"I remember Soupy [Brian Campbell] being out there with a great poke check right there. He was in on the winning goal," he says.

"Are you one of those coaches who remembers games verbatim?"

"No, it'll come back. I remember some key things. I remember we were a four-line team. It was a tremendous lineup. There are six or seven or eight or nine guys who are in the league that all end up getting paid off of this. They're all good players. Soupy is hitting. You've got Hammer [Niklas Hjalmarsson], Mr. Reliable, as good as any defenseman in the game, defensively. He could do it all."

Over the years, the hockey world has gained an appreciation for Hjalmarsson. (Enough so that I even spelled his name correctly on the first try right there.)

"He was so underrated," Quenneville continues. "He was so smart. Dave Bolland, another smart player, a hard guy to play against. He was a warrior type."

He turns his attention to the Flyers.

"They had the one big line, eh? That played great against us. The Fin who got paid…"

"Ville Leino."

"And Hartnell and Briere—were they good against us. That was the most dangerous line. Everybody else worked hard and their defense was pretty responsible. The goaltending in this series wasn't great."

"From the outside, there was never any doubt that you guys were going to win this series. Did you have that same confidence?"

"We were still a very young team. The year before we got a great lesson, playing Detroit. We played them pretty well. And then, in 2010, we had some interesting series. We got a break in the first round where we scored short-handed."

He's referring to Chicago's first-round matchup against Nashville. In Game 5 of that series, Patrick Kane scored the game-tying goal with 13.6 seconds left in the third period. Then Marian Hossa, who'd been serving a five-minute boarding penalty, streaked out of the penalty box and won it in overtime.

"Was it Nashville in the first round? I think it was the first round where they made—I don't want to say dumb—I'll say a fortunate play for us to the slot. I'm going to think of who made that play. Don't tell me. Shit. Who was the guy? He was in Arizona at the end. Traded to Washington."

"Marty Erat."

"It was Erat. Yeah. We got a break on that play. We all have interesting calls that can be defining moments."

Over the years, what I've learned to really appreciate about the Blackhawks is their ability to finish off a series when given the chance. Under Quenneville, they're a team that gets better as the playoffs progress. If they're down in a series, they usually find a way back into it.

That's not to say there weren't plenty of butterflies flying around in the hours before this Game 6.

"We played a great Game 5 [against Philadelphia]," Quenneville says. "But you know what? It's nerve-wracking as heck trying to prepare the night before and the day of when you have to go win the Cup that night. It's the toughest thing in the world."

Especially this first Cup. Sharp said the next two clinching games, in 2013 and 2015, were more settled for him, probably because he'd already gone through it.

This first one? It was chaotic. The young Blackhawks had heard all the stories about how players can go their entire NHL careers and never get an opportunity like the one they would have on that night. At the time, they had no idea they'd be playing in these games every other season for the next five years.

Sharp roomed with Adam Burish on the road, and before this game the two laid on their beds, staring at the ceiling, talking about just how close they were to winning a Stanley Cup.

"I remember being nervous for basically the whole Final. It was the first time I felt the nerves and the anxiety," Sharp said. "I just remember so much going on…You're so worried about everything else, it's like, 'Oh yeah, let's go play a hockey game.'"

During a team meeting in the visitors' dressing room, Quenneville asked veteran center John Madden to speak about what the team was facing. Madden had two Stanley Cups under his belt, winning twice with the Devils, in 2000 and 2003.

The room got quiet as Madden began to talk.

"Mads didn't miss a beat. He went right into it," Burish said. "'Yeah, you're going to be nervous, but find a way to understand this is just another game. Understand we're the better team. If we do these things, we're going to win the game.'"

"That influence can help a young team, knowing that you can't sleep. You can't rest. You're nervous. You can't wait to play. You think of a million things except what you really need to think about," Quenneville says. "He put a lot of things in perspective, having been through it all. That helped stabilize us."

Madden remembers looking around the room as he spoke to his teammates and realizing just how few had ever been in this moment. These Blackhawks were confident and played with plenty of swagger, but they were also so young.

"I echoed what Joel said. 'This is ours to take if we just bear down,'" Madden said. "'Let's keep our swagger. Let's be loose. We were loose all year.'"

As the players catch Quenneville's attention on the screen, we're both reminded of how deep this 2010 Blackhawks team was.

He notices Troy Brouwer, a guy who spent time on the fourth line.

"Look at the lineup we had," he says.

"The salary cap on this team, if we took the salaries now, it would be $100 million."

"I know. It's unbelievable. Yeah. Easy. Do the numbers."

Later, I did the numbers.

If you take the highest average salary the 22 players on the Blackhawks roster from the 2010 Final have or had made in their careers, the total salary cap charge would be $109.8 million. At the time, the NHL's salary cap was only $56.8 million. So basically, the retail price of this Blackhawks team was double the cap that year.

They were good. It's a team that would be impossible to reconstruct in the salary cap era.

They also have a coach in Quenneville who is one of the best of his era. But back to Game 6.

"Are you anticipating plays now?" I ask.

"Yeah. I'm almost playing the game…We give the guys a lot of freedom offensively. We try to encourage them to keep the puck. Move before they touch it. Don't stand still. Basically, if you stand still before you touch it, when you're touching it, it's too late. You've got to start moving. Then you can protect the puck. Then you have it. I like to play fast. I want the puck."

Quenneville has a knack for knowing quickly if a player is going well during a game or not. He's not afraid to mix things up if he doesn't like what he sees. For example, Sharp has it going in this game in front of us.

"You can tell right away," Quenneville says. "You can see with guys, they have patience with the puck. They have good play recognition. They have speed. They come up with loose pucks, which is the best measurement of a hockey player to me, and they come up with it in a battle tight area."

He pauses for a moment to take a phone call. As he does, his team on the screen in front of him is taking control of the first period after an even first four minutes. Five minutes in and the Blackhawks have opened up a sizable advantage in shots on goal. By NBC's count they have a 2–0 edge in scoring chances.

The play is nonstop and the speed is breathtaking. It's a pace the series hadn't seen until this moment.

The Blackhawks go on the power play, and Duncan Keith rips a shot from the blue line that is deflected before ringing the post.

"Look at that one," Quenneville says. "Hits the post. Wide-open net. We had a bunch of these."

He starts chatting about his pregame strategy.

"I just give them pointers technically. 'This is what we want to do. Boom. Boom. Boom.' We have the best leader in the game in Tazer. That whole group, they all get rewarded. They were well prepared. They're great pros. They want to be as good as they can, game in and game out. They're individually motivated and wired the right way."

It was a fun group to follow during the playoffs. Even in the mass chaos that is being a part of the media during the Stanley Cup Final, you got the sense the boys were having fun. Whether it was Dustin Byfuglien balling up tape and firing it at teammates or Kris Versteeg singing, there were glimpses of the kind of fun they were having behind the scenes.

Occasionally you'd see them out on the streets of Chicago at night or at a restaurant. It was a great time to be a young Chicago Blackhawks star.

Quenneville created an atmosphere where they were allowed to have that fun. The night they eliminated the San Jose Sharks in the Western Conference Finals, the players were out celebrating until 4:00 AM. Quenneville didn't care, as long as they showed up at the next practice ready to go.

"After every single round, we had a big party," Burish said. "We were out late nights. Late, late nights. Every round was like that. He kept it loose, kept it fun. He was focused, dialed in. There were no gray areas with him. You knew what you had to do. You knew your job."

Quenneville also has a way of keeping everybody involved. Burish wasn't seeing a ton of ice time during the playoffs but he left that team feeling as if he contributed as much as anyone.

Before the first round against Nasvhille, Quenneville did something he'd never done before with this group. Instead of having the coaching staff prepare Chicago's scouting reports, he assigned each Blackhawk a corresponding Predator and asked them to prepare reports and present them to the team.

Guys didn't know what to expect. Some didn't want to do it, not exactly comfortable stepping in front of the group.

Burish decided to put his own spin on it. He brought a guitar to the rink and when it was his turn to give the scouting report on Jordin Tootoo, Burish sat on a stool in the center of the dressing room and sang his scouting report, a song about Tootoo to the tune of Tom Petty's "Mary Jane's Last Dance."

Quenneville and the team loved it.

"I was dying laughing," Madden said. "It was just a real classic moment."

Before playing the Canucks in the next round, Burish did it again, this time singing a scouting report on Alex Burrows to the tune of Petty's "Free Fallin'."

Quenneville upped the stakes for the Western Conference Finals. When the team arrived at its hotel in San Jose before Game 1, the coach asked Burish to compile a scouting report on every single player on the Sharks.

Burish went back to the hotel and wrote a long poem, assigning different parts to be read by different players on the Blackhawks. It couldn't just be funny, it had to have useful information, something he took seriously, calling people he knew in hockey to provide scouting tips.

One of the parts of the poem was to be read by Quenneville. It was about him yelling at the referees.

Before the Stanley Cup Final, Quenneville told Burish he had to go for a grand finale.

For the Flyers scouting report, Burish got the Blackhawks video team involved. They went around Chicago with Burish dressed as different teammates, wearing their jerseys as he imitated them on camera.

Nothing was sacred. He dressed as Patrick Sharp—known for his good looks—standing in front of a mirror primping himself while giving a scouting report on Danny Briere. He was Dustin Byfuglien at a bar. Dave Bolland sitting in a Lamborghini. Jonathan Toews, waking up crabby from a nap. Patrick Kane in the back of a cab.

Nothing was off limits.

On the night before Game 1 of the Stanley Cup Final, a screen was lowered and the video was played. If the team was nervous or tight, those feelings quickly disappeared. The video absolutely killed.

When it was over, Burish was told to destroy all copies of it.

But the gambit worked. Rather than Quenneville giving some motivational speech or overloading the team with information on the Flyers, the video did exactly what he had intended.

"He was genius that way," Burish said. "He had a lot of goofy guys on that team, crazy personalities. He embraced that. He was demanding of us but he understood us. He realized guys like it. Giving up a little of that control is hard for some coaches. He knew these guys know what they need to do to get ready. I always tell people, he's as big a reason for the Stanley Cup as Kane or Toews."

* * *

The first period of Game 6 is playing out at a frantic pace on the screen in front of Quenneville. With about seven minutes remaining in the first period, Brent Seabrook absolutely flattens Ville Leino, crushing him into the boards. The hit comes moments after Scott Hartnell, flying around like a wrecking ball, smashed Jonathan Toews.

When there's finally a break in the action, Doc Emrick speaks for everyone watching the broadcast when he says, "Wow, this is good."

Quenneville loves the hit on Leino, as Leino's helmet goes flying. He doesn't like that the Flyers want a penalty called.

"Look at that hit there. They're complaining about that hit. It's a perfectly clean hit," he says.

Then he starts giving his play-by-play as the Blackhawks are buzzing, all in short, staccato phrases.

"We're pressuring.

We're playing the right way.

F2 is jumping.

F3 is in the middle.

Great stick, Sharpie.

Another good stick.

Quick to the puck.

Good coverage down low.

We're fast.

We're on the puck.

Now they're looking at the referee.

They're using the crowd."

Finally, the Blackhawks break through and get the goal they deserved in this period. It starts as so many scoring plays do for the Blackhawks, with Toews winning a battle along the boards. It ends with Dustin Byfuglien banging home the rebound on Toews' shot. The Blackhawks celebrate a 1–0 lead.

"There we go," Quenneville says as it happens. "Buff was so important for us in this playoff series. Against Vancouver, he dominated. Buff was gigantic. He was unreal. That presence in front of the net. It's like, pick your poison—you want Buff pounding the puck from the point? Or Buff hanging around at the front of the net, quick hands for a big man?"

As we're talking about Byfuglien, Seabrook catches Hartnell with an elbow. Hartnell helicopters in a few circles, then goes down to the ice holding his head.

"Look at him diving there," Quenneville says. "Show it again. He falls. [Seabrook] didn't even touch him. Pretends he got hit in the head."

Quenneville can't help himself. He knows how this game turns out and he's still mad about the calls on the ice.

His team is dominating the shot count. The Flyers have only managed three shots on goal in the period, and they don't get one on the power play either. After the penalty kill, Patrick Sharp grabs the puck and is up the ice like he's been shot out of a cannon.

"Flying!" Quenneville nearly shouts. Then a whistle blows.

Brent Sopel is called for interference on Ville Leino.

"Look at that dive. Holy fuck. What kind of call is that?"

It only takes 27 seconds for Hartnell to tie the game on the ensuing power play.

"We got fucked on two calls in a row. Two dives. Now it's 1–1. You know it's not going to be easy. It's a tough building to win in. They're coming. The building is rocking. They're hitting everything that moves. Keep our composure. Finish this period well. Don't take a dumb penalty."

The period ends and the video goes right into the second period. Toews is back at center ice, taking another faceoff to start things off.

Quenneville is into it.

"Tazer right from the faceoff, let's go. Let's do it right. Let's win it. Let's start with the puck."

Toews loses the faceoff. Moments later, Marian Hossa turns the puck over at center ice, leading to a Simon Gagne breakaway.

"Oof, what a start. Big save. Is that Tomas Kopecky who lost that puck? Hoss wouldn't do that," Quenneville says, smiling, but I think he knows the truth.

Seeing Hossa is a reminder that at this point in history, there was a real debate about whether or not he could win the big game. He'd advanced to the two previous Stanley Cup Finals and lost them both, first with Pittsburgh and then with Detroit.

But in Chicago he was playing for a coach who is known for getting the best out of his stars, a coach who leans on them in the most crucial moments.

"I don't care if the numbers say Marcus Kruger should be out there for every faceoff, Joel Quenneville is not going to lose a hockey game with Marcus Kruger there," said longtime Blackhawks analyst Eddie Olczyk. "He's going to lose with Jonathan Toews taking faceoffs. He's going to go big or go home with his guys."

Olczyk also credits Quenneville for his willingness to make changes the moment he senses something is off.

"Joel shortens the bench. He's not afraid. It drives fans crazy how much he changes the lines over the years, but it's proven. You have to trust what he's thinking."

"He doesn't look at the bad in players. He finds a way to bring the best out of every player," said Sharp. "If Player A is good at this or bad at that, he's going to put that player in situations to be his best. That's what makes him a great coach."

"We try to encourage guys positively. Reinforce the positive side. We never embarrass anybody," Quenneville says when I bring this up. "I feel that if you put them in good situations, they'll do their thing. Treat them the way you'd want to be treated. That's basically our approach. The difference is the top guys play more."

"How do you find that balance, when you want the fourth line and the third pair to stay involved?"

"It's tough when you have guys playing four or five minutes…that's a balancing act. The guys who don't play regularly, not dressing, you have to be careful—especially in the playoffs. As you go along you don't want anyone being a negative around the team, that their body language doesn't get anybody off or down."

Burish is a great example of that. He played five minutes a game but at times he felt like he was the captain. Quenneville gives me another example.

"We've got Brouwer playing on the power play. The units are pretty even. Kris Versteeg, he was really good there for us. He was tricky, great with the puck."

Just as he says that, Versteeg loses the puck.

Quenneville lets out a big laugh.

"As soon as I say that, he lost it."

Another reason players love playing for Quenneville is that he provides a layer of protection between them and the public. You see it in the way he assesses players after the game. He's never critical. When he says a guy played "just okay," that's about as close as he gets to being critical.

But it's more than that, said Kelly Chase, who played for Quenneville in St. Louis. He covers up for his guys.

"That guy has sat on more swords for more shit that has gone on," Chase said. "It's not talked about."

I relay Chase's words to Quenneville while we're watching the second period.

"Whether it gets out or whatever, I'm never going to embarrass a player," he says. "I'm never going to say anything negative about them in the media. I try to be positive with people. Very respectful that these guys are all pros and professional."

At this point, I explain to him how I've been collecting stories about his efforts to help players reach their bonuses at the end of the year. He smiles and then goes right to the Pavol Demitra story, letting out a good laugh while telling it.

On the screen, Scott Hartnell's skate clips Duncan Keith's as the Flyers are approaching the Blackhawks zone. Keith goes down hard and the Flyers suddenly have a 2-on-1 with Leino and Briere, two players who have been great in this series. Leino feeds Briere for the quick shot that beats Chicago goaltender Antti Niemi.

The crowd, a sea of orange waving white towels, is now going absolutely crazy. The Flyers, despite being outplayed by the Blackhawks, are now up 2–1.

Quenneville is steamed. It's the middle of the summer six years later and this still angers him.

"How do you think Duncan fell? I'm not sure about that play. Did he get picked? Did he get tripped? What happened?" he says. "Yeah. He got tripped. Watch this play. This was fucking brutal what's going on in this game. Watch Duncan. Yeah, he toe-picked him. It's almost like they were looking to do that, drag their back foot."

"You think it was intentional?"

"Oh for sure, it was 100 percent intentional."

There's a quick replay of the goal. Then a replay of Mike Richards absolutely crushing Kopecky earlier. It's a reminder of just how good Richards was in this era.

"What a hit," Quenneville says. "He knew he was getting him in that shift. We played against Richards in L.A. three years in a row, too."

Those Blackhawks and Kings series were the best. The 2014 Western Conference Finals was one of the best in league history. I'll go to my grave believing that. I share that opinion with Quenneville.

"When they beat us in Game 7? That hurt," Quenneville says.

"Sorry, I didn't mean to bring up a loss. You would have gone back to back. You would have beat the Rangers in the Final."

"That would have been back to back to back."

He's right. I forgot just how close the Blackhawks came to winning three consecutive Stanley Cups in this era, which is ridiculous since the league is built for parity and they had to partly dismantle this 2010 team we're watching. The Kings beat the Rangers in five games in 2014 and I'm confident the Blackhawks would have done the same thing.

"I think we would have been alright. It wouldn't have been easy though. I don't think we would have beaten them as easy as L.A. did," Quenneville says.

Halfway through the second period, with the two teams playing 4-on-4 hockey, Sharp gets the goal he deserved in this game. It's not the prettiest but it evens things out.

Quenneville hoisted the Stanley Cup for the first time in 2010. He'd repeat the moment in 2013 and 2015. (AP Images)

The broadcast cuts to an interview between Pierre McGuire and Quenneville. He manages to get a shot in about the officiating. He's really hung up on it. Still is.

I've always wondered whether coaches even listen to the questions in these midgame interviews. They can't be fun to do.

"I'm pretty vanilla," Quenneville says. "I remember one time, Joe Micheletti was asking me something right after Hossa got ran over by fucking Raffi Torres. I just about chewed his head off. I know Joe, he's a former defenseman partner. He basically said, 'Okay, I'd better cut this short.'"

On another night, Ray Ferraro was working between the benches and there was a disputed goal. Quenneville was up on the bench and letting the referees have it. He was screaming and yelling, his arms waving all over the place.

With the benefit of replay, Ferraro noticed that the refs called it right. Quenneville was on the wrong side of the argument.

Ferraro caught Quenneville's eye in the middle of the rant.

"I go, 'It didn't go in.' He goes, 'Oh, I know.' And he goes right back at it," Ferraro said, laughing.

The game enters the third period. The Blackhawks have now taken a 3–2 lead after Andrew Ladd tipped a shot from Niklas Hjalmarsson past Flyers goalie Michael Leighton. During the previous intermission, Quenneville told his guys to keep doing what they were doing. They'd just played the best five periods of the Final. They were 20 minutes away from winning a Stanley Cup.

I offer to jump ahead to the point where the Flyers tie it.

Quenneville has another idea. He wants to jump ahead to the point where Jonathan Toews got hurt.

I didn't know that part of the game existed.

Toews won the Conn Smythe Trophy that year. He was a force for the Blackhawks in the postseason. This is where he heightened his reputation as one of the game's best leaders. Part of that leadership was playing through a severe knee injury suffered in the final minutes of this Cup-clinching game.

"Jonny gets hurt in this game with less than 10 minutes to go in regulation," Quenneville says. "He can't really go. Thank God we scored early [in overtime]. I think it would have been impossible for Jonny to play Game 7."

Wait. What?

This was all news to me. Later, I relayed the Toews injury story to John Madden. He said the players had no idea.

"I do recall taking a lot more faceoffs," Madden said. "I was like, 'Uh, I must be playing better.'"

Quenneville and I go looking for the moment Toews gets hurt. With just over 11 minutes remaining in the third period, the Blackhawks are up one goal, closing in on their first Stanley Cup in decades, desperately trying to keep the Flyers off the board.

We're still looking for Toews but it's Dustin Byfuglien who catches our attention, chasing a puck down the center of the ice like a runaway freight train. Philadelphia's Kimmo Timonen has to make a diving play to prevent Byfuglien from a breakaway. When Braydon Coburn goes to retrieve the puck along the boards, Byfuglien hammers him.

Quenneville is cheering him on as it happens. I get a sense of exactly what it's like to be next to Quenneville during a game.

"C'mon Buff! Go Buff! Big hit Buff!" he yells.

We're watching every shift closely, looking for any sign that Toews is laboring. He's still getting regular shifts as Quenneville starts leaning on his best players to close out the game. He's mostly playing four defensemen. The Flyers are making their push and Quenneville is trying to will his team on from the future, almost as if he can impact the outcome, maybe get a regulation win this time.

Toews takes another faceoff in the defensive zone with 4:23 left, up by one goal. He's 22 years old but you'd never know it from the weight of responsibility he's carrying.

The Blackhawks clear the zone and Pronger gains control of the puck, with Toews skating in on him to apply some pressure. It looks like he's moving fine.

Pronger works the puck over to Leino, who takes it the length of the ice. The rush looks harmless enough until Leino gets to the goal line and sends a backhanded pass toward the front of the net. The puck richochets off Brent Seabrook's stick, then off Marian Hossa and somehow past Niemi. The Flyers have tied it, with Scott Hartnell getting just enough of his stick on the puck to be credited with the goal.

Making things worse for Chicago, we see a collision in front of the net between Hartnell and Toews. Toews is clipped in the knee, with Briere falling on top of him.

"There. He got hurt," Quenneville says. "That's exactly what happened. He got hurt on that play. Watch, he gets crosschecked into the goalie."

The crowd is going absolutely crazy. The game is tied and Quenneville is being notified by Blackhawks trainer Mike Gapski that his captain just got hurt, too.

Then there's another moment that's been lost in history. Flyers forward Jeff Carter has a chance to give the Flyers the lead and probably a win in regulation.

Quenneville can't finish a thought without appreciating the effort of both teams. He lets out another big laugh. He's enjoying this.

"Very physical game, isn't it? People thought they could intimidate this team. But it was as tough a team as you could ever have," he says.

There's 2:35 remaining in the game when Toews resurfaces. He takes an offensive zone faceoff against Mike Richards. He loses and is laboring a bit when the puck is worked around the boards.

"Jonny is out there," Quenneville says. "He said, 'Let me go. I gotta go.' Let's see what he does."

Toews and Hossa are in the neutral zone, heading toward the Flyers goal with 2:14 left. Toews' teammates have no idea how serious the injury is at this point.

"It wasn't until midsummer. I remember talking to him, he was still having problems with his knee," Sharp said. "That's when I was like, 'Holy shit, we wouldn't have had Tazer in Game 7.' That just shows you the margin of winning and losing is so small."

In this moment, Hossa has no idea how banged up Toews is. He taps the puck back to Toews as they enter the offensive zone. Flyers forward Darroll Powe bumps him off the puck and the threat is wiped out. The Flyers are headed the other way.

"Yeah, he can't go. Left leg, can't really go," Quenneville says.

He's now talking to Toews through the television.

"Get off the ice."

Just imagine the lift the Flyers would get if they realized that not only had they tied the game and possibly forced a Game 7, but the Blackhawks' most important player was injured. Quenneville realized this. He was hoping to play Toews just enough to throw the Flyers off the scent.

"He gets that shift, so everybody knows he's fine. Okay, this is Carter. Watch this chance he gets."

Claude Giroux finds a wide-open Jeff Carter, who spins and fires a puck that Niemi somehow saves.

I'm stunned at how close the Blackhawks came to losing this game.

"What a chance he had," Quenneville says.

"That would have made it it 4–3 and you're going back without Toews in Game 7."

"Every one, we got lucky."

That's a part nobody ever wants to talk about when winning a Stanley Cup. Luck is such a big part of it.

In this moment, the Blackhawks have luck on their side. Quenneville calls a timeout after an icing call to give his guys a breather. There's a shot of him on the screen, staring straight ahead while his assistants Mike Haviland and John Torchetti talk on either side of him. On screen, he actually looks a little stunned about what had just happened.

"What's the conversation there?"

"Probaby saying, 'How the fuck is that guy so wide open? Why was Carter so wide open?'"

He laughs.

At this point, Quenneville has told Toews he's going to use him, he's just not sure how much. They'll monitor it after each shift.

Regulation ends with Hossa, Sharp, and Kane on the ice for the Blackhawks. The Flyers' late charge means there's overtime.

Quenneville's message after regulation to his players was simple. Until that final push, the Blackhawks had dominated play for five periods and the start of the sixth. They just needed to settle down and return to that level of play.

In the visitors' dressing room, Sharp broke away from his teammates and headed into the bathroom for a moment alone.

He started talking to himself.

"'Let's just win this game. We've got to win this game,'" Sharp said. "I remember almost praying to get this done."

There's a promo from NBC on the screen for a potential Game 7. It would be a Friday night game in Chicago, maybe a game for the ages. Overtime will now determine whether or not it's necessary.

The extra period starts. There's a clean sheet of ice and Jonathan Toews is in the center taking another big faceoff. He wins it, sliding the puck back to Brent Seabrook. He loops around and starts skating down the left side of the neutral zone.

"He's trying. He's trying. I think he gets another shiiiii…," Quenneville says.

As he's saying the word "shift," Duncan Keith turns the puck over to Mike Richards, causing Quenneville to stretch out the last word in his sentence.

"Duncs! What the fuck are you doing? They had another chance to win it."

The Flyers had no shortage of opportunities to win this game. The puck finds its way to Claude Giroux, who gets a shot off that Niemi turns aside. The Flyers have had the last few really good chances.

"Niemi has made a couple good saves for you," I say.

"Yup. The Carter one was great. They're coming. You think Toews gets another shift?"

"Who is monitoring him? Are you?"

"Or Gapski. I might ask Jonny, 'How'd it feel?' He'll never tell me."

Seabrook makes a diving play in the defensive zone to separate Hartnell from the puck. He's quietly had a really good game.

With 17:27 remaining in overtime, Toews hops over the boards for what would be the last time that season.

"This is his second shift. I think it's his last shift. There's no way to not get him out there," Quenneville says. "He's going to say, 'I'm alright.' Gapper is going to say, 'I don't know.' Let's watch this shift, see what he does. He's skating alright there. I think he felt better there at the end of the period."

Toews wins another faceoff, this one coming in the defensive zone. He wins a battle up the wall and helps gain the zone by working the puck up to Marian Hossa. He does look a lot better; whatever treatment he received before overtime, paired with his adrenaline, has worked.

Patrick Kane's line jumps on the ice, with his linemates Andrew Ladd and Patrick Sharp. Kane gets the puck at center ice with speed, just how Quenneville instructs. Quenneville is watching closely.

Kane gains the offensive zone and spins back to create some space. He fires a shot that bounces wide, one that Sharp sends back behind the net to try and maintain possession.

The Flyers have a chance to clear it. Darroll Powe gets the puck behind the goal line and, after some pressure from Sharp, sends it up the wall. Brian Campbell is there waiting for it, regaining possession for the Blackhawks. Quenneville notices Campbell's play, one the rest of us have long forgotten.

"What a play keeping that puck in," he says.

Campbell slides it over to Kane, who puts a couple of jukes on future teammate Kimmo Timonen. Kane skates wide, toward the goal line, and fires a shot.

Two people in the building immediately know this shot beats Michael Leighton to make the Blackahwks Stanley Cup champions: Kane and Sharp. There's no goal light. No horn. There's no immediate call from Doc Emrick on the broadcast we're watching. It's a surreal moment as Kane, Sharp, and eventually the rest of the Blackhawks start celebrating during the confusion.

The rest of the Blackhawks jump onto the ice but even some of them are not sure. Madden remembers thinking at that moment how stupid he'd feel if there was no goal and his gloves were at center ice. He had no idea what became of his stick.

Andrew Ladd turns to Burish and asks him if they should go back to the bench. Nobody wants to be penalized for having too many men on the ice.

But Kane knows the goal is good. Eventually the rest of the team realizes it.

"What an anticlimactic ending," Quenneville says, watching. "It's an awful ending. It should have been way better."

The Blackhawks' Stanley Cup drought is over. One of the league's most storied franchises is back on top. It's the start of a dynasty for some of the greatest players of this generation.

Quenneville, in the moment, still wasn't sure it was a goal.

"How long until after he scores are you waiting to celebrate?" I ask.

"I stood on that bench for a long time. A long, long time. And then [video coach] Brad [Aldrich] came out with the video and said it's in the net."

Kane skates down and hugs Niemi. His teammates pile on.

There's an overhead replay of Kane's goal. Back and forth, rewound and replayed. It's clearly a good goal, the puck stuck in the side of the net, somehow beating Leighton at an impossible angle.

"How does that go in the net?" Quenneville wonders aloud. There's a shot of Kane, with his mullet and shaved side of his head, swinging his arms in celebration. "That's got to be the worst goal to win a Cup on, huh? The best or the worst, whatever way you you want to look at it."

It may have been an unusual goal but these Blackhawks proved that none of their success was a fluke, winning two more Cups with this core group in the next five years.

But the first one was special. They were all kids. They were all having a great time. This was a roster that could never be duplicated, not in today's NHL.

This was the group that started it all for this era in Chicago.

"It was a fun team to coach," Quenneville concludes. "They were competitive. They were tough. Young. All fun. Awesome."

• CHAPTER 8 •

KEN HITCHCOCK

Game 6 of the 1999 Stanley Cup Final

I was driving along I-70 through downtown Indianapolis, heading home to Detroit after sitting down with veteran NHL coach Ken Hitchcock, when my phone made a noise I'd never heard it make before.

It was the high-pitched buzzing sound of the Emergency Broadcast System.

On the screen was a warning triangle and message that left little ambiguity. There had been a tornado spotted in the vicinity and I was to take cover immediately. Like, right now.

In elementary school, I'd been well trained on what to do during a tornado. You got under your desk and put your hands over your head. At home, you go to the lowest point in your house.

In this moment, I wasn't sure what the protocol was for taking cover when you're doing 65 miles per hour on the highway during a storm. I turned on the radio and the news didn't get any better.

"For those on I-70 between exits 85 and 90, seek shelter immediately," warned the voice on the radio. By my best estimate I was smack in between those exits. The sky was a swirling mix of gray and pea-soup green.

I opted to plow on. I didn't know where to take cover anyway, and figured I could be past exit 90 in 10 minutes at my current pace.

My heart was beating fast as I navigated traffic, looking for funnels to drop out of the sky at any moment. The guy on the radio was talking about where they'd been spotted in counties and cities nearby.

They reported that the town of Kokomo had just been crushed by a tornado, with winds up to 165 miles per hour. I had no idea where Kokomo was, as I headed north in an attempt to change directions. Of course, Kokomo was north of where I was.

Eventually, I stopped. I went to a Jimmy John's and grabbed a sandwich. My wife was at home on the computer tracking the radar and trying to help me find my way back to Michigan safely.

It was touch and go for a while there—and I regretted none of it.

Ken Hitchcock is always worth the trip. Every time.

He's a storyteller and a teacher. He's also still a bit of a salesman, left over from his days working for Wilf Brooks at United Cycle in Edmonton.

And he's crazy about the sport of hockey. When we first sat down to talk for this book months earlier, he grabbed a chair in the media room and started talking about how he spent his lunch break for 12 years while working at the sporting goods store growing up: he'd sit in the stands at the University of Alberta and watch legendary Golden Bears coach Clare Drake run practice. The only other people in the building besides the team were joggers running around a track.

Hitchcock and I would eventually watch the legendary Game 6 of the 1999 Stanley Cup Final between his Dallas Stars and the Buffalo Sabres, a triple-overtime classic still remembered today because of its controversial ending. Something we'd get into much later.

During this first visit, I was in St. Louis, where Hitchcock was the head coach, to witness the NHL debut of a young phenom named Connor McDavid, a kid many expected to transform Edmonton. As Hitchcock talked, it was fascinating to hear about another kid from Edmonton, this one taking a completely different path to the NHL.

It was the story of a coach who started at the bottom and worked his way up to become a Stanley Cup champion.

Hitchcock's path to the top began in that university arena, watching Clare Drake practices. He'd get lesson plans from Drake and the coaching staff so he could follow along with the drills. Then the coaches would tell him afterward why they did everything they did.

"What Clare did for a group of us was he moved us into understanding positional play. It went from 'everybody work hard, everybody compete hard, everybody battle hard' to structure on the ice," Hitchcock said. "'This is how to play your position. This is how to teach positional play. This is how to teach a system.' He organized ice hockey for thousands of coaches."

Watching Drake conduct practice, Hitchcock couldn't have been further from the NHL. He was just learning about discipline in his life.

When Hitchcock was 14 years old, his father passed away. As a kid, the coach who now demands self-control and discipline had neither.

"I was out of control," he said. "Crazy. Set up to crash and burn. I go to golf reunions with guys I played junior golf with, and the biggest surprise isn't the record I have or the championships or medals. It's that I'm alive. That's the shock."

Hitchcock's life and success is an example of the power of mentorship. He's living proof that investing in talented, if troubled, kids can really pay off.

Drake poured into Hitchcock all his knowledge about hockey and systems and the details that go into winning. Wilf Brooks, his boss at the sporting goods store, taught him about leadership. Another friend, Chuck Geale, gave his life structure. They became his father figures.

From Brooks, Hitchcock learned the value of giving people control over their part of the world. In Hitchcock, Brooks saw a natural salesman.

"One of Ken's greatest gifts is his ability to get people to buy into what he's thinking," Brooks said. "It doesn't matter if it's a reporter he's talking to or his players or 1,000 people in the room. Ken has a gift to reach out to them."

I met with Ken Hitchcock in St. Louis to watch the triple-overtime classic between the Dallas Stars and Buffalo Sabres from the 1999 Stanley Cup Final.

From Geale, Hitchcock learned how to act, how to treat people. When Hitchcock started coaching locally, Geale would watch Hitchcock lose control behind the bench. He'd see him throw things onto the ice and get ugly with the media. He'd see him berate players.

Hitchcock had a passion for hockey but sometimes that passion was misplaced.

"He would get really upset," Geale said. "Throw sticks on the ice. I'd say, 'Who the hell are you trying to impress? You're not impressing anyone. You have to show yourself as a person who is always in control.'"

One time he saw Hitchcock really get after a player on his team.

"I said, 'Hitch, a hockey player is not a piece of meat. A hockey player has a heart, a soul, they cry, they laugh,'" Geale said. "'You're hurting his soul.'"

These were lessons Hitchcock had to learn, and he did. His teams were successful on the ice and he was the king of Sherwood Park. He could have settled in and done that for the rest of his life, be the big fish in a small frozen pond. When he turned down a promotion to coach a junior team in Medicine Hat, it looked like that might be the case.

He still wasn't exactly positive he could make the jump from midget to junior hockey. Hitchcock was worried about losing his job in the sporting goods store. Brooks was a surrogate father and he wasn't eager to walk away from what he had.

Geale helped give him the push he needed.

"'You have to be more than working in a sporting goods store the rest of your life. You have a talent. Go. You're going to make it. You're going to be great. You have to convince yourself you're going to be great,'" Geale said, relaying what he told Hitchcock. "It took confidence to break from Sherwood Park and Edmonton, where he was king. Everybody knew Hitch."

Geale's message was simple: don't look back. Ever. When you get to Kamloops, start looking for an opportunity in the American Hockey League. When you get to the AHL, start looking ahead to the NHL. Always be planning the next step in your life.

Geale believes the position we are in today is merely training for the next one. It's about never settling in.

Hitchcock, as it turns out, didn't settle at all.

He was returning from the midget championships when he decided to apply for the Kamloops job on a whim. He called from an airport pay phone to let them know he was coming. He was told he needed to bring a résumé, so he grabbed a pack of lined paper and wrote down his coaching records. That's what he handed them.

"I believe I got my job in Kamloops because I was willing to work for less than anyone else," Hitchcock said. "I don't believe I got it on merit."

He had no idea how to run a junior team. He was probably heavier than he should have been. There was so much work to be done.

A few Kamloops players stuck around to watch his first press conference, including future Oilers goalie Daryl Reaugh. A reporter asked Reaugh what he thought of the new coach.

"Daryl said, 'I don't know anything about him, but looking at him it looks like we're going to eat well on the road,'" Hitchcock said with a laugh.

That was where it all began. Just about 15 years later, he was raising the Stanley Cup as the head coach of the Dallas Stars.

* * *

It's late August and I'd just spent the previous day with Joel Quenneville, whose Blackhawks team Hitchcock's Blues had eliminated from the playoffs that spring.

An afternoon drive down I-55 got me to St. Louis from Chicago in about five hours. There were no tornadoes yet, which helped.

Hitchcock wanted to get started early, so I was in his office at 9:00 AM.

A few moments later, in walks Hitchcock. He's gearing up for the season and planning on having a meeting with Alex Pietrangelo later that afternoon to talk about the captaincy vacated by David Backes, who had signed as a free agent with the Boston Bruins.

He's wearing a black polo shirt and sits down at a shared conference table in the middle of the Blues coaching offices. He's ready to go.

I hook up the equipment and we dive right in. The game took place on June 19, 1999, so the video is less than ideal. The players are fuzzy on the big screen. It's a game from another time, certainly before high definition television.

"When was the last time you watched this?" I ask.

"I never watched a second of this or the controversial goal until this came out on NHL Classics four or five years ago," Hitchcock says. "Now, I'll bet you in the last four years, I've seen it 10 times."

"What do you remember about your first viewing?"

"How nasty the game was, how vicious it was. The thing that really stuck out to me was how many penalties would get called if this was played today."

At that point, Mike Yeo walks in the room and sits down at a desk behind us. Yeo had just been hired as an associate coach under Hitchcock. As it turned out, Hitchcock was fired in February of 2017 by GM Doug Armstrong, who then elevated Yeo to be his replacement.

But if there's anything uncomfortable about the relationship between the two on this day, months before those events, I don't sense it at all. Hitchcock greets him right away.

I had gotten to know Yeo while covering a series between his former Wild team and the Colorado Avalanche. That Avalanche franchise played a big part in helping shape the Stars teams from the Hitchcock era. Even now, Hitchcock remembers more about those incredible series between Dallas and Colorado than the Stanley Cup Final he won.

"The two series in '99 and 2000 that we played against Colorado, I watched those games a lot. They were classic hockey. Both teams were still not beat up like we were here," he says.

At that time, getting out of the Western Conference was a battle of attrition. If you beat the Stars, the Blues were waiting. If you beat the Blues, the Red Wings or Avalanche were waiting. It was an absolute gauntlet.

Then you had to go and beat the Eastern Conference winner with half your team in the trainers' room.

That's what Hitchcock remembers most about this Game 6 against the Sabres. Before the overtime session, Hitchcock met with his coaches because they were running out of players.

"In Games 5 and 6, we had a lot of guys who were taking needles and trying to play through stuff and the doctors were getting involved because they had to," he says. "We were laughing after this game because we would not have been able to field an NHL team to play Game 7."

Then Hitchcock started to list some of the injuries he recalls.

Brett Hull had a Grade 3 MCL tear.

Joe Nieuwendyk had a separated shoulder.

Mike Modano had a broken wrist.

Pat Verbeek had a pulled groin.

As we're watching, the injury to Brett Hull is apparent as Hitchcock cycles through forwards to play with Modano and Jere Lehtinen. Hull is in bad shape, bad enough that the conversation with Hitchcock and the doctors continues throughout the game.

How much more can he go? Can he take another shift?

We skip right to the first overtime with the game tied 1–1. After the first 60 minutes, the decision was made that Hull was done. The coaching staff had every intention of sitting him for the remainder of the game, no matter how long it went. Then two more Stars players went down and Hull was forced back into action. It was a decision that would change the course of hockey history.

"Hully had missed some shifts and the decision was, 'You have to get out there,'" Hitchcock says.

"What did he say to that?"

"Hully is a really tough guy. He took the knee injury and rather than have surgery, the decision to play through was made. It was a Grade 3, which is a six-to-eight-week injury. He opted to play through it."

As it turns out, it was a career-changing decision.

When the Final began, the feeling internally was that the Stars were the better team. But as the series continued, Hitchcock sensed the pendulum shift to the Sabres' favor. By the last game, Buffalo was the better team. The toll of coming out of the West had all but crushed the Stars. If this series had gone seven games, the Sabres probably would have won.

"Look here," Hitchcock says, pointing to the screen as the Modano line hits the ice. "That's Jere Lehtinen and Mike Modano and Blake Sloan. That's not Brett Hull. He couldn't play all the time. It was Blake Sloan, it was Pat Verbeek, it was Benoit Hogue. It was some of Brett Hull. This starts the overtime. We're mixing and matching. We're in trouble."

"You're taking on water."

"We're really taking on water. Modano—that's a full broken wrist he's playing with."

We start to talk about the path Hitchcock took to get that moment. The coach behind the bench in this game is the end result of the mentoring he got in Edmonton, along with the experiences he gained after breaking away.

He began to understand that the process was more important than the result. That was a big change for him, having come from a midget program that rarely lost.

The result often takes care of itself if the process itself is sound, and to achieve the best results, it's best when the players take ownership of that process.

It certainly happened in 1999 with the Stars.

In January of that year, GM Bob Gainey approached Hitchcock about letting the players run practice.

"That's good," Hitchcock responded. "I'll just sit and watch."

"No," Gainey answered. "You're taking two days off. You're getting out of here. You're driving everybody nuts. You're pushing it. They got the message. You need to go for a walk."

So he did. For two days, Hitchcock left the team alone. The players ran practice on their own, away from a coach always searching for perfection.

"I always said that Hitch made sure everybody was on the same page. The same page was, you were all so pissed at Hitch," said Dave Reid, a forward on this championship team. "I swear, if Hitch thought someone was happy with him, he would piss that guy off just to make sure that player wasn't criticized by his teammates for being happy with the coach."

He instructed and coached but Hitchcock left the meetings to the players. For about a two-year stretch, Hitchcock had players pushing each other harder than any coach ever could.

"It's the perfect scenario," Hitchcock says. "Before the coaches would get in there, they would take care of their own business."

It seems like such a crucial achievement for a coach, or any leader—to get the people they lead to take on full responsibility and accountability, without daily input or oversight. That it only happened with three groups in Hitchcock's long career to that point shows how tough it is.

"How do you implement that mentality?" I ask.

"To me, it's the relationship you have with your leaders. It's the relationship and responsibilities your leaders accept. There's a change in your team that happens when your team goes from being friends to teammates. When that change takes place, that's when accountabilities fit in. When accountabilities fit in, it's like gold."

"You coach the leaders and you instruct everybody else."

"The relationship you have with your leaders has to be without consequences. They have to feel comfortable coming to you and being critical of you, and you have to be willing to accept it. The conversation has to be continual both ways. There can't be any sensitivity toward your relationship with your leaders. It has to be candidness without consequences."

If the players are mad at Hitchcock, he wants to know. He's learned not to take it personally.

"You've got to be willing to accept blame and criticism, same as they are," he says.

"You had that with this group?"

"They laugh at me still. If I go sit in a locker room with this group now, they would have no issues busting my balls. They're all over me. I was the target. You'd better be willing to laugh at it."

"I think some coaches would have a hard time with that."

"Yeah, they would. In this business, I find that if you want to last, you'd better take what you do really seriously but you'd better not take yourself seriously…When you're asking people to do things that are really uncomfortable, it gets old after a while. They get tired of you."

In the 1999 Western Conference Finals, the Stars lost to the Avalanche in Game 5 to fall behind 3–2 in the series. Hitchcock's coaching instinct was to go after the pride of his players and appeal to their emotions. Instead, 38-year-old Guy Carbonneau met with him and said the players would take care of it. All they wanted from Hitchcock were very clear instructions about how to play, and what they look like when operating at their very best.

Hitchcock found video clips that showed exactly how the Stars group looked when they were clicking. He skipped the emotional appeal and just instructed. The players only needed that reminder.

"Then we went out to Colorado and we won, played our best game," Hitchcock says. "That was the best game I'd seen. The response was great. The players took care of all the emotion. The players took care of all the effort. We went back to our structure and that followed through to Game 7."

That only happened because Carbonneau and the other veterans on the roster felt comfortable going to Hitchcock and telling him to ease up. It only happened because Hitchcock was willing to listen.

"Guy Carbonneau was really good at being a bridge," said Mike Modano, the Stars' young superstar at that time. "We just had a ton of veteran guys that had been there. They all had some success with the Stanley Cup. They all played the way Hitch was preaching. It really wasn't a big change on their part, how they were asked to play. Their big thing was telling us what Hitch was telling us."

Not that Modano didn't hear from Hitchcock often. He did. It was Modano's transformation as a player that helped the Stars ultimately stack up against the other great teams of that era. His performance in the game being played on the screen in front of us was a long time coming.

Before the 1996–97 season, the Stars coaching staff decided they were going to start playing Modano exclusively against the other team's best players, rather than trying to get him favorable matchups against second or third lines.

Their thought process was simple: they liked their star player better than the other star players in the league at that time. They thought he could win that battle or at least play to a draw. The rest of the lineup in Dallas was so deep, they reasoned, the Stars could grind their opponents down.

"We were going to bite the bullet and he was going to play Mark Messier, Wayne Gretzky, whoever Mike had to play against," Hitchcock says.

The Stars played one home game and then hit the road on an East Coast swing through New York. During that stretch, Modano was matched up as often as possible against the best players on the ice.

"At the end of the day, he didn't have a lot of points but we won all the games," Hitchcock says. "Our whole structure about becoming a 200-foot team changed because Modano saw the value of being really good in his own end to help us. He figured out if he was even, we were going to win games, because we didn't need him to do everything. At the end of the day, he took real pride in being good against the other team's top players."

"Was that something you had to pitch to him?"

"I pitched it to him all summer and it wasn't getting bought."

"What were those conversations like?"

"They were candid. He didn't see that happening. He didn't see how that could equal a win. He felt he needed to do everything. I said, 'If you're even, we should be able to have an advantage here with the way we're built.' When he saw it take place, he bought in."

During his time in Dallas, Hitchcock convinced star Mike Modano to adjust his playing style. The result was a Stanley Cup championship. (AP Images)

Modano had to change the way he played. Until that point, he liked to constantly be on the move. When he played on the move against the best players, the puck often ended up in the net—either the Stars' or their opponents'.

Hitchcock tried to convince Modano that he'd get more scoring chances playing the right way against the best players.

"That's the part he didn't believe," Hitchcock says. "When you play against offensive players, you get odd-man rushes. When you play against top players, you get odd-man rushes. He didn't believe that. Then it started to happen. All of a sudden, he's got the same point total and he's a plus-30 playing against the other top players. Not bottom feeders."

Part of Modano's reticence was probably because there still needed to be trust built between the American superstar and the coach trying to change the way he played.

"Over time, I learned to like him," Modano said of Hitchcock. "At the start, we had issues. As a guy being asked to change or add a little bit to your game, there's no promises what the outcome is going to be. At the end of the day, what guarantee do you have? You're going on what they suggest."

Then the success started coming. Modano played better and better. He helped shut down top players. His point totals didn't nosedive. His plus/minus numbers during this era are staggering. He was a minus-12 in 1995–96 and then a plus-43 in the following season.

The change took discipline. Modano had to fight through bodies to get to the areas of the ice Hitchcock wanted him patrolling. He had to be more of a traffic player rather than a perimeter player.

"It was being more of a hunter than the hunted out there," Modano said. "I always felt I needed to keep my speed to give me separation from the defender. Hitch was like, 'Have you ever watched when you stop and start? You can still get going pretty good.' That took a lot of time to beat into me."

"It took time," Hitchcock says. "He wasn't a first-year player when I got to Dallas. He'd played six or seven years in the league already. When he bought in, it was good."

At that moment on the big screen in front of us, Sabres defenseman James Patrick nearly ends the game we're watching. He comes millimeters away from sending this series to a Game 7, a game the Stars probably weren't winning. Millimeters away from changing the course of Buffalo sports history, and possibly the career of Ken Hitchcock.

"There's Patrick hitting the crossbar. Holy cow," I say.

A replay is shown on the screen. Stars goalie Ed Belfour goes down slightly as the puck sails up. It ricochets off the crossbar and into the stands. About as close as one can get to ending the game.

"That's the one. That's the one where I thought it was over," Hitchcock says. "That shot made a funny sound. The sound on the bench was back bar, not front bar."

"You can tell the difference?"

"Yes."

The game goes on. At that point, it looked like the Stars had nothing left.

"Benoit Hogue was beat up. Hully was on one leg. Half our defensemen were hurt," Modano said. "They were the younger team. They seemed like they were starting to come at us more often. Physically, it's tough. You only have one good rush, then you're off the ice. You really couldn't counter or go back on the offensive. You're waiting for that one hiccup. Plus, you're dealing with the old rules. It was pretty much prison rules out there."

The players grind on. Hitchcock is eager to jump to the conclusion of the game.

There's now six minutes remaining in the third overtime, and the players on the ice aren't trying to make plays anymore. It's like they're moving in slow motion, trying to skate on a sandy beach.

There's a shot on the screen of the Sabres bench, and as the camera pans from right to left, there are nothing but completely blank stares on the players' faces. They're all looking straight ahead, almost as though talking to the guy next to them might use energy they need for a fourth overtime. They're absolutely drained.

There's a similar shot of the Stars bench. It's almost impressive that Brian Skrudland has enough energy to chew gum.

The action resumes and Modano loses a faceoff. Sabres defenseman Richard Smehlik gains possession and tries to make a pass to Joe Juneau. Brett Hull intercepts the pass and sends the puck across the ice as the Stars enter the offensive zone. They work the puck around a bit until Jere Lehtinen fires a shot toward Buffalo goalie Dominik Hasek.

Hasek makes the save but is on his stomach when the rebound slides toward the front of the net.

Hull is there. He kicks the puck to his stick and bangs in into the empty net.

Ken Hitchcock, the kid from the Edmonton suburbs who friends thought might not live past the age of 30, was a Stanley Cup champion.

The NHL had a rule on the books that season that disallowed a goal if a player's skate was in the goal crease when a puck crossed the line. Hull's goal was ruled a good one because he kicked the puck to his stick while outside the crease, and the effort to score the goal was seen as a single possession. At least, that's the explanation that was given afterward.

Buffalo fans still argue otherwise. The rule was removed the following season, making this goal one of the most notorious in Stanley Cup Final history.

If there was controvery on the Buffalo side, Hitchcock was oblivious to it all. He was too busy celebrating.

"I never knew anything about anything until we went in the locker room after the celebration," he says. "I never saw what was happening on their bench or anything. There was a celebration. The trophy came out. We were going around the ice. I still saw people on their bench. I never saw anything until I went into the little coaches' office an hour and a half later."

Then he saw the replay. He watched it for a second and dismissed it.

"Quite frankly, I didn't think anything of it. There wasn't dialogue. It wasn't debate. It wasn't anything other than, 'What are they going to do, take the trophy away?'"

The moment Hitchcock remembers more than any controversy surrounding the goal was what happened in the dressing room after the game, as the celebration was settling down.

The family members had left, heading for the charter to take them back home to Dallas. The only people left were the players and the coaches.

Bob Gainey had just won his sixth Stanley Cup, this time as the general manager of the Stars. He stood up in the dressing room and shared what it meant to him personally to win this Cup.

Then another player shared his story. Then another and another.

Brett Hull was still in his gear, sitting on top of the locker room stall, his feet dangling, sharing what that moment meant to him.

"That was like gold for me," Hitchcock says. "Somebody has a video of that. I don't know who it is but somebody has a video of that."

It was an emotional moment for Hitchcock, to hear the sacrifices each player made to get to that moment. Asked for specifics, Hitchcock wasn't giving any. He wants to leave those stories in that room.

"I'd rather not say," Hitchcock says. "It was bonding, bonding for years."

"There was a seriousness but it was also the giddiness because it's 2:30 in the morning," Dave Reid said. "You just played six periods, you're dehydrated, and the first thing they give you is champagne and beer. You're drunk after two sips. I just remember the one-liners from Mike Keane—his ability to make light of things in a serious way."

The Stars thought they could have won it all in 1998 but were beaten by the Detroit Red Wings. There were players on the 1999 Stars team who seriously wondered if they'd ever win a Stanley Cup after falling short the previous season.

"To see all the work we put in, it meant a lot to everybody," Hitchcock says. "When you look at this group, we were a hockey team that had captivated a Dallas Cowboys city. We were, for a short period of time, on equal footing."

Nearly two decades later, in the same city, Ken Hitchcock went back to try it all again.

• CHAPTER 9 •

CLAUDE JULIEN

Game 7 of the 2011 Stanley Cup Final

This was it. The last coach on my list. A journey that began in Dan Bylsma's living room in April of 2015 was ending at the Bruins' new practice facility in Brighton, Massachusetts, 18 months later with Claude Julien.

So close to completing the journey, I realized that only a technical snafu or some outside force could screw it up.

I tried to eliminate any and all conceivable variables. I found a hotel five minutes away from the practice facility. I could walk if I had to. Even then, I woke up early and made sure I was the first one there. The Bruins had played in Montreal the night before, so the practice facility was empty when I arrived.

There's something beautiful about being the only one at a rink. The glimmering ice reflected the large rows of windows surrounding it. It's a practice facility but the championship banners still hang from above, including the one earned in the game Julien and I were going to watch—Game 7 of the 2011 Stanley Cup Final versus the Vancouver Canucks. It's the best Final I've ever covered in person. It's also my favorite.

I had double and triple checked everything. The NHL graciously provided a copy of the game when I couldn't find one anywhere online. I had that covered. Wireless wasn't going to be an issue. I'd heard from the Bruins that morning that we were good to go.

Nothing could get in the way. Just to be absolutely sure, I pulled out my digital recorder, one that I purchased just for this project because it had hours and hours of room on it. The battery was a little low so I unzipped my backpack, pulled out a fresh battery, and swapped out the old one.

I set the digital recorder on a railing overlooking the ice and walked to a nearby garbage can to toss the old battery. I grabbed my backpack and headed for the Bruins offices down the hall. I couldn't wait to watch this game.

Eric Tosi, who worked for the Bruins public relations department, led me down to a theater room where the players and coaches break down film. There are four rows of black chairs, each with its own cupholder. On the front wall is a huge screen. To its right is a podium where the laptop controlling the game would sit. Julien was on his way so I pulled out my notepad full of questions and unzipped my backpack to grab the digital recorder.

Only it wasn't in the first pocket I checked. Or the next one. Or the side one. Or the front one. I checked my pants pockets, my jacket pockets. Nothing. I began frantically pulling things out of my backpack.

I excused myself left the room. Maybe I left it on the counter in the bathroom? I started there. Nothing.

I hustled down to a vending machine where I'd bought a breakfast bar. Wasn't there either.

I mean, I had just had it in my hands. I was going crazy but knew I didn't have the time to turn the place upside down. I ran back to the viewing room, checked my bag again. Or course, it wasn't there.

My phone was my backup plan. I had an app that records voice memos. I'd used it in a pinch before but I had no idea if there were length limits. I didn't even know if I had enough space to record an interview as long as the one I was about to do. But it was all I had.

So I hit the giant red record button on the app, set the phone on the armrest of a seat in the second row, and hoped for the best as my digital recorder sat quietly on the railing in the hallway, right where I'd left it.

* * *

As Julien gets settled, we start chatting about the film room.

"This is awesome. This is really nice," I say.

"We come here, do our meetings, power play, penalty kill, pre-scout, whatever video we have. It's a good setup," Julien says.

"I love this series, between you and Vancouver. Have you seen this game since it ended?"

"I watched it once, shortly after, in the summertime. It's almost like there was so much going on after we won. I've never had a chance to sit like this and watch it."

Until this game, the home team had won every single game in this series. It was a crazy Final from start to finish. Canucks forward Alex Burrows bit Bruins center Patrice Bergeron in the third period of Game 1 and that pretty much set the tone for the rest of the series.

Boston's Nathan Horton was leveled by Vancouver's Aaron Rome, earning Rome a suspension for the rest of the Final. The goalies had an exchange in the media, where Roberto Luongo famously wondered when Tim Thomas was ever going to compliment him, or "pump his tires," the way Luongo had done for him in the past.

The night before Game 3 in Boston, the Canucks went for a team dinner at Grill 23, a Boston chophouse. Bruins fans found out and took turns interrupting the Canucks' meal.

"People are just giving it to you," said Andrew Alberts, who played on that Canucks team. "Seriously? We're just trying to eat."

Covering this series was an absolute circus. After every game there was something crazy to write about.

Brad Marchand punching the Sedin twins.

Riots in Vancouver after Game 7.

Sometimes we even wrote about the games themselves.

We blew everything out of proportion because it was the Stanley Cup Final. For their part, the players did their best to use it to their advantage.

"You jump on anything you can for motivation," said Shawn Thornton, the Bruins' bruising, outspoken fourth-liner in this series. "If you can use it, why wouldn't you? If it affects the other team, you hope, in a negative way? Any advantage you can get in the playoffs."

You'd better believe that Thornton was giving it to Luongo on the ice before Game 6, following his comments about Thomas.

"We chirped Lou," he said. "We were aware what he said was taken out of context but they made a big deal out of it, so we jumped on it."

The series was exhausting, too. The travel back and forth between Vancouver and Boston was grueling even for those of us who weren't doing anything more physical that watching games, asking questions, and then having a few beers afterward.

There were 4:00 AM wakeup calls, cross-country flights, overtime games, and time-zone changes back and forth between the East Coast and British Columbia.

By the time we got back to Vancouver for Game 7, we were all spent. I can't imagine what the players were feeling.

"It was fucking exhausting," Thornton said. "I know I did media one day and someone took a picture of me in the stall in my big beard. I saw the picture a couple years later. I look absolutely exhausted."

Entering Game 7, Julien noticed the Canucks were starting to crack. They were the more talented team. They were the one with the bigger stars, more regular season points, and the favorite to win the Stanley Cup.

But mentally? The Bruins seemed to have an edge the longer the series went on. Part of that was likely due to the Canucks' inability to close out the series when they had the chance, in Game 6 in Boston.

"I think it affected us mentally," Vancouver center Ryan Kesler said. "We were in full control and it just turned on us and went the other way. Game 7, I don't think we responded well. You feel the pressure of playing in Canada, you feel the pressure of the city, and everything crumbles."

Boston probably had a physical edge, too.

"They were starting to run into injuries," Julien said as the video gets underway and we start reliving the series.

Kesler had injured his hip on a routine play in Vancouver's Western Conference Finals series, against the Sharks. He could barely walk by this time, let alone skate, and would have surgery after the playoffs were over. Dan Hamhuis was another important player for the Canucks struggling with injuries.

Julien sensed his opponents' discouragement—and maybe some desperation—on the day before Game 7. The Bruins were supposed to practice at 5:00 PM but when the Canucks canceled their practice, Julien tried to get his guys on the ice early so they could be finished earlier.

The Zamboni driver told the Bruins staff that they weren't allowed on the ice even a minute before 5:00. It was just another sign of how petty things had become between the two franchises.

"To me, there was a sense of, 'You know what? We may be getting a mental edge here before Game 7,'" Julien says.

The Bruins, meanwhile, seemed to be taking things in stride. Perhaps concerned about how they'd be received in public by the Canucks fans in Vancouver, they had a quiet team meal together, a private buffet. That night, Mark Recchi invited Thornton into his hotel room to share a glass of wine from a bottle Recchi had brought for the occasion. Win or lose, the next game was going to be Recchi's last as an NHL player.

"That meant the world to me," Thornton said.

On the afternoon of the game, Zdeno Chara, Patrice Bergeron, and Andrew Ference went for a walk in downtown Vancouver to try and clear their heads before the game. At one point, they came across a media member doing a live radio hit on his phone. Just as they were approaching

Claude Julien took the Bruins to two Stanley Cup Finals during his run in Boston, winning the Cup in 2011.

him, the voice on the other end asked him for a prediction on the game that evening.

He picked the Canucks to win.

"We all looked at him," Ference said. "Now, he's on the radio, stumbling around, and he actually switched it. He goes, 'On second thought, it's the Bruins.' We were all laughing."

There were two memorable moments for the Bruins leading up to that game, both involving assistant coach Geoff Ward.

The first started during a phone conversation Ward had with an old college friend before the team left for Vancouver. They were talking about how well the Bruins had played at home in this series when his friend asked, "Why don't you take some of the home ice with you?"

It was a brilliant suggestion. Ward had ice from TD Garden scraped into a green Gatorade bottle, labeled with white tape. The plan was to pour it onto the ice in Vancouver. Ward had Bruins strength and conditioning coach John Whitesides ask Nathan Horton to do the honors.

Horton was happy to do it.

"Nathan Horton had been such an emotional part of our run," said Ward. "For example, we'd been giving out an old Bruins jacket to the player of the game after every game we won. Nathan had won it and then got injured. The guys decided that they didn't want anybody to pass the jacket out. I remember the moment he showed up after his concussion to present the jacket after a win at home. That was an emotional, powerful moment."

As it turns out, so was the pouring of the water. Horton, wearing a black Bruins hoodie, casually walked to the bench, looked both ways, and then started sprinkling the TD Garden water onto the Vancouver ice before Game 7. He even unscrewed the top and shook out every last drop.

"I thought we were in the right place [mentally]," Julien says, reliving those events. "You saw Nathan Horton, who poured the water on the ice, bringing the water from the Garden. That kind of stuff. Everybody was enjoying the moment."

Earlier that day, Ward sat down and wrote a letter to his kids. He was doing it, in part, to pass the time before Game 7. But the words started to pour out of him. He wrote about what it takes to win and be successful. He wrote about how times like a life-changing game can remind you about the people who helped get you to that moment.

He showed the letter to Julien, who loved it.

"I thought it was pretty powerful," Julien says. "I asked Geoff if he would read it to the team, and he did. It was kind of neat—about the opportunity, where he'd come from, having the opportunity in Game 7 and having an opportunity to win the Stanley Cup for his kids, his family, and the support they'd given him through all of that."

Ward remembers reading it to the players, who were totally locked in. All eyes were on him as he read it. It was more emotional than he intended it to be, but that's what happens in these moments.

"Guys are in their last preparations before a Game 7, they all know what it's about, what it represents. They were tuned in and I just started to read," Ward said. "I remember Patrice Bergeron saying after, the part about the other voice we all listen to was a big thing for him. Sometimes in athletics, it's an emotional thing. It's a game played with passion and emotion."

Just before Game 7 began, then-Bruins GM Peter Chiarelli couldn't get cell service to text his coach, so he wrote out a note and gave it to Bruins PR executive Matt Chmura to pass along to Julien. The note was later reprinted in the Bruins' team-produced championship book:

CLAUDE,

I DON'T KNOW WHAT MADE ME THINK OF THIS, BUT CAN YOU REMIND Z THAT SIMPLE IS BEST FOR HIM?

—PETE

Chiarelli brought this note up when we later chatted about Julien. He spoke glowingly about his former coach from his current office in Edmonton, where he was trying to win another Stanley Cup as the GM of Connor McDavid and the Oilers.

He loved the way Julien never placed himself above the team. There was never an ego there. Julien reminds his teams often about the importance of staying humble and he leads by example. Chiarelli admired Julien's work ethic, one that was honed while working for his dad's roofing company in the off-season.

Whenever there was a problem, Chiarelli watched Julien roll up his sleeves and find a solution.

"He's not a complicated guy. I'm not a complicated guy. It's about work ethic and preparation," Chiarelli said.

"Humble" is a word often used to describe Julien. Most coaches, most leaders, have an ego. They want to be in charge. They want people to follow them. They're confident in their abilities to take a large number of people and achieve something great. That usually takes a healthy ego.

It honestly doesn't seem to be the case with Julien.

"It's the way I've always been," Julien says. "I've said it many times before—if I could do this job and walk out of the rink and nobody knew who I was, I'd be the happiest guy on earth. I don't need that in my life."

The other word often used to describe Julien is "resilient." Just look at his playing career. He played in Oshawa, Windsor, Port Huron, Salt Lake, Milwaukee, Fredericton, Quebec, Baltimore, Halifax, Kansas City, and Moncton.

That resilience and humility come from the same place.

"My upbringing growing up, and I'm proud to say it, is a very modest background. My family is roofing contractors," he says. "Back in those days, you didn't have the whole summer to work out. I had to make money somewhere. I had to work as a roofer, work in the hot weather, the hot tar and all that stuff. It was great exercise, all that stuff you had to carry up there."

But even more than staying in shape, he realized it wasn't something he wanted to do for 12 months. He had great respect for the guys putting in the work, he just preferred to channel that same work ethic into hockey. Sometimes the best lesson a job can provide is showing you how not to spend the rest of your life.

"If anything, it helped me to appreciate the opportunity I was having, even if I wasn't in the NHL very long or for very many games," Julien says. "Just playing it was awesome."

* * *

There's 5:27 remaining in a scoreless first period in front of us, with both teams playing pretty well.

Boston's Brad Marchand gets the puck along the wall and flips a backhanded pass toward the slot, where Mark Recchi and Patrice Bergeron are both creating traffic in front of Luongo. Bergeron bangs at it and beats Luongo for the first goal.

This moment, and Marchand's play on the wall, were just a hint of what was to come in his career, where he'd establish himself as a big-game player.

Doc Emrick's voice fills the room:

"They scoooooore! A lot of traffic in front and Patrice Bergeron has gotten the first goal of the game!"

For a Bruins team that was winless in this building, getting a lead was huge. It also built on Julien's belief that Boston had all the momentum and the cracks were starting to show in the Canucks.

"We did a great job there in managing the puck," he says. "At the same time here, I'm going to say it's a little bit of luck. It goes through a bunch of skates. Sometimes you have to be lucky to be good. Sometimes when you're good, you're lucky."

Before this game got too far along, I wanted to get into one moment in this series that is still talked about today: Alex Burrows biting Patrice Bergeron's finger in the third period of Game 1. The incident occurred as players from both teams gathered around the end boards following a whistle. When Bergeron's gloved hand got near Burrows' mouth, it appeared to everyone that the Canucks winger intentionally bit down on it. Burrows was not suspended or fined by the league.

The playoffs had already taken an emotional toll on the Bruins coming into the Final. They had survived a seven-game series against the Canadiens in the first round. They had an emotional revenge sweep of the Flyers in round two, after the Flyers had come back from a 3–0 deficit to beat the Bruins the previous season. The third round was another seven-gamer, with Boston advancing against the Tampa Bay Lightning.

For Ward, the moment Burrows bit Bergeron ignited an emotional reaction that might not have come otherwise.

"The biting incident got us emotionally attached to that series. Our guys, when backs were to the wall and they got angry, they were pretty good," Ward said.

The Bruins viewed themselves as a team that played on the edge physically but in a way that was respected in hockey. The Bruins would hit you early and often, and if you wanted to fight, they were ready to go.

They didn't feel the same way about the Canucks. The more they played Vancouver, the more they resented the way the Canucks behaved.

"We had that old-school hockey style, which was respectable compared to the b.s. that was going on on the other side—biting, flopping, some of the more cheap shot stuff," Bruins defenseman Andrew Ference said. "It wasn't in-your-face toughness, it was sneaky toughness. That dislike came really early. There was a lack of respect from us to them and vice versa."

The lack of respect for that Canucks team didn't just come from the Bruins. In the days leading up to that series, Julien received phone calls from friends around hockey wishing him luck and letting him know they were rooting for the Bruins in this series.

Julien even got insider tips on the Canucks from people around the league.

"I'll give you one. I was told by someone to watch during every TV timeout, one of the Sedin twins would be talking to the refs looking for a power play, and to make sure that one of our players was right there. It was just little things like that, little things to watch. That tip came from a very respectable person," Julien says.

The players were getting phone calls, too. There's not a bigger rival to the Bruins than the Montreal Canadiens but even that feud was put on hold when the Bruins faced these Canucks. Ference got calls from Montreal players letting him know they were pulling for Boston to win.

That's how much these Canucks were disliked around the NHL.

"We knew we were disliked but we felt it was because we were so dominant. That was probably one of the most dominant teams I played on," Vancouver's Ryan Kesler said. "We didn't fold. We didn't make mistakes. We'd get up 2–1 and end up winning 6–1."

And if they were diving or doing things that irritated other teams, it was done in the name of trying to win a Stanley Cup.

Aside from their feelings about the Canucks, people in the hockey community had plenty of reasons to pull for Julien. The guy known for his humble nature had gone through a lot to get to this point.

There was a belief that an early exit in these 2011 playoffs would cost Julien his job. Even he believed as much and you can understand why he never felt 100 percent secure. As the head coach in Montreal, he led the team to the second round of the playoffs in 2004. He was fired in January of 2006.

In New Jersey, it was even worse.

In 2007, the Devils were in first place with just a few games left in the season when GM Lou Lamoriello called him into his office. Julien assumed it was going to be a chat to discuss how they'd approach the playoffs.

Instead, Lamoriello let him know he was being replaced.

"I was surprised," Julien says. "More than anything else, what bothered me most was that this was my second firing in two years. As a young coach, I was really worried about my career. I'd never been fired. I started coaching in 1994 and had never been fired. Now, in two years, I got fired and I had a winning record both times. I'm trying to figure it out. I think the worry was, where was I going to end up?"

Coaches only get so many chances in the NHL, and Julien had blown through two head coaching jobs in two years.

It turned out he needn't have worried. He was getting calls within the next week.

Improbably, that scenario repeated itself in 2017, when Boston fired Julien in February despite the team's 26–23–6 record. One week later, he was hired by the Bruins' most hated rivals, the Canadiens, and promptly led Montreal to a first-place finish in the Atlantic Division.

Those experiences have given him a great deal of compassion for other people going through similar situations. After losing a job, it sometimes feels like another opportunity will never come. Usually one does, so his advice to those going through it is to use the time they now have to do something they normally couldn't do. Spend time with family. Experience something your job wouldn't allow you to do otherwise. Have faith the next opportunity is coming.

When Lindy Ruff lost his job in Buffalo in 2013, Julien called him and offered that same advice. He's done it with other coaches. He's been through it and come out the other side.

By the time this game rolled around, he had evolved as a coach. Players saw a coach who didn't micromanage as much as he did earlier in his tenure with the Bruins. He wasn't afraid to turn things over to his team, as he did during a crucial moment in the first round against the Canadiens.

Boston dropped the first two games of that series, both at home, and faced a 2–0 deficit heading to Montreal. It wasn't the ideal place to be for a coach who suspected he might not survive a first-round exit.

After the second loss, Julien turned the room over to Mark Recchi.

Geoff Ward shared what happened next.

"He said, 'Boys, we're down 2–0. There's nothing we can do about it. We have to embrace it as a team. We can't forget that it happened. We have to own it. We have to take ownership that we're down 2–0. All we need to do is go to Montreal and play one good game. That's all we need to do. One good game in Game 3 in Montreal,'" Ward said.

Recchi pointed out he was in a similar spot with the Carolina Hurricanes and ended up winning the Cup in 2006. It's moments like this where the experience of one player can be so critical.

It also takes trust and confidence from the head coach to let it happen.

Bruins GM Peter Chiarelli felt Julien was in complete control at all times. Chiarelli said in previous seasons there were conversations with Julien about the kind of composure it takes to win. If a coach becomes unglued on the bench, it trickles down to the players.

During this championship run, Chiarelli saw the composure behind the bench needed to win a Stanley Cup.

"A lot of it is just experience," Julien says. "Every little thing that happens, it's, 'Next time, I'll know better. Next time, I'll do it differently.'"

For example, one part of the job that Julien noticed his own improvement in was his ability to talk honestly and directly with players, no matter their stature in the game. That was an important development, because he had some big names and personalities dropped onto his teams at various points in Boston, including guys such as Recchi and Jaromir Jagr.

"I don't care if you're a Hall of Famer or just traded to the team, you're going to play our team game," he says. "Making them understand there's only one set of rules here, we should all respect that part of it. Maybe the first few years, you're giving them a little bit more space than you should, you don't want to ruffle feathers. You don't have the same confidence. That comes with time."

Then, Julien stops. He notices where the play is headed on the screen in front of us.

"Watch this goal here," he says.

Brad Marchand, just as he did on the Bruins' first goal, gets the puck along the wall and starts working, showing an ability to make plays in a tight space. He ends up sliding the puck up to defenseman Dennis Seidenberg, who fires a shot from the point.

Luongo makes the save but there's another rebound there for Marchand to pounce on. He does, picking up the puck and quickly skating behind Luongo for a wraparound. Marchand's shot deflects off a diving Luongo and it's 2–0.

There's 7:45 left in the second and the Bruins are up two goals. Marchand now has 10 goals in the playoffs, an unreal rookie debut.

"This is where Brad was so good around the net area," Julien says, watching.

"This is him at his best."

"Absolutely. He was so good. Watch him go to the net. He was so good at getting to those loose pucks around the net and being strong on it. He was so good in tight. Even off draws, he would just sneak in there, grab the puck, and score. He scored a lot that year that way."

"Did you know what you had in him?"

"He was a good skater. What I liked about him was that he was a competitor. He was in everybody's face."

Marchand certainly showed that ability in this series. In Game 6, he grabbed Daniel Sedin by the jersey and punched him a good six times in the face without any retaliation.

When asked after the game why he did it, Marchand's answer was simple.

"I felt like it," Marchand said.

Marchand arrived on the scene as a player who pushed the limits of what should and shouldn't happen on the ice.

"To be honest with you, I had chats with Brad before almost every game of that series," Julien says. "He was really, really playing on the edge there. It was important for me to stay on him."

There's 2:36 remaining in the second period and the Canucks are on the power play. The game is still 2–0 but this is a critical point. Vancouver has 43 seconds remaining on the man advantage and a goal would be an absolute game changer.

Instead it's Patrice Bergeron scoring a short-handed goal for Boston. It's his second of the game. It's just about the moment we all realized the Bruins were going to win this thing.

"The way we played, for them to score four to beat us, our team was really good with protecting the lead in those days," Julien says. "I felt confident but it was so important to keep our eyes focused. Even at that point, we're half a game from winning the Stanley Cup."

During the intermission heading into the third period, Julien came out of his office at his usual time, with eight minutes remaining before retaking the ice.

He saw a team that was dialed in.

"Guys, we'll remember this forever if we do it right," Julien told his players.

Julien didn't want the players to feel like this was different than protecting any three-goal lead. But they all knew it was. Their lives would be forever linked if they held this lead.

Julien could hear the players talking and realized they didn't need much more from him.

"They were not going to let this slip away. They were there talking about, 'This is the most important 20 [minutes] in our lives here,'" he says.

He had so much trust in these players at that point. Before we sat down for this conversation, Julien took out a sheet of paper and wrote down the names of the players on this team that he knew he could count on every single night.

On a young, inexperienced team, that list might only go five or six deep. In 2013, the year the Bruins played the Blackhawks in the Stanley Cup Final, he felt he had 13, maybe 14 guys who fit the description.

This Bruins team?

"I think there were between 14 and 16," he says. "You knew they were coming. They didn't always play great but you knew they were going to come to play."

A shot of Johnny Boychuk, later traded to the Islanders in a salary-cutting move, shows up on the screen. You can tell Julien misses him. There were no concerns whether or not Johnny Boychuk was going to show up to play.

"We all loved him," Julien says. "We had to make tough choices as an organization through the years with the cap and all that. Obviously it hurt us."

The third period begins and the Bruins are building a defensive wall to protect the lead. The players are standing on the bench, yelling instructions to their teammates on the ice. They've completely clogged up the neutral zone while the Canucks show further signs of cracking.

Julien feels his ability to communicate to his players has improved over the years. It paid off for Boston in 2011. (AP Images)

Vancouver winger Jannik Hansen tries to draw a penalty from Tim Thomas, skating into his stick and flopping to the ice. There's no call.

A couple minutes later, leaving the ice, Hansen drills Andrew Ference with the puck nowhere near the play.

"See what I mean?" Julien says as Hansen is called for an interference penalty. "They were starting to unravel there."

One of the byproducts of this series was a change in the relationship between the two coaches behind each bench. Julien and Vancouver's Alain Vigneault were former teammates and friends leading into the Final.

"We were teammates in Salt Lake City and St. Louis' farm team…As the season was going, we were texting each other. 'Good luck. Good luck moving on. Maybe we'll see ourselves in the Final.' Stuff like that," Julien says. "Once the series started, that obviously stopped. As the series went on it just got more intense. And uglier. We still talk and all that stuff, but there's something there. There's a scar that's been left. I gotta admit, there's a scar. It's unfortunate."

The game is winding down. The Bruins' victory is looking inevitable. But with five minutes left Julien is still focusing on matchups. He's trying to get Zdeno Chara and Dennis Seidenberg out there against the Sedins as much as possible. He's taking nothing for granted.

Roberto Luongo looks to the bench with about 3:40 left in the game, wondering when Vigneault will pull him. Thirty seconds later Luongo is off the ice. The Canucks have an empty net.

Julien interjects.

"I found out later they had asked our owner and the people upstairs to come down when the score was 3–0, and as they were walking toward the elevator, they hear a goal scored and some sort of cheer. Now, they're thinking that Vancouver scored and they've jinxed us by coming down too early," he says.

But it wasn't a Canucks goal. It was Brad Marchand, again. His empty-netter with 2:45 left made it 4–0 and iced it for the Bruins. The celebration was on.

Marchand is mobbed on the ice by Mark Recchi and Patrice Bergeron. The microphones pick up the reaction from the Bruins.

"Yeaaaah! Oh my god!"

They're going to win a Stanley Cup.

Making it even better, they now have nearly three minutes of play to let it sink in.

Andrew Ference said it was the first time the players started to let their guards down all postseason. They'd worked so hard to be emotionally stable, not to let the highs and lows of the playoffs get to them. Now, the emotions came rushing in.

Assistant coach Geoff Ward remembers the talk on the bench. Players had the rare opportunity to reflect on their paths to this moment, on the verge of a championship.

"I remember Andrew Ference talking about his mom, players relating stories about people they were connected to during their lifetimes who helped them get to that moment," Ward said.

Ference thought of his former Calgary Flames teammates. He'd been on the other side of a game like this earlier in his career, losing to the Lightning in Game 7 of the 2004 Stanley Cup Final. Nobody celebrates the team that goes just as far as the champion, the one that falls one win short of immortality.

It's funny the things that pop into your head in these moments.

"You get a tinge of regret of not being able to do it in Calgary, with those teammates," Ference said. "Oh man, how good would that have felt with those guys? You also think that it's the ultimate way to pay back your parents, all the time and money they spent getting you around. That was the big thing. That makes it worth it. It's such an odd moment. You have 1,000 things going through your head."

In the final seconds, Julien's focus is on making sure Recchi is on the ice when the final horn sounds. Julien is moments away from achieving the ultimate goal as a coach and he's thinking about someone else. That captures who he is as a coach.

There's 30 seconds left and the celebration is breaking out on the Bruins bench. There's a shot of Tim Thomas smiling behind his goalie mask. He was brilliant in this series.

Bergeron leaves the ice for a final time, getting a big hug from Chris Kelly as he hops over the boards. Marchand is next to leave the ice, getting a hug from a young Tyler Seguin as he joins him on the bench. Recchi stays on the ice with the Bruins' fourth line to close out the game.

The Bruins had won four of five games in this series against a team that was considered the best in hockey. There's a mass pileup of players, all smiling through overgrown beards and injuries, the grind finally over.

"It's amazing," Julien says, watching his players celebrate. "It's been so long. You kind of forget about that. There's a lot of good people in there that aren't here anymore."

Then there's a shot of the disappointed Canucks, taking a knee with their heads bowed. A devastated Ryan Kesler is looking off in the distance, eyes glassy.

Kesler remembers that moment all too well.

"It's such a terrible feeling. It's probably the hardest thing I've ever done, put your body on the line and to play until June 6 or something, to come up with nothing, it sucks. It's terrible," Kesler said.

Even after this hate-filled series, Julien felt for them.

"It's got to be tough," he says. "There was part of me that put myself in their shoes and really understood how they felt. You're the best team in the league and you get to Game 7 of the Final, you're at home, and you run just short. All that work, all that effort in every area put into that season, it's got to be tough to swallow."

It's clear that Julien's compassion isn't just for his hockey players, it's for all hockey players.

Five years after this loss, Kesler and Kevin Bieksa were in Boston for a game against the Bruins. They got together with Andrew Alberts, and the three sat at the bar of a Boston steakhouse, watching the Bruins on television.

They reminisced about that run in 2011, about how much the league has changed. They laughed about the time Bieksa, during a roadtrip, said, "Fuck it, boys, let's go win 20 in a row." The Canucks won 12 of their next 13 games. They were just that good that season.

Bieksa went back to the team hotel and watched highlights from the 2011 Stanley Cup Final for the first time in years. Immediately the memories rushed back. The pain returned.

"You start to second-guess things," Bieksa said. "Could I have done this better? Should I have done this instead? You're so tired, you're not thinking clearly at the time."

The pain of that Game 7 has faded some for the Canucks but it doesn't take much for it to resurface. Kesler gets emotional talking about it. He says the pain will never leave him. Bieksa is the same way.

"It's the worst feeling in the world," Kesler said. "It was a bitter, bitter pill to swallow. It was tough to play the Bruins the first couple years after that, knowing they took that away from us."

With Julien, the memories are so different. We're watching the celebration when Patrice Bergeron walks into the room we're sitting in. He sees what we're watching and gives us a huge smile.

"You come in for treatments?" Julien asks.

"Yeah," Bergeron answers, watching his teammates passing around the Stanley Cup. "The games are fun but that part is the best."

Julien laughs.

He's enjoying catching glimpses of different people celebrating this championship. There's a shot of defenseman Tomas Kaberle, acquired in a trade with Toronto.

"There he is, there's Kabby. He served a purpose. That was a great trade, because when you win the Cup there's no such thing as a bad trade."

"Exactly."

Forward Michael Ryder is shown on the ice, celebrating.

"He was always a great playoff performer," Julien says. "He had the nickname Easy Ryder every once in a while, but he was a good player. There is Nathan Horton. See? All the players are so happy for him."

"That hit on him turned the whole series around."

"Yeah, it did."

I'm always conscious of overstaying my welcome in moments like this, so I start winding things down.

"I've taken enough of your time. Anything else about your experience?"

"I remember to this day that we had to go into overtime against Montreal in Game 7 in the first round, because they called a high-sticking penalty on Bergeron. Then they score a power play goal," Julien says. "I know at that point, if I don't get through here, I could be coaching my last game as well—not that that scares you."

"But it's the reality of the situation.

"Yeah, that series we were down 2–0. We'd lost the first two games at home then went to Montreal and won the next two."

"That's crazy."

"I was supposed to be fired already. We came back and I still remember having to score that overtime goal to advance. You talk about adversity or that place you're in where it can go one way or another. It went our way and we just took off from there.

"It's an amazing sport that a career can hang in the balance of one bounce or one game or one goal."

"I guess the older, more experienced you get as a player, a coach, or whatever, those things matter less. When you're young, when you're starting your career, those things weigh heavy on you. This is what this game is all about. It goes back to the GMs who ended up firing me—there's no reason to have ill feelings, because that's the way the game is."

It's a perspective that can only come from experience. Maybe it's an easier one to have with a Stanley Cup ring in your collection but it's still valuable. There are outside forces that are completely out of anyone's control that can help determine one's fate or future.

Julien has learned not to let those moments define him, and they don't. He's a Stanley Cup winner but his bigger accomplishment may have been managing a group of players that reflected his core beliefs.

"The team was high character. It was humble," said Ward of his former boss. "If you know Claude, he always stresses it's very important to be humble. It was a high character team. Just like him."

EPILOGUE

It's impossible to sit with leaders such as the coaches included in this book and not walk away changed, or at least inspired. Each coach has a story of perseverance and risk-taking that reveals what is required to accomplish something great.

Greatness requires leaving your comfort zone. It requires discovering the profession that best aligns with your passions and then pouring everything you have into it. These aren't stories of individuals either. The greatest successes don't come from one person. They come from each person involved—players and coaches, in this case—sacrificing for a greater cause.

After winning a Game 7 in Colorado during one playoff run, Bob Hartley and his coaching staff took off their suits, ordered pizzas, and stayed up the entire night watching film and preparing for the next series, one that started in two days.

There's no time to celebrate successes when the ultimate goal hasn't been reached yet. Every coach in this book has a version of that story, and they wouldn't do it if their job didn't align with their passion.

But to get there, as Mike Babcock says, you have to be comfortable being uncomfortable.

Babcock passed on a comfortable job in business to stay in coaching. He walked away from a comfortable job with the Red Wings to take on the monumental task of building a winner in Toronto.

Hartley left what could have been a lifetime job at the windshield plant. Ken Hitchcock walked away from his job at the sporting goods store. John Tortorella took a job that paid him next to nothing, even when his wife had one that could have set up his young family for years. Todd McLellan answered a job posting in the classified ads, even when he knew little about how to coach.

They persevered.

Every single one of them has been fired.

Claude Julien was fired in New Jersey on the verge of leading a team to the playoffs. He believes he was one loss away from being fired in Boston before winning a Stanley Cup.

Joel Quenneville failed to win it all in St. Louis and Colorado before guiding the Blackhawks to three Stanley Cups.

Mike Sullivan had to wait a decade between head coaching jobs. He had to start all over again in the AHL after being fired with Tortorella in Vancouver.

Even a guy like Dan Bylsma, who skyrocketed to success immediately as an NHL head coach, only got there because he refused to quit as a player.

At one point Bylsma and close friend Davis Payne were sitting shoulder to shoulder as young hockey players on the ECHL's Greensboro Monarchs, and they weren't playing. They were two players with NHL aspirations and were two levels away from making it. Riding the bench.

"You are essentially a million miles away at that point," Bylsma said.

In that moment, the two made a pact that they would do whatever it took to make it in the NHL.

It meant uncomfortable conversations with the coaches, facing the problem head on. It meant putting in extra work on and off the ice. They understood they had to get in a fight at least every five games. Whatever it took.

"He went on to play over 400 NHL games and carve out a career he was able to parlay into coaching," Payne said of Bylsma. "I see him, the way he approaches life, it's about hard work and it's about being optimistic. They go hand in hand."

I get those two things.

I'm an optimist by nature. I grew up in the Midwest, where hard work is ingrained in the culture. My parents were public school teachers. They were up early every weekday morning to be among the first ones in the building.

The parents of my best friends worked on the assembly line in the auto industry. You put in the work.

But in these coaches, I saw what could be accomplished when work ethic is mixed with risk taking. They ripped themselves out of comfort zones or avoided them altogether. They sacrificed normal lives, passed on taking the jobs of least resistance, passing on safe careers to take on ones that aligned with their destiny.

I never asked any of them if they were scared along the way. But they had to be. They had families, children who depended on them. All the things you and I worry about.

There was no doubt when they raised that Stanley Cup or reached the pinnacle of success in what they'd set out to do, it was worth it. The sacrifice, the risk—it was all justified.

It was justified because they were doing exactly what they were called to do.

For two years, I saw up close the payoff that comes with that kind of sacrifice. I saw the payoff that follows risk taking and hard work. I saw the payoff of living exactly the kind of life you were meant to live.

When it was done, I couldn't help but wonder what my life would look like if I did the same.

ACKNOWLEDGMENTS

Let's not overthink anything here.

This book doesn't happen without great cooperation and flexibility from the coaches in these pages. A huge debt of gratitude to Dan Bylsma, Ron Wilson, Mike Babcock, Bob Hartley, Todd McLellan, Mike Sullivan, John Tortorella, Joel Quenneville, Ken Hitchcock, and Claude Julien. Not only were all of you gracious with your time, you were interesting and bought into the idea. Thank you.

A first assist goes to Todd Sharrock, Adam Rogowin, Eric Tosi, and everyone else on the team media relations side who helped convince people in these pages to participate. Same goes for Jim Nice and everyone at CAA. You guys are the best.

And thanks, Sidney. Your perspective was invaluable.

I owe Scott Burnside, Joe McDonald, and Pierre LeBrun beer for life for their assistance in lining up contacts and, in some cases, vouching for the project with a source they were close to. I can't imagine a better group of guys to work with. My editors at ESPN, notably Chad Millman, Dan Kaufman, and Tim Kavanagh, deserve credit for green lighting the project and allowing me the time to pull it off.

Bob McKenzie hooked me up with agent Brian Wood and Brian somehow found a taker for this crazy idea from a writer who'd never written a book. Thanks, guys.

Thank you to Mitch Rogatz, Adam Motin, and everyone at Triumph Books for taking on this risk and then making this concept a reality.

Lastly, a word about my family. Having a hockey writer for a husband and a dad means he's gone for long stretches. It means sometimes he's at Game 2 of a second-round series between the Blues and Stars instead of a concert or Little League game.

The kids—Calvin, Cameron, and Cormac—never complain. They open presents over FaceTime so dad can see. They send video clips and text updates from the biggest games. Usually we have our summers together and this book even cut into that. Instead of complaints, I got, "How's your book coming, Dad?"

Thank you, kids. I love you.

Cassie, I know this book meant you had to carry the burden of raising our family more than you normally do. The fact that our family is perfect shows how amazing you are. I love you.

ABOUT THE AUTHOR

Craig Custance is a journalist who spent the last decade covering the NHL as a national hockey writer, including six years with ESPN.com and *ESPN The Magazine*. He left ESPN to join The Athletic, a San Francisco–based sports media startup. He is currently an NHL Insider for The Athletic and editor-in-chief of The Athletic Detroit. Before working at ESPN, Custance wrote for *The Sporting News*. He spent the first 10 years of his writing career with the *Atlanta Journal-Constitution* after graduating from  Michigan State University. He lives in Clinton Township, Michigan, with his wife, Cassie, and three children, Calvin, Cameron, and Cormac. You can follow Craig on Twitter @craigcustance or read more of his work at www.craigcustance.com.